# WALL STREET'S INSIDERS

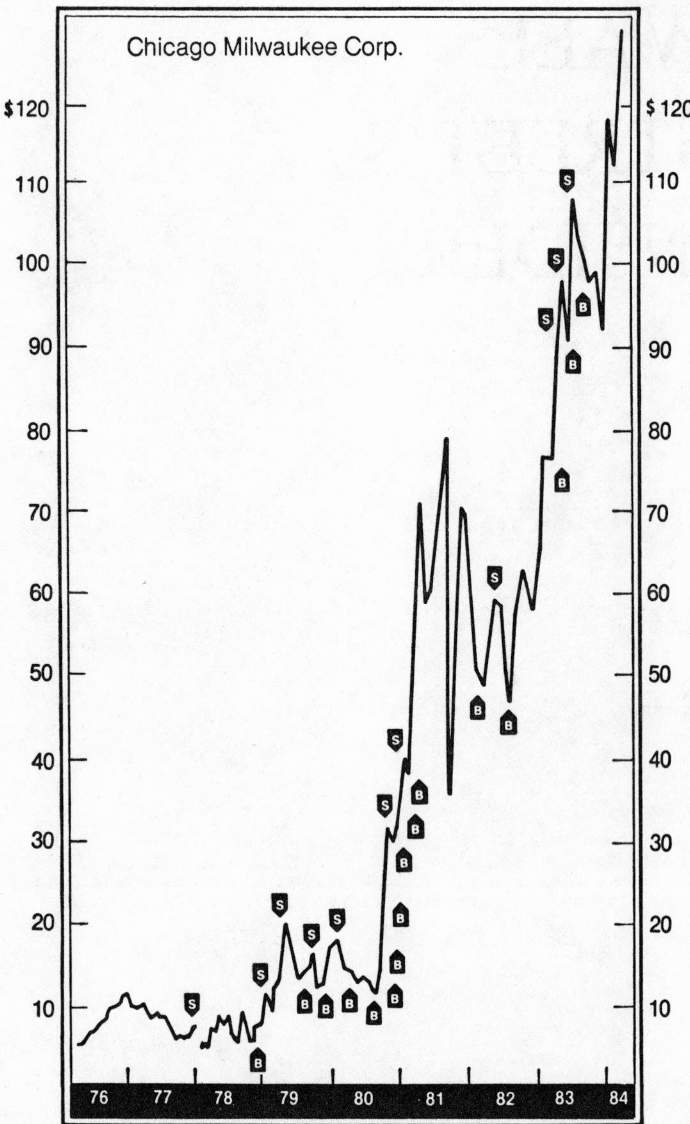


**Chicago Milwaukee Corporation—a stock that insiders bought.**

# WALL STREET'S INSIDERS

## How You Can Profit with the Smart Money

by JOHN C. BOLAND



*William Morrow and Company, Inc.*
*New York*

Charts by Joe LeMonnier



Library of Congress Catalog Card Number: 84-62023

ISBN: 0-688-03872-7

Printed in the United States of America

First Edition

1 2 3 4 5 6 7 8 9 10
BOOK DESIGN BY PATTY LOWY

*for Mira*

# ACKNOWLEDGMENTS

# ACKNOWLEDGMENTS

Several people took time from their own pursuits to offer helpful suggestions on the manuscript. I'm grateful to James Grant, editor of *Grant's Interest Rate Observer,* in New York; Jack P. Kneafsey, vice-president Prudential-Bache, in Baltimore, and Daniel R. Long III, president of Corbyn Associates and the Greenspring Fund, Village of Cross Keys, Maryland. The book's deficiencies belong solely to the author.

# CONTENTS

## INTRODUCTION

# *Insiders Know Things You Don't*

Prudent investors don't count on fair play.

Despite decades of regulation, the stock market remains a game in which the insiders of Wall Street and the corporate boardroom wield the upper hand. Their knowledge makes them winners. Consider recent history:

- The stock of a small fast-food company jumps in heavy trading. Hours later, the company announces that it may be taken over.
- The son of a mining company's director pays $3,000 for options entitling him to buy the company's stock. Two days later, an oil conglomerate's bid to acquire the firm makes the options worth $427,000.
- Officers dump a video-game company's stock hand over fist for weeks. Twenty-three minutes after the last sale, the company discloses that its machines are gathering dust in warehouses, and the share price plunges.
- Funneled through Swiss banks, orders pour into the market for seemingly worthless options on an oil-drilling contractor's shares. A week later, the company agrees to a takeover by a Persian Gulf firm.
- A group of professional investors quietly scoops up bonds in a bankrupt railroad. They double their money, roll the

profits into the common stock, and reap another tenfold gain.

- ✔ Wall Street bogeyman Carl Icahn closes in on a department-store chain, buying undervalued stock and threatening a battle for control. Two months later, the chain's managers leap into the arms of another suitor, who buys the entire company. Icahn and his associates split a trading profit of $4 million.
- ✔ Former Treasury Secretary William E. Simon invests $330,000 in a greeting-card company. Eighteen months later, the company goes public and his stake is worth $70 million.
- ✔ As the worst postwar business recession deflates stock prices in the summer of 1982, hundreds of officers and directors buy their companies' shares at bargain-basement prices. On August 13, while the public worries about a depression, the stock market embarks on the opening leg of a new bull market.

You may have witnessed some of these escapades or recall others in which insiders and their friends walked away with full pockets. Often they do so at the expense of the average investor.

## The Insiders

The pages ahead will look at these cases and others. Some are legal, some criminal. All fit under the heading of ''insider trading''—the buying and selling of stock by officers, directors, major shareholders, and other people with an ear to the boardroom door. In theory, trading stocks on confidential inside information is illegal. In practice, it's done more often than most investors imagine.

This book has two objectives. The first is to address the realities of the stock market. Despite assurances by the brokerage industry and securities regulators that insider trading can be curtailed, it never will be. Insiders' use of their privileged information is a fundamental fact of life in the stock market. It's a fact investors must come to terms with in order to act intelligently.

The second objective is to help the average investor close part of the information gap that gives insiders such an advantage. This means watching the investment moves of corporate officers and top professionals. It also means learning to think the way they do. Much of what they do is legal—or close enough to legal that few suffer prosecution. Much of their trading goes on in broad daylight. We'll discuss what to look for:

- ✔ How insiders can help you know when the stock market is cheap.
- ✔ How to find stocks that insiders buy—including takeover candidates.
- ✔ How to spot a company in trouble.
- ✔ How to double-check insiders' judgments.

Though they have no interest in doing so, insiders can help you make profitable investments. Many of their favorite stocks have climbed steadily through bear markets. Many have lain cheap and neglected for months after insiders bought, giving outside investors ample time to climb aboard.

When you read this book, the Dow Jones Industrial Average may stand at 1,500 or at 900. Business may be buoyant or dragging. Whatever the market's health, there are stocks that insiders are buying right now. Here's how to find them.

*To speculate in Wall Street when you are not an insider is like buying cows by candlelight.*

—Daniel Drew

*If you've got a secret and more than six people know about it, it doesn't stay a secret.*

—unidentified managing director,
Lehman Brothers Kuhn Loeb Inc.

# ONE

## *Insiders' Credo: You're Guilty Only If You're Caught*

To anyone browsing the New York Stock Exchange for bargains on the morning of March 10, 1981, many stocks must have seemed at least as appealing as St. Joe Minerals Corporation. The price had been drifting lower for months, as traders sniffed the demise of a natural-resources boom that had lifted the fortunes of St. Joe and other mining companies. On an average day, 30,000 to 40,000 St. Joe shares might change hands without disturbing the price by more than a half-point. There was talk of lower inflation in the year ahead, even a rare whisper that a bout of deflation might loom—not the kind of musings to excite interest in a lead and zinc producer.

But strange things were happening at Post 12 at the exchange, where a specialist with M. J. Meehan & Co. was charged with making a market in St. Joe. A day earlier, volume had suddenly swelled and the price closed ahead a half-point at 27¾. Now orders were rolling in, and most of them were to buy stock—not just a few hundred shares, but thousands. The price jumped and still found buyers. At the close, St. Joe stood at 30⅛, the New York Stock Exchange's third best performer of that day, with a gain of nearly 9 percent. The volume was the session's sixth largest, 604,000 shares.[1]

The trading currents in stocks often seem inexplicable. Flurries of buying and squalls of selling buffet prices for a short time but prove of fleeting significance. Today, money-managing institutions might be crowding into the market, clumsily bumping prices as they add to portfolios. Tomorrow, profit-takers might dominate. Or perhaps a rumor is making the rounds. The market's sages on March 10 settled on the last answer, a rumor. Less than a week earlier, another mining company, the giant Amax Inc., had gotten a takeover offer from Standard Oil of California. Though the public's buying frenzy in resource stocks had calmed, corporate interests were still prowling the market for wealth in the ground. If Amax could draw an offer, so might other companies.

Elsewhere, St. Joe's leap was causing consternation. At the Philadelphia Stock Exchange, traders who made markets in the issue's options were taking a beating. The March "call" options, which entitled the holder to buy the common stock at various prices, were due to expire in eleven days. As usual, professionals had been betting that nothing would happen in the meantime and had sold a lot of the calls short. Doing so seemed an odds-on strategy with the stock around $27. For the March $30 calls to be worth anything, St. Joe common would have to rise 11 percent in two weeks. If that didn't happen, the calls would die worthless, and the short-sellers would pocket their profits. On the previous Friday, the option had been quoted at 3/16 of a point, just 18¾ cents. But as the common stock suddenly broke above $30 on Tuesday, the call was transformed from a long-shot bet into sure money. In two days, its price jumped tenfold, to $2. Every time the short-sellers entered the market to limit their losses, they pushed the quote higher. More than 6,000 calls, each covering 100 shares of the common, traded in Philly on Tuesday. The pros' short sales in St. Joe were turning into a disaster.

There was consternation, too, in Montreal, at the headquarters of the Seagram Company Ltd. Security had been unprecedented at the Canadian distilling company's offices, but here was St. Joe stock leaping ahead in heavy trading. Could there have been a leak?

Edgar Bronfman, the burly-browed chairman of Seagram, was determined to pull off a natural-resources acquisition and hadn't made much secret of his thinking. The previous summer, Seagram had raised $2.3 billion by selling its U.S. oil and gas interests to the Sun Company, and in December Bronfman had tapped a group of banks for $3 billion in Eurodollar credits. The war chest was bulging. The only question was where Seagram would strike.

Bronfman had settled on St. Joe Minerals Corporation. It was a well-run company that had diversified beyond cyclical base metals and now boasted oil and gas stakes in Canada, the Gulf of Mexico, and the North Sea. On the earnings record and growth prospects, Bronfman viewed St. Joe as a solid investment. He had hired a cadre of financial advisers, lawyers, consultants, commercial banks, stock-forwarding agents, financial printers—the usual crowd surrounding a merger proposal—to lay the groundwork for his campaign.

One of Bronfman's advisers was an Italian-born investor well known to Wall Street's inner circles. Giuseppe B. Tome, fifty-one, had helped run the international business of two major U.S. brokers, E. F. Hutton Company and the Bache Group, and now was representing a third firm, Baird Patrick & Co., in Geneva. Though they had known each other less than a year, Bronfman and Tome were fast friends. The European was a card-carrying cosmopolite, well liked and regarded as an astute businessman. He had signed on to advise the distilling company on its foreign-currency positions and on European affairs. But soon Bronfman had given him investment control over $10 million in Seagram funds plus some of Bronfman's own money, which Tome deployed mainly in currencies and gold. "We see each other a great deal socially," Bronfman testified later, ". . . and we talk about a lot of things in a business nature."[2]

On the weekend before Seagram was scheduled to announce its offer for St. Joe, Tome and his wife flew from Switzerland to New York, where Bronfman was giving a dinner in Tome's honor. Sunday evening, Bronfman took the adviser into his confidence. That coming Thursday, Seagram would make a play for control of St. Joe Minerals Corporation. The distiller's bid, naturally, would offer a substantial premium over St. Joe's market price, to attract public investors and institutions to sell their stock.

Confidential information. Highly secret, all but priceless. Once word of Seagram's offer became public, the price of St. Joe stock and options would soar. Tome had three days before that happened—Monday through Wednesday—to make a killing. If such an opportunity fell into most investors' hands, they would have little chance to capitalize. Heavy buying just before a tender offer would invite government scrutiny. If an investor's broker didn't turn him in, officials at the stock exchanges would most likely run up a flag, and the Securities and Exchange Commission, the federal agency that oversees the securities markets, would force repayment of the stock gains. It was even possible that the Justice Department would launch a criminal prosecution. Not inviting odds.

Giuseppe Tome had an advantage. A financial sophisticate, he had done business for years through Swiss banks, known for their formidable secrecy about clients' dealings. When the time came to cash in on Edgar Bronfman's confidence, according to the government, Tome had just the mechanism to improve his chance of getting away with it.

Acting through Banca della Svizzera Italiana, based in Lugano, Tome jumped into the market, according to court records. On March 10 alone, the bank transmitted an order for 1,400 call options, controlling 140,000 shares. The buyer not only wanted the calls but seemed to want them badly. Within ninety minutes, the bank raised the price it was willing to pay.[3] Its broker, the Geneva branch of A. G. Becker Inc., managed to buy 1,055 of the contracts. Meanwhile the alarm was rising at Seagram headquarters. Officers couldn't believe that there could have been a leak, but watching St. Joe's price jump, they decided to act. Rather than wait until Thursday to announce the offer for St. Joe, Seagram unveiled its intentions on Wednesday. It would pay $45 a share for all of St. Joe's 45 million shares, an offer worth just over $2 billion.

The common stock soared. Tuesday it had closed at 30⅛. By Wednesday's finish, after 677,800 shares changed hands, the price was 51 percent higher, 45½. In Philadelphia, the action in the call options was explosive. The March 30s that had been worth 18¾ cents the previous Friday and $2 at Tuesday's close rocketed to $15.50—a gain of 8,267 percent in three trading days. Even for some of the best-capitalized market makers, the loss from being caught short was horrendous. But for Giuseppe Tome, the situation was rosier. As near as the SEC investigators could determine, Tome's inside information had netted him and his clients on the order of $3.4 million in two days. Their outlay was probably less than one-tenth of that sum.

Others profited as well. Ballooned by foreign orders, volume in the common stock on March 9 and 10 totaled more than 750,000 shares, the equivalent of more than two weeks' normal trading. If even a third of that activity came from buyers privy to Seagram's plans, illegal profits in the common stock alone totaled more than $4 million.

Giuseppe Tome was camping at New York's Pierre Hotel when he got wind from a Wall Street contact of the SEC's investigation. He caught a plane and a day later was safely back in Switzerland.[4] Although the SEC succeeded in freezing $2 million in assets of the Banca della Svizzera Italiana, most of the profits got away.

Among other losers in the raid were hundreds of private investors who weren't in on Seagram's plan and who sold their stock just before the price rose.*

## No Secrets on Wall Street

As spring approached in 1981, Edgar Bronfman's enthusiasm for natural-resource companies was shared by other corporate chieftains. Fluor outbid him for St. Joe. Standard Oil of California made a $4 billion pitch for Amax. Standard of Ohio bought Kennecott Corporation for $1.77 billion. Within months, industrialists with 100 percent hindsight to the previous decade's inflation would be bidding top dollar for Conoco (Seagram losing out again, to Du Pont), Marathon Oil, Santa Fe International, and Texasgulf. As word of the takeover schemes leaked from law offices, investment banking houses, consulting firms, and

*Seagram was technically a loser, as St. Joe rejected its $2.03 billion bid as "grossly inadequate" and succumbed to a $2.73 billion offer from Fluor Corporation. Shortly after, lead and zinc prices tumbled; presumably Seagram's disappointment was bearable.

brokers, well-wired stock traders seized the advantage. At times it seemed as though anyone who owned a telephone and had a friend at a big oil or mining company might get the early line on who was next in the takeover parade.

Seven months after the St. Joe affair, the secretive Swiss connection sheltered buyers who got the jump on another takeover. This time, the target was Santa Fe International Corporation, an oil-drilling and engineering company headquartered in California. Kuwait Petroleum Company, owned by the government of the Persian Gulf state, planned to buy Santa Fe for $2.5 billion cash—equivalent to $51 a share, more than twice the stock's market value. It was probably the worst-kept secret of the year. For more than a week, orders for Santa Fe stock and options poured in from odd corners—Switzerland, the Kuwait office of Merrill Lynch, a small Washington, D.C., brokerage house. From about $20 a share, Santa Fe stock jumped in five days to $24.75. On the Pacific Stock Exchange, one Santa Fe option leapt sixfold in a day, from 6¼ cents to 37½ cents.

By the time the buying binge was over, hundreds of thousands of shares had changed hands, two market makers on the Pacific Stock Exchange options floor were broke, and the Securities and Exchange Commission was digging into a case that produced charges against more defendants than any other insider affair.

The trail stretched coast to coast, to Kuwait, China, and the Alps. In all, more than a score of people were accused by the SEC of buying stock or options on inside information. Among them: Darius N. Keaton, a Santa Fe director who bought 10,000 shares through a Swiss bank account thirteen days before the takeover announcement. Keaton settled with the government a year later by agreeing to turn over his profit of $278,750. Ronald A. Feole, the general counsel of a Santa Fe subsidiary, allegedly telephoned his broker from China, where he was on a business trip for the company, and bought 20 call options eight days before the merger. Feole and five relatives and friends, according to the SEC, netted $787,000.

Then there were two Dallas-based vice-presidents of Santa Fe subsidiaries, who had been asked by the company to value its mineral reserves for use in merger talks; their profits totaled

$116,700. On down the line, a Seattle accountant, asked by a Santa Fe director to compute the tax liability from a sudden capital gain, guessed right and bought Santa Fe options; the government put his profits at $1.1 million. (He drew a jail term after spiriting his assets out of the country.)

In Washington, D.C., a lobbyist for Santa Fe got word of the deal and tipped a friend, who gave him $500 after allegedly cashing in to the tune of $250,000. Eight brokers at Bellamah, Neuhauser & Barrett Inc., a small firm at which the lobbyist's chum did business, snapped up options for 12½ cents a share, according to the SEC complaint, and made a one-week killing of half a million dollars. From Kuwait, a multimillionaire named Faisal al Massoud al Fuhaid bought 50,000 Santa Fe shares the month before the merger. From Switzerland, half a dozen other traders using secret bank accounts bought 35,000 common shares and 3,000 call options. Their profits may have topped $5 million.

To keep the money from fleeing the country, the SEC persuaded a federal judge to freeze assets held by a total of nine foreign and U.S. financial institutions allegedly used in the raid. Some of the names were familiar on Wall Street: Chase Manhattan, Citibank, Credit Suisse, Drexel Burnham Lambert, Lombard Odier & Co., Morgan Guaranty, Moseley Hallgarten Estabrook & Weeden Inc., Swiss American Securities, and Swiss Bank Corporation. About customers' identities, the Swiss banks were characteristically silent, until the SEC last year won disclosure in the Swiss courts. In all, the Santa Fe takeover gave insiders and their friends and relatives gains of perhaps $10 million, proving that the right information can be worth more money than most people earn in a lifetime.

## Thayer and Reed

Insider scandals ended the careers of two high-ranking officials in the Reagan Administration. Paul Thayer, the deputy defense secretary, resigned in 1984 after the SEC charged that he had tipped friends of pending takeover attempts he learned about while chairman of LTV Corporation and director of several other companies. Among the targets: Campbell Taggart Inc. and Grumman Corporation. A Dallas stockbroker, a couple of his customers, and their girlfriends allegedly profited by $1.9 million. Also among Thayer's alleged tippees was a former LTV receptionist who, as the SEC delicately put it, "maintained a private personal relationship" with her ex-boss. Thayer denied the charges and was fighting the SEC in court. One of his contentions: he hadn't profited personally from the tips.

By contrast, another Reagan Administration appointee made a bundle—and got to keep much of it—when Standard Oil of California tried to buy Amax Inc. Thomas C. Reed, a forty-seven-year-old San Rafael real estate developer, was well connected in California Republican circles, an asset that would soon help him win a national security post. But more important just then was a family connection: he was the son of Gordon W. Reed, a longtime director of Amax.

Within two days in March 1981, Tom Reed parlayed a $3,000 plunge in the options market into a profit of some $427,000. He did it by purchasing 500 contracts that gave him the right to buy 50,000 Amax common shares at $50 each. To a casual onlooker, Reed's chance of making money must have seemed slim. The $50 exercise price was a long yard above Amax's latest quote on the New York Stock Exchange, 38⅞. The options were valid only until March 21, after which they would become waste paper. For Reed to make out—indeed, for him not to lose his entire $3,000—something had to propel Amax stock ahead 29 percent in less than three weeks.

What an outsider couldn't know—but Reed did, according to the SEC—was that a company that already owned 20 percent of Amax wanted to buy the rest. On March 5, trading was halted and Amax announced that it had gotten a takeover offer worth $4 billion from Standard Oil Company of California. The price was equivalent to about $78.50 a share—twice the market value. Thomas Reed's options, worth 6¼ cents each the day before, overnight became worth $9. His profit was about 14,100 percent.

For several days, Reed's identity as buyer remained shrouded. But the heavy volume in the calls and the too-lucky timing were a tip-off that someone had known too much. The bruised seller, a prominent Chicago firm, filed suit alleging insider trading violations. The American Stock Exchange, where the options were purchased, launched an investigation. And so did Dean Witter Reynolds, the brokerage firm that put through the orders. Soon Reed's name surfaced.

When a director's son loads up on calls just before a takeover, it strains everybody's belief in coincidence. The pattern of Reed's buying—bad on the surface—looked worse as details emerged. It turned out that SoCal and Amax had been talking for months and that Reed had been buying calls during much of the time. He picked up his first 500, according to the Securities and Exchange Commission, in January and February 1981 for $40,000. On January 26, SoCal had made a merger proposal, which Amax's chairman relayed on February 5 to the board of directors, including Gordon Reed. The following Sunday and Monday, Tom Reed visited his father in Greenwich, Connecticut. During the visit, the SEC alleged, the Reeds discussed SoCal and Amax. The elder Reed opposed the oil company's expanding its role.

Not much happened for a month except that the value of Tom Reed's 500 calls sank as their expiration date neared and Amax common's price slid from the 40s into the 30s. By March 2, the calls had lost 90 percent of their value. But over the next couple of days, Tom Reed chatted several times with his father, according to telephone records subpoenaed by the SEC, including two calls to Barbados on the morning of March 4, while the senior Reed was vacationing. Three minutes after the third talk with his father, Thomas Reed called his broker in San Rafael and ordered him to buy 500 more Amax calls. The next day, SoCal's bid became public.

Coincidence? The SEC staff decided there was too much coincidence. In its complaint, the commission alleged that Tom Reed had obtained inside information "directly or indirectly from persons associated with Amax."

It wasn't entirely a family affair. Three hours after Reed's purchase, an old college chum and business associate, Frank M. Woods, joined the act. Woods, president of a Reed company, bought 50 Amax calls, which turned him a quick $48,971 profit. Also buying were Reed's broker at Dean Witter, the broker's office manager, several of their colleagues, and even two wire operators.[5] It seemed they recognized smart money.

That December, both Reed and Woods settled with the Securities and Exchange Commission. They agreed to give back their profits—$427,000 in Reed's case—and not to violate the securities laws in the future. Four weeks later, Tom Reed was hired as a temporary consultant by President Reagan's National Security Adviser, William Clark. His job was to advise on MX missile deployment, and he stood in waiting, according to Washington gossip, to take over as head of the National Security Council if his friend Clark got promoted.

A year later, however, Reed's career at the NSC landed on the rocks. A magazine published by a Washington political lobby revived the issue of his insider culpability. In a long article based on SEC files, *Common Cause* charged that Reed had gotten a sweetheart deal from the regulators. For one thing, the SEC didn't try to force Reed to return the profits from the calls he bought in January and February. Only his March purchase was challenged. And while it's normal for a defendant settling with the SEC to agree to neither admit nor deny the charges—a sort of "I won't say whether I've violated the law this time, but I promise not to violate it in the future"—Reed wasn't so restrained; in public statements, he denied the allegations even as he turned over his profits.[6] A long adaptation of the article appeared in *The Washington Post,* and CBS Television shelved a *60 Minutes* segment it had planned for that weekend to take a close look at the Thomas C. Reed affair. Congress demanded explanations—an insider-trading culprit on the National Security staff?—the SEC denied soft-pedaling the case of a President's man, and critics demanded Reed's ouster. Some of them hadn't much liked the advice he was giving Reagan, anyway. *Common Cause* pictured Reed with missiles thrusting from an open cranium and a ticker tape spilling from one eye. Reed resigned.

There's an ironical footnote to all this. By early 1983, shareholders in Amax probably didn't care much about Reed's profiteering or his stand on the MX. True, the people who had sold him the options—and suffered big losses—were still pushing their claims of foul play in court. But a number of Amax shareholders felt they had a bigger beef with the company's board of directors. Unlike the boards of St. Joe and Santa Fe, which yielded to offers promising handsome profits to their public shareholders, the directors of Amax had balked.

SoCal's bid, worth twice the market price, was inadequate, announced French-born chairman Pierre Gousseland. Caught short by the rebuff, SoCal dithered awhile and then backed off. There were rumors of other suitors waiting in the wings, but none stepped forward, and as a recession took hold, Amax's price began a long slide. For investors, the bottom line was this: Thomas Reed's raid cost them less than half a million, by the SEC's count. As Amax common slipped to $17.50 a share, the board's spurning of SoCal cost its shareholders almost 8,000 times as much: $3.2 billion.

## Bad News Is Old News

Trading abuses in mergers often involve an "outsider" like Tom Reed—a person who isn't an officer, a director, or a major shareholder but gets wind of inside information. By far, most of the cases brought by the SEC fall into this category. That's not necessarily because corporate insiders are more honest. Rather, perhaps, it's because they're more careful, buying through relatives' accounts or behind other cover.[7] Many of their transgressions, moreover, fall into a "gray" area where enforcement is difficult. This is true whether insiders buy before good news or sell before bad news ("before the rain," in the jargon of the Street). The SEC rarely intervenes, and shareholders must fend for themselves.

A few weeks before Christmas 1982, there was a particularly garish episode of insiders' selling on the eve of bad tidings. Warner Communications Inc., a $4-billion-a-year entertainment conglomerate, had been one of the New York Stock Exchange's brighter stars. Movies, recordings, and, more recently, home video games had turned Warner into a growth company, and since 1974 its stock had risen thirtyfold. Thanks to its Atari Inc. electronics division, Warner was booking huge profit margins selling Pac-Man games and computers. Given the company's jump on the competition, Wall Street analysts who talked with management expected Warner to earn more than $5 a share in 1982 and $6.75 the next year. By that measure, with the stock market rising and investors turning more optimistic, Warner shares trading in the high 50s hardly looked overpriced.

Yet more than a dozen executives of the company, including two top officers in the Atari unit, had been selling stock.

If investors knew it, they paid little heed. From the stock's low of $34 in early September, buyers in three months drove the quote up 75 percent. One of Warner's biggest fans—and later among its bitterest critics—was analyst Lee Isgur of Paine Webber Mitchell Hutchins. Word on Wall Street had Isgur "staking his considerable reputation" on Warner's performance and looking for the company to earn $7 a share in 1983.[8] That would have been twice its profits of two years earlier, but Isgur was confident. "All the evidence we have," he said, "continues to indicate strong domestic sales for Atari . . . hardware for at least two more years and cartridge sales growth well beyond that time."

Bulls had grown adept at shrugging off doubts about the company. Isgur dismissed the specter of competition, arguing that the electronic-games market offered plenty of room for everybody. More basic questions about Warner management's integrity also got short shrift. Analysts loved Warner's style. Chairman Steven Ross, a tall, silver-haired millionaire in his mid-fifties, had built the company in twenty years from a small string of funeral parlors (his father-in-law's business) into a high-profile showbiz group. By far his greatest coup appeared to have been the 1976 purchase of Atari for $28 million—a move that five years later was bringing Warner a quarter of its annual sales and $145 million in profits. Befitting a winner, Ross lived well—Park Avenue apartment, East Hampton waterfront home—and enjoyed hobnobbing with his Hollywood friends Frank Sinatra and Steven Spielberg. He could afford luxury on one of corporate America's fattest paychecks, approaching $3.7 million in 1982.[9]

But Ross's image wasn't all glamour. The latest cloud, in November 1982, was a federal-court trial in Manhattan that was creating ugly headlines. Solomon Weiss, Warner's assistant treasurer, was answering bribery charges stemming from a scheme to have Warner Communications buy stock in a Westchester theater firm linked by federal prosecutors to organized crime. Already two former Warner executives had been found guilty and were testifying against Weiss, whose legal fees were being paid by the company he stood accused of betraying. Perhaps the most alarming thing wasn't that scandal had reached so close to the top of Warner's executive heap but that the federal prosecutor was pointing his finger still higher. The real culprit in the bribery scheme and slush fund, said Assistant U.S. Attorney Nick Akerman, was Warner chairman Steve Ross.

On Monday, November 29, after a jury convicted Weiss of accepting $170,000 in bribes, Warner stock briefly touched its high for that winter—59⅝—before losing 2¼ points on 459,000 shares. But a little thing like an officer's conviction didn't discourage investors for long. The next day Warner snapped back to 59½ on twice the prior day's volume. To many Warner fans, a slush fund apparently fit the image of go-getter management.

But then the stock sold off again. It fell 3⅛ on Wednesday, ⅜ on Thursday, and 1⅝ on Friday. After a brief rally the following Monday, the shares plunged again on Tuesday and early Wednesday. The selling pace was rising, and by midafternoon on Wednesday, December 8, about a million shares had crossed on the New York Stock Exchange. That was when the bad news struck. The company announced that competition was cutting deeply into sales and profits at Atari, which had provided more than 60 percent of Warner's 1981 income. Eight minutes after the revelation crossed the tape, a flood of sell orders swamped the specialist and trading was halted. But in the over-the-counter market that afternoon, Warner shares plunged to $40. And when trading resumed late the next day on the New York Exchange, the quote sheared to 35⅛. That represented a 32 percent loss in the company's market value in little more than twenty-four hours.

Not known for several weeks were the heavy stock sales by corporate insiders—more than $40 million worth—that had preceded the disclosure. Securities analysts meeting with Warner executives on December 13 asked about rumors that insiders had been selling. An officer was quoted as saying that to his knowledge there had been no significant insider trades. A crestfallen Lee Isgur complained later, "Warner deliberately lied. . . . I will never again trust the people who now run Warner."[10] It was Isgur's second sandbagging by management; he said he had talked to a Warner executive on December 7 who confirmed that 1982 earnings should top $5 a share. The next day, the company admitted that Atari was short-circuiting.

Perhaps it was a matter of definition of what constituted "significant" sales. The executive quoted was Warner's co-chief operating officer, Emanuel Gerard. A month before the discussion with analysts, Gerard sold 2,000 shares at $57, a couple of points shy of the top. Between March and July, he had sold 71,000 shares, moves a company spokesman said were for tax reasons.[11] In all, his selling brought him $3,624,310.

Heavy sales by corporate insiders aren't always cause for alarm. Executives who have been well rewarded with options often cash in part of their holdings, especially when stock prices are rising. Seldom does disastrous news befall their companies soon afterward. But when bad news does follow, angry public shareholders, Wall Street analysts, and government regulators look back on those timely sales and ask: "What did they know and when did they know it?"

Between August and November, as Warner's price nearly doubled, at least ten officers sold hundreds of thousands of shares. The biggest blocks, $29 million worth, were disposed of by the company's chairman, Steve Ross. But Ross had announced the previous April that he intended to lighten up on Warner stock for tax planning.

The timing of sales by two other executives, however, was harder to explain—though a company spokesman once more trotted out "tax reasons" in a game effort. The sellers were Raymond E. Kasser, the chairman of Atari, and Dennis D. Groth, executive vice-president. Kasser came closest to the wire, dumping 5,000 shares at 2:41 p.m. on December 8, twenty-three minutes before Warner let the bomb drop. The Atari chief, who received 52⅝ per share, had seen all the gloomy numbers, according to an SEC complaint filed a year later. He knew that sales had stalled and profits were in a tailspin.[12] When the dismal news hit the wire, according to a Warner spokesman, Kasser tried to call back his sale, but it was too late. Kasser settled with the SEC, accepting an injunction without admitting or denying guilt but agreeing to pay $81,875 to the investors who had bought his shares.

Groth allegedly got an early glimpse of Atari's troubles at a Chicago trade show. In his first day at the show, where Atari products won a chilly reception, he sold 10,900 Warner warrants on the American Stock Exchange for about $208,000. Two days later, according to the SEC complaint, Groth phoned from Chicago to his broker in Palo Alto, California, directing the sale of 5,000 shares of common. The stock went across the NYSE tape at $58. Less than two weeks after that, as disappointing sales figures arrived, he let loose 3,800 more shares at 58¼ and 2,576 shares at 58⅜. In three weeks, Atari's executive vice-president had unloaded more than $870,000 worth of stock and warrants.[13] Settlement with the SEC eighteen months later cost him $270,000. Although Kasser and Groth were the only Warner-Atari executives named by the SEC in complaints, a private class-action suit by shareholders accused chairman Steven Ross and other officers of having issued glowing reports despite signs of Atari's malaise. Part of the purpose, according to the suit, was to inflate the stock price so that insiders could unload.[14]

The depth of Atari's problems emerged slowly. In the annual letter to shareholders in early 1983, Ross warned that the new year's profits would fall "far short" of 1982's. That assessment turned out to be optimistic. The stock broke below $20, and in 1983 Warner lost $417 million. That was more money than it had earned the year before.

There was a sense of *déjà vu* in these travails. Allegations that executives "sold before the rain" had struck Franklin Mint, a Pennsylvania "collectibles" marketer that Warner bought in 1981. The SEC said Franklin executives had learned from confidential internal reports in 1976 that the company faced slower earnings growth. Rather than disclose the bad tidings, Franklin's chairman, president, and two other executives sold thousands of shares of stock—and only later announced the gloomy outlook. The SEC figured the insiders garnered unfair profits of $283,738.

The Franklin case highlighted officers' ability to keep a lid on bad news. Franklin allegedly padded sales and earnings for the final part of 1976 by counting shipments that didn't go out until 1977. If year-end reports had reflected actual business trends, the public might have smelled the trouble sooner and sold its own stock—just the thing insiders don't want.

For investors, there's faint consolation in the hope that the SEC might eventually catch up with wayward insiders (it took five years in the Franklin case). But this is usually the only consolation. Chances that an individual will recoup losses are faint. A handful of incidents from recent years attests to the pervasiveness of insider abuses.

## Rogue's Gallery

**Beating the Tender.** When a company wants to buy some of its own stock, it may announce a tender offer, inviting outsiders to sell their shares to the company at a price above the market. That's bullish news. When it gets out, the market quote usually jumps toward the tender price. Sedco Inc., an offshore-oil-drilling contractor, decided to make a tender offer and told an assistant treasurer to update its financial forecasts. On February 17, 1982, just hours before the announcement, the executive bought 1,200 shares of Sedco. His profit a day later: $5,850.

**Lawyer's Privilege.** For thirty-one months, according to federal sleuths, Kenneth Rubinstein, a young lawyer with a New York law firm (Fried, Frank, Harris, Shriver & Jacobson) specializing in mergers, fattened his income on the side by buying shares of takeover targets. Among them: Brookwood Health Services Inc., Cenco Inc., Ludlow Corporation, Texasgulf Inc. Profits allegedly totaled $620,000.

**Going Private.** The week before Metromedia Inc. management unveiled its plan to take the company private in December 1983, the price rose on volume eight times the preceding weeks' pace. As secret talks on a leveraged buyout ripened at National Can Corporation in January 1984, the stock tacked on 7 points.

**Thanks, Son.** Adrian Antoniu, a thirty-four-year-old Romanian émigré, was a merger specialist for two top-ranked investment banking firms, Morgan Stanley & Co. and Kuhn Loeb Inc. When he was accused in 1981 of having peddled secret takeover information for years to an international ring of traders, some

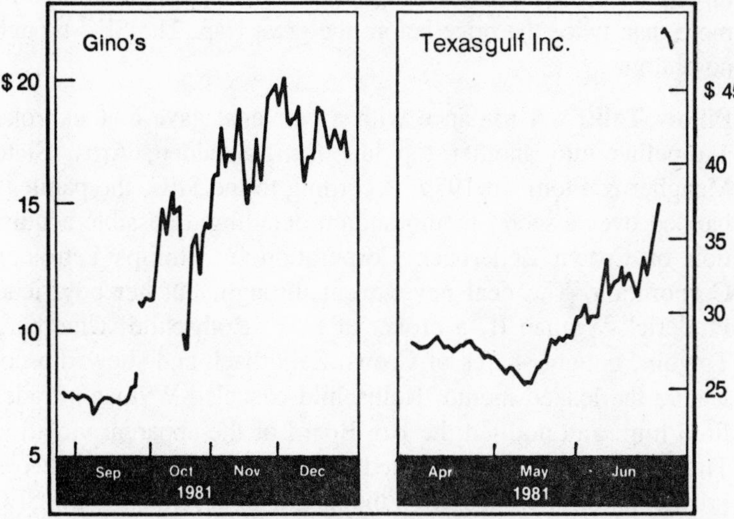


**Figure 1. Poorly kept secrets. Texasgulf Inc. rose 50 percent in the seven weeks before a tender offer in 1981. Gino's leaped 25 percent hours before an announcement.**

people might have thought he just wanted to finance his own high living. But no. His widowed mother had gotten into debt, his lawyer pleaded, and Adrian needed money to help her out.

**Stoolie.** Four New York City policemen were charged in 1983 with profiteering from inside dope on tender offers. Their source: a leak at another prominent New York law firm. Among the deals were Mobil Corporation's unsuccessful pass at Marathon Oil Company in 1981 and Allied Stores Corporation's acquisition that same year of Garfinckel, Brooks Brothers, Miller & Rhoades Inc. Other defendants included several relatives of one police officer, a New York lawyer, and a former president of a Teamster's local.

**Private Feast.** In September 1981, shares of a small fast-food chain, Gino's Inc., leaped 25 percent one morning on the New York Stock Exchange. When the exchange asked management if something was happening at the firm, the company confirmed that it had been "approached" about a possible merger. The suitor turned out to be Marriott Corporation, which bought Gino's for more than twice the price before the great leap. The SEC brought no charges.

**Pillow Talk.** A romance with a paralegal gave a stockbroker a pipeline into another top law firm, Skadden, Arps, Slate, Meagher & Flom. In 1979, according to the SEC, the paralegal handed over a secret memorandum detailing a possible acquisition of Crown Zellerbach Corporation by Phillips Petroleum Corporation. The deal never went through, but her boyfriend, Frederick Wyman II, a broker at L. F. Rothschild, Unterberg, Towbin, bought shares of Crown Zellerbach and showed a colleague the leaked memo. Rothschild canceled Wyman's trades, fired him, and notified the Big Board of the apparent violation. The leaks, however, continued. Wyman's father, a well-heeled private investor, cashed in on the next one, according to the SEC. Word came that Blue Bell Inc., a Southern apparel company, was planning a tender offer for Jantzen Inc. The senior Wyman bought 14,900 Jantzen shares in November 1979, and on December 5, Blue Bell launched its takeover campaign. Wyman's profit: $99,168.

Time and again, Wall Street law firms and investment banking houses have had their secrecy breached as inside information proved too valuable to contain. Even Morgan Stanley's famous combination-lock wastebaskets haven't kept their secrets. Traders have been caught when they were flagrantly careless, but those employing a bit of discretion have escaped detection for years.

Consider the case of Adrian Antoniu, the fellow who did it for Mom. He and a former Morgan Stanley colleague, E. Jacques Courtois, Jr., were charged in early 1981 with leaking information on seventeen takeovers from 1974 to 1978. The two merger specialists, who had been classmates at Harvard Business School, collected a percentage of the profits as three coconspirators, operating through bank accounts in Switzerland, Luxembourg, and the Caribbean, bought the shares of takeover targets, including Anaconda, Marshall Field, Occidental Petroleum, and Seven-Up. The heavy buying tripped alarms, and eventually investigators discovered that the companies that were being bought were clients of Morgan Stanley and Kuhn Loeb. But because Antoniu and Courtois didn't trade for themselves, it took years to uncover the scheme. By the time the government brought charges, Antoniu had decamped to Italy, Courtois to Bogotá, Colombia.

Or consider Carlo M. Florentino's profitable career as a Wall Street lawyer. Again, a blue-chip firm (Wachtell, Lipton, Rosen & Katz) noted for its expertise in the takeover game provided an unwitting base of operations. Between 1977 and 1981, according to the government, Florentino cashed in on nine takeover bids, among them NCR's pass at Applied Digital Data Systems, Allied Corporation's acquisition of Fisher Scientific Company, and a French firm's takeover of Texasgulf Inc. He also was accused of picking up a stake in Curtiss-Wright Corporation, knowing the firm planned a tender offer for its own stock. When Florentino came before a federal judge in October 1982, the sentence was one year in jail—suspended. He had agreed to return $450,000 in profits, and psychiatric reports found an emotional disorder behind his investments. Less than a year later, a typist at the same firm was charged with a five-year string of illegal trades involving twenty-nine companies and $2.7 million in profits. And so it goes.

We've been looking at high-profile, big-money scams—the kind that justify regulators' attention. People on the inside track who are less flamboyant and less greedy get away with using their information to outtrade the public. Word passes on a golf course, and a friend buys. An executive sells 600 shares two weeks before poor earnings and a regulator shrugs: "I wish I saw more shares."[15] A money manager gets early word from a broker that a name to reckon with, Warren Buffett, has bought more R. J. Reynolds. A broker sniffs out a bullish magazine article in the works and alerts friends. The typical use of inside information is a small, valuable confidence. "It looks like we're going to land a pretty good spare-parts contract." "Have you heard my brother-in-law's outfit isn't paying its bills?" "Old man Sikes is thinking about selling out."

Can the SEC keep a lid on such stuff?

It's folly for the public to assume so. The stakes are too high for players to follow silly old rules.

# TWO
# *The SEC's Hopeless War*

Wall Streeters have long recognized that some of the best money is made by removing it from the pockets of less astute traders. At the turn of the century, the game knew few bounds. Pools run by professional traders bid up the prices of stocks, aided by glowing business reports issued by company insiders, and when the gullible public was lured into buying, the manipulators unloaded. Jesse Livermore, the boyish veteran of Boston's bucket shops, was famed for this sort of "marketing" to the public of Mammoth Oil, Piggly Wiggly, Tobacco Products, and other shares on behalf of prosperous clients. In the same league was Mike Meehan, whose brilliant management of a Radio Corporation pool added $15 million to the wealth of such gentry as auto magnate Walter P. Chrysler, steel tycoon Charles M. Schwab, and Mrs. David Sarnoff, wife of Radio's chairman.[1] "The way to sell stocks to the public," declared James R. Keene, an expatriate Englishman who knew his business, "is to manipulate them to the highest point possible, then sell them on the way down." Some of Keene's fellows and later manipulators might have quibbled with his details; Jesse Livermore insisted on selling into a rising market. But few would have disputed the basic theme. The public lived to be skinned.

More finesse is employed today, but selling pumped-up stock for insiders is still part of the broker's bread and butter.

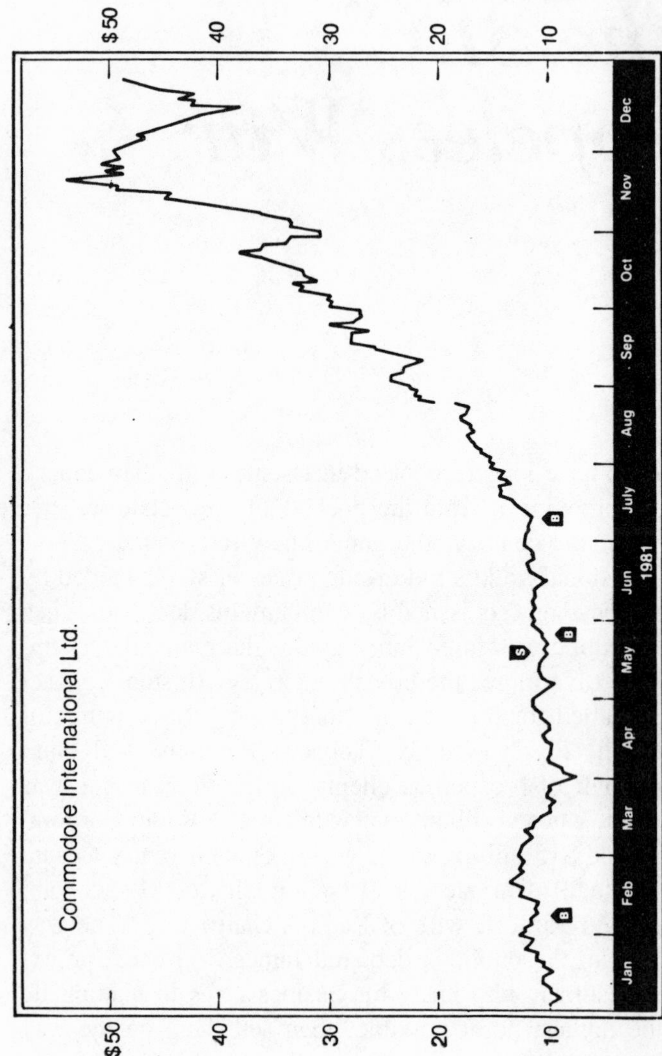


**Figure 1. A director's buying in Commodore International in 1980 preceded a fast quintupling of the stock. From this temporary peak, the computer maker's shares more than tripled again.**

As is evident from the Radio pool, the profiteers weren't low-bred scroungers. Rather they were among the pillars of Wall Street. An outstanding example of their style was the debut in 1901 of United States Steel Corporation, the creation of Pierpont Morgan. Lured by booming business, record earnings, and generous dividends, the public chased after the newly issued stock even as insiders, knowing the good times couldn't last, sold heavily. When business fell off, Steel cut and then suspended its dividend. The public turned bitterly pessimistic, the share price crashed, and Morgan interests reclaimed stock at a fraction of the old prices. "From the standpoint of the great manipulators," judged a contemporary market watcher named Thomas Gibson, "it was beautifully done."[2] Reporting record earnings and raising dividends were actions for which the Morgan crowd could never be called to account. The reports were genuine. But the public, eyes fixed on the present bounty, failed to anticipate the future correction. The Morgan syndicate "knew what the effects of their actions would be and acted accordingly," Gibson observed.

Leaving little to chance, the Steel crowd helped its scheme with devices that would be illegal today, at least in their boldest form. To promote the shares, the group hired Jim Keene, who stirred up interest by crisscrossing massive blocks on the New York Stock Exchange. As an unwary public saw this heavy trading and began bidding, the shares jumped from $24 to $55. Keene meanwhile unloaded large amounts of syndicate stock. Each day, according to a floor broker who joined the sport, the pool would "sell 100,000 shares to the public and buy back only 10,000."[3] All told, trading profits and management fees netted the Morgan syndicate more than $57 million, and at the bottom, three years later, Steel sold for $8.86 a share.

So prevalent was this sort of gentlemen's piracy that a popular investment book in the 1920s devoted four of its first five chapters to the subject of manipulation, which typically involved the collusion of insiders. Counseled the authors: "Manipulation need have no terrors for the intelligent speculator who will take the trouble to learn its ways: he should in fact profit. . . ."[4] Newspapers flashed rumors of campaigns to bull this or that security. The public loved pools, John Brooks notes, because "it thought it could turn them to personal advantage; someone else would be the sucker. Bona fide market letters . . . would confide to ordinary brokerage-house customers that the inside information was that General Motors or Radio was to be 'taken in hand' at 2 p.m. The customers . . . would rush to climb aboard in hopes of taking a short ride to profit with the big money."[5] Pool operators clearly had their work made easier by this enthusiasm. No need to tease the suckers in subtly; they came running.

## INSIDERS AID MANIPULATION

The most successful schemes enjoyed the cooperation of the target companies' officers and directors. As early as 1837, when a clique of brokers set out to break the notorious short-seller Jacob Little by cornering the stock of the Erie Railroad, directors of the Erie were among the group bidding the price higher.[6]

When politicians were let in on a deal, they proved as untrustworthy as financiers. In expanding the New York and Harlem Railroad, Cornelius Vanderbilt acted as any astute industrialist of the 1860s would have done. He needed a franchise from the New York City Common Council to extend track into lower Manhattan. So he cut the council and Boss Tweed of Tammany Hall in on his accumulation of Harlem stock. Once the franchise was granted, all the insiders stood to profit handsomely. But Vanderbilt's archrival, a religious philanthropist and financial cutthroat named Daniel Drew, saw a different path to fortune. With Tweed's help, Drew mounted a bear raid on the Harlem. Tweed had the Common Council repeal the Vanderbilt franchise, while Drew and the politicians sold Harlem short, hoping to ride it from $100 down to $50. To crush the scheme, Vanderbilt bought every share of Harlem offered and forced the short-sellers to settle on harsh terms.[7] The titans' collision whipsawed share prices, ruining smaller traders caught on the wrong side of the swings.

In the late 1860s, Vanderbilt and Drew clashed again. When Vanderbilt set out to wrest away Drew's control of the Erie Railroad, the battle marked only the latest episode of raids and insider manipulations that earned the Erie the soubriquet "the Scarlet Woman of Wall Street." As a director of the Erie, "Uncle Daniel" ruled the rail line and the stock price in league with two notorious allies, Jim Fisk and Jay Gould, authors of a later campaign to corner gold. When Vanderbilt began buying Erie stock, Drew and his sidekicks sold short massive amounts—notwithstanding Drew's role as an Erie director, supposedly answerable for the welfare of the company and its investors. Prices swung 20 points in a day. When Vanderbilt seemed about to triumph, the Drew faction got the Erie board to vote a huge issue of new convertible bonds—which Drew promptly swapped for stock to be dumped on Vanderbilt. Not even Vanderbilt's fortune could absorb all the watered shares.* To restrain the mutual bloodletting, the four financiers eventually struck a truce.[8] Commented a chronicler sixty years later:

> Vanderbilt, Drew, Gould and the rest recognized few of the present-day rules. Judges, legislatures, officials, even governments were legitimate allies. Bribery, perjury and forgery were not uncommon tools. And yet the men, in private life, were by no means rogues. Vanderbilt did not feel his Wall Street life inconsistent with his firm ideas of fair play and sportsmanship; Drew did not think that religious endeavor precluded his right to legitimate stealing; nor did Gould feel that a ruthlessness below Canal Street was unbecoming in a man exceptionally gentle and kind in his family life. It was a game, and there was never a time when the game was more merciless or cruel.[9]

Recognizing that coattail riders were eager to profit from their market operations, both Drew and Gould were famed for dropping "poisoned tips" on their plans. Jay Gould, according to one account, was approached by the pastor of a wealthy church for investment advice. Gould not only touted Pacific Mail but also promised the preacher that if the speculation failed, Gould would make up his losses. The trade turned into a disaster, but Gould was as good as his word. He paid the preacher for his

*A similar tactic, employing preferred stock, was adopted in the 1980s by companies trying to discourage takeovers.

loss. When the churchman asked about the massive losses of his parishioners, to whom he had passed along the tip, Gould is said to have replied, "They were the people I was after."

That the manipulators mistrusted one another was a product of expensive lessons. The more participants in a pool, the more chance of a traitor making his fortune by selling out his fellows. Jim Keene and a consortium that included former President Grover Cleveland were double-crossed in the 1890s when they teamed up with insiders in buying shares of the Distilling & Cattle Feeding Company. Two members of the pool, Nelson Morris and J. B. Greenhut, turned on their associates and, instead of buying Distilling to support the price, dumped stock on the Keene group. As the price sank, Morris and Greenhut reaped a profit of $1.5 million. Greenhut, as president of Distilling, was trading not only against his confederates but also against the public shareholders in his company.

A year and a half later, Morris and Greenhut once again put together a pool to bull Distilling, and once again Keene and his friends came in. Old habits die hard when they're profitable; Morris and Greenhut again began to sell stock into the pool. Alert to double-dealing, Keene wired the two, crying treachery, and in two days threw 200,000 shares onto the market. To prove their good faith, Morris and Greenhut bought all the stock offered and discovered only later that their first sin hadn't been forgiven: Keene and his associates had sold them 100,000 shares short. Two of Keene's group, who between them netted $1.7 million at the expense of Morris and Greenhut, also were insiders at Distilling, a second vice-president and a director.[10] Given the insiders' mutual backstabbing, it was hardly surprising when in 1895 the company entered receivership.

By these operators' standards, the routine insider abuse of trading on advance knowledge of earnings and dividends was the equivalent of good behavior.

Even short of such mischief, it was easy to outtrade the public. Financial disclosure by corporations was seldom elaborate unless to further an insider campaign in a stock. In 1899, *The Wall Street Journal* complained that "in 95 cases out of 100 the stockholder in an industrial company is obliged to take the word of the managers—with all that that implies—for the company's net earnings."[11] The legality of insiders' using their knowledge for trading profits was a murky issue. But of sixteen court cases decided from the mid-1800s through 1909, the outcome in eleven favored the insiders. "Fraud and 'active or intentional' concealment of information were illegal," writes a biographer of Bernard Baruch, "but directors and other insiders could generally trade as they liked with the knowledge uniquely at their disposal."[12] A critic vented his indignation at the state of affairs in the *Michigan Law Review* in 1910: "That a director may take advantage of his position to secure the profits that all have won, offends the moral sense; no shareholder expects to be so treated by the directors he selects; . . . that the law yet allows [a director] to do this, does more to discourage legitimate investment in corporate shares than almost anything else. . . ."[13] As late as 1923, another writer examining legal precedent found little to support the claim that insiders' trading should be limited by a fiduciary responsibility to public stockholders.[14] Even Baruch, later confidant of presidents, found nothing amiss in trading on inside information.

## THE END OF THE PARTY

As prices broke in the fall of 1929, rumors swept the financial district that the great bear himself, Jesse Livermore, was on the prowl, orchestrating selling campaigns against stocks. Livermore issued a statement denying any scheme to drive down prices—he wasn't involved in one, he said, and he didn't know of anyone else who was. Whether the bogeyman of the bulls was believed in those panic-filled days is debatable. Anyone who credited the denial, however, might have found more cause for alarm: prices were plunging not because of manipulation but of their own weight.

The Crash marked the end of much in America, including, among symbolic footnotes, Livermore's career as a market force. Also ended, or at least restrained, were Wall Street's days of legal freebooting. High Barbary below Canal Street had captured imaginations when prices were soaring. But when the receding tide swept away paper fortunes from the common folks on Main Street, they demanded public hangings. A few rascals were jailed. Another basked in luxury at a suburban asylum safe from pursuit. Many others suffered the ultimate humiliation of going broke.

With the New Deal, national regulation came to the securities markets. Two pieces of reform legislation—the Securities Act of 1933 and the Securities Exchange Act of 1934—outlawed much of the high-spirited pillage, including pools, market manipulation, and a variety of frauds. Companies hoping to sell securities or to have them listed on an exchange were forced to provide financial details so that investors could judge the issues' worth. A syndicate of financiers still could distribute watered stock to the public, but it had to disclose the soggy numbers.* Set up to write and enforce rules of fair play was a new agency, the Securities and Exchange Commission, presided over by a veteran stock manipulator named Joseph Kennedy, father of a future President, who had enjoyed a last game with the shares of Libbey-Owens-Ford before turning to public service.

Corporate insiders suffered other setbacks. Under the Securities Exchange Act, they were forced to forfeit any profits they made on their firms' stocks through short-term trades. That largely nulled the incentive for such insider stock-kiting as old Henry Havemeyer regularly staged in American Sugar.

But the problem remained of insiders' taking unfair advantage of their knowledge about their companies' prospects—or passing information along to friends who took advantage. Neither the 1933 nor the 1934 act directly outlawed such practices. Nor, really, did a new rule that the Securities and Exchange Commission adopted in 1942. At least that wasn't the initial impact of Rule 10b–5. The edict had grown out of a section of the 1934 act dealing with stock fraud and broker deception, and for years, according to legal scholar Henry G. Manne, Rule 10b–5 was used mainly in disciplining brokers.[15]

*Subsequent generations of new-issue promoters have not found this a great impediment.

## CURBING THE INSIDERS

Let's look at how the rules on insider trading developed. An investor who understands their objectives—and failings—will have a better idea of the perils encountered in today's stock market.

In 1951 there was an important decision extending the antifraud principle to insiders trading on nonpublic information. In *Speed* v. *Transamerica Corporation,* a federal judge ruled: "It is unlawful for an insider, such as a majority stockholder, to purchase the stock of minority stockholders without disclosing material facts affecting the value of the stock, known to the majority stockholder by virtue of his inside position but not known to the selling minority stockholders. . . ."[16]

This was new ground. Transamerica, the controlling shareholder, had devised a liquidation plan to capitalize on another company's greatly undervalued tobacco inventory. When it offered to buy out that firm's minority holders, it kept the liquidation plan to itself.[17] The court found that this silence on a material fact made Transamerica's other statements misleading—a case of telling part of a story but leaving out the punchline. That, the judge said, violated 10b-5 subsection (b).*

*When Congress and the SEC drafted their rules, grace wasn't high on the agenda. Section 10(b) of the Exchange Act states:

> It shall be unlawful for any person, directly or indirectly, by the use of any means or instrumentality of interstate commerce or of the mails, or of any facility of any national securities exchange
>
> . . .
>
> (b) To use or employ, in connection with the purchase or sale of any security registered on a national securities exchange or any security not so registered, any manipulative or deceptive device or contrivance in contravention of such rules and regulations as the Commission may prescribe as necessary or appropriate in the public interest or for the protection of investors.

Rule 10b-5, adopted under that provision, states:

> It shall be unlawful for any person, directly or indirectly, by the use of any means or instrumentality of interstate commerce, or of the mails, or of any facility of any national securities exchange,
>
> (a) to employ any device, scheme, or artifice to defraud,
>
> (b) to make any untrue statement of a material fact or to omit to state a material fact necessary in order to make the statements made, in the

Another legal benchmark was set in 1961, when the SEC decided that a director of Curtiss-Wright Company had violated Rule 10b-5 after the company's board voted to cut the dividend. The director, an official at the New York broker Cady, Roberts & Co., quickly phoned the word to his firm, which sold stock—some of it short—before news of the dividend cut reached the stock exchange. The phone call constituted illegal tipping, according to the SEC. The Cady, Roberts ruling established the agency's claim that persons with a "special relationship" giving them access to material inside information on a company must disclose the information or refrain from trading the stock.[18]

Four years later, the government brought a major insider-trading prosecution, the Texas Gulf Sulphur case, and won a landmark decision. The implications of the Texas Gulf ruling, handed down by a federal appeals court in 1968, were vague in many respects. But one thing was clear: suddenly, trading that had been taken for granted for decades might be judged illegal. The notion shocked corporate officers and Wall Street professionals alike.

Texas Gulf Sulphur was in the right business for having important secrets. The New York–based company, a major minerals producer, routinely shipped exploration teams out to remote areas to search for new ore deposits. In late 1963, word began leaking out of a potential blockbuster of a discovery in Timmins, Ontario. Among the earliest to sense something big was a young geologist who commanded the work crew at the drilling site. Looking over the rich core samples, he was excited. More drilling would be needed for anyone to be certain, but evidence at hand pointed to an ore body of considerable value. He shared his opinion with a woman friend in Washington, D.C., and her mother, and they passed the word to other friends. In short order, the geologist, the girl, the mother, and other persons in the chain had bought thousands of shares of Texas Gulf stock and options.

Drilling supported their hopes. By early 1964, Texas Gulf

---

light of the circumstances under which they were made, not misleading, or

(c) to engage in any act, practice, or course of business which operates or would operate as a fraud or deceit upon any person, in connection with the purchase or sale of any security.

shares had climbed from the high teens into the low 30s. As the size of the lode grew apparent, other insiders—an engineer and the corporate secretary—also bought stock. By then rumors were spilling out of Canada into the American press that the strike was mammoth—valuable beyond all expectations. After playing down the reports, the company arranged a press conference in mid-April, and the news was out: Texas Gulf had brought in a world-class mine. In two weeks, the stock leaped from the high 30s to just under $60.

For the geologist and others who had bought in late 1963, it was a six-month bonanza. The stock price had tripled, and the call options had done even better. But from the SEC's perspective, those profits were gleaned at the expense of public investors who hadn't shared the buyers' information. The agency brought an unprecedented case, alleging the early buyers had known the Canadian property's worth and thus had defrauded investors who had sold them stock and options unaware of the discovery. The defendants countered that they hadn't *known* the ore body was a major mine—only later drilling had confirmed the deposits—but had simply speculated on sketchy data. For a time their argument prevailed, as the trial judge found in favor of most of the defendants. Only the engineer and the corporate secretary who had bought in April were convicted. By April, the judge argued, evidence pointed strongly to a major ore discovery, and those buyers acted on information, not educated guesses. But he said that the earliest birds—the young geologist and others—lacked enough hard information to have violated the law.

If that judgment had stood, much of the next decades' securities regulation might have been different. On appeal, however, charges against all defendants were upheld, and the shrewd guessers were found guilty. Pronounced the Second Circuit Court of Appeals in 1968: ". . . Anyone in possession of material inside information must either disclose it to the investing public, or . . . must abstain from trading in or recommending the securities . . . while such information remains undisclosed."[19] In the next fifteen years, that decree proved the undoing not only of corporate insiders but also of securities analysts and outside investors.

But the SEC's reach in Texas Gulf was even broader. It brought complaints against two directors of the company who, by most accounts, acted shortly *after* the Timmins discovery was announced. One director phoned a broker and bought shares for a family trust he controlled; another, Thomas S. Lamont, passed word of Texas Gulf's good news to an employee at Morgan Guaranty, who bought stock for a hospital trust. More than two hours later, well after news of the press conference had reached brokers' offices over the Dow Jones wire, Lamont bought 3,000 shares for himself and his family.

The directors had violated 10b-5's antifraud provision, according to the SEC, because they hadn't waited long enough after the public disclosure before tipping and buying. Declared the SEC counsel: "It is the Commission's position that even after corporate information has been published in the news media, insiders are still under a duty to refrain from securities transactions until there had elapsed a reasonable amount of time in which the securities industry, the shareholders, and the investing public can evaluate the development and make informed investment decisions. . . . Insiders must wait at least until the information is likely to have reached the average investor who follows the market and he has had some opportunity to consider it."[20] The suitable amount of time would "vary from case to case," said the SEC counsel. In other words, an insider wouldn't know whether he had violated the law until the SEC brought a complaint—or until an appellate court spoke. This far-reaching claim by the SEC wasn't fully tested in Texas Gulf. In 1966, the trial judge found for the two directors. The case against Lamont was dropped when he died shortly after, but the appeals court found that the other director, who had called his broker within minutes after the discovery had been revealed, had indeed acted too soon.

## The Pursuit of Virtue

Texas Gulf laid a legal minefield. The rules were vague or in flux. Who had an obligation to disclose inside information? What kind of data met the standard of "material information"? When was such information "available" or not to the public? The court urged the Securities and Exchange Commission to draft a code "to provide some predictability." Instead, the agency left the rules vague while time and again over the next decade, without specific grants of new authority from Congress, it went to court to extend the perimeter of the insider trading prohibition.

Merrill Lynch was the next major target. In 1966, the commission charged that the brokerage house had illegally tipped institutional clients of earnings problems at Douglas Aircraft. Merrill had obtained the information as prospective managing underwriter for an issue or the airplane builder's stock. The duty to "disclose or abstain" applied not only to corporate insiders, according to the government, but also to investment professionals such as underwriters with access to inside information. Also charged by the SEC were Merrill Lynch salesmen and fifteen institutional clients who sold Douglas Aircraft stock—or sold it short—on the brokerage house's word. Settling the case with the Commission cost Merrill, by one estimate, $1 million.[21]

So far regulatory judgments and case law had stuck to a reasonable if murkily defined assumption: that corporate insiders or their hirelings—people with a "special relationship" giving them access to confidential information—had a duty to outside owners of stock not to take advantage of their privilege.[22] Insiders' fiduciary roles, in other words, barred them from acting against the company or against its owners.

But in the early 1970s, the SEC embarked on litigation to extend the taint on nonpublic information to anyone, whether or not an insider and regardless of how the information was obtained. The first defendants were a top drug-stock analyst and the chairman of Bausch & Lomb. The analyst had smelled trouble in the company's soft-contact-lens business and doubted that profits would match expectations. When he put his doubts to the chairman, he got back a glowing report: all was well, earnings looked fine. Instead of accepting that assurance, the analyst trusted his nose and told his firm's clients to sell Bausch & Lomb stock. It was a smart move. Later that day, the chairman checked his numbers and found the analyst was right. He called the analyst, to set the record right, and *The Wall Street Journal* so the news would be widely reported. Even though the analyst said "sell" before the chairman confirmed his pessimistic hunch, and even though nobody at Bausch & Lomb bought or sold stock on the information, the SEC brought charges that the analyst had been using inside information.

Life had certainly changed on Wall Street since Jim Keene's day. Here was no obvious piracy, no rape of the shareholder by insiders. By conventional standards, the analyst was doing his job: watching companies, forming judgments, advising clients. If the Securities and Exchange Commission could discern "material nonpublic information" in the Bausch & Lomb affair, how might the agency rule on any other contact between a corporate officer and an analyst?

If the SEC's aim was to encourage fair distribution of information in the market, the sally looked counterproductive. Fearing prosecution, corporate officers might be reluctant to talk to analysts. Diligent analysts would live in perpetual jeopardy of being charged as lawbreakers. (To whom did they owe an obligation to report their discoveries? To the public? Or to their employers and clients who provided the incentives for research?) If less total information reached the market, it would be the small investor who suffered. The insiders, after all, already *knew*.

More to the point, what liability would fall on outside investors who came by material nonpublic information?

Critics who had no stake in letting insiders run wild accused the SEC of overreaching, of expanding its authority by making a legal no-man's-land of the market. The agency brushed off the complaints. As lawyers pressed for legal definitions, a top SEC official said a formal code "would only enhance the substantial premiums guile and subtlety already command. . . . All you wind up doing is putting a premium on some crook's ingenuity."[23] The response neglected a principle of equity: that a citizen—even a stockbroker—should be able to know *before* he acts whether the action is illegal. The disagreement among federal judges in the Texas Gulf case underscored the ill-defined risks. A trial court found information not to be "material"; an appellate court found it "material." A trial court found that a press conference had made information "public"; an appellate court found the information remained "nonpublic."

The commission's pattern in attacking insider cases was repeated in other enforcement activities, prompting former commissioner Roberta S. Karmel, appointed during the Carter Administration, to issue a stinging critique of "the SEC's proclivity to formulate policy through litigation that expands the agency's jurisdiction."[24] Karmel also complained: "My basic criticism of the SEC's enforcement program is that it lacks standards for the initiation and prosecution of cases. Investigations and enforcement actions are begun and maintained out of an emotional reaction to particular factual situations. . . ."[25] She wasn't describing the agency's prosecution of insider cases, but she might have been.

After four years of litigation, the Bausch & Lomb case was dismissed.

Two major insider trading cases have reached the Supreme Court in recent years, and the SEC's view of the stock market suffered major setbacks in both. The impact on investors looms large.

The first rebuke grew out of charges against Vincent Chiarella, an employee at a financial printing firm who moonlighted buying takeover targets' stocks. The companies' names were blanked out in the financial papers that reached Chiarella, but he gleaned enough facts to guess identities. The SEC, in *United States* v. *Chiarella,* contended his purchases violated 10b-5. But in 1980, the Supreme Court said no. In contrast to the SEC's vague doctrine, the court put a narrow reading on who mustn't use inside information. The printer had no fiduciary relationship to the shares' sellers, the court noted; he wasn't in a position of trust or confidence as an officer or director of one of the companies. And he had not made misrepresentations to the sellers, which might qualify as fraud. Therefore, the court decided, he had no duty to disclose what he had guessed. As a group of SEC staff attorneys analyzed the ruling: ". . . the Court held that mere possession of material nonpublic market information does not impose a duty to disclose prior to trading."[26]

That was a body blow to the SEC's stance. The Securities Exchange Act, the agency's forty-six-year-old mandate from Congress, and Rule 10b-5 didn't impose the restrictions that the SEC believed they should. Cases the agency had won through settlements with defendants might have been lost under the *Chi-*

*arella* standard. The SEC's response to the new legal obstruction was educational for anyone who believes that law in Washington is made by Congress. Rather than assent to certain uses of nonpublic information, as the court seemed willing to do, the SEC adopted a new rule, 14e-3, which explicitly outlawed practices that the Supreme Court said weren't illegal under 10b-5. Rule 14e-3 forbids anyone who knows that a tender offer is about to be made from trading the target's stock until the offer becomes public knowledge.* The rule also bars the passing of tips about tender offers. In effect, the SEC overruled the court's *Chiarella* decision, writing into regulatory law the agency's view of what should be permitted in the stock market. And it persisted in prosecuting outsiders who came by inside information—not only lawyers and investment bankers, but also analysts and private investors.

## The Dirks Fiasco

Another Supreme Court setback to the SEC may have a far-reaching impact on investors. The ruling didn't make it legal for insiders to cash in on their knowledge. But it made it safer for outside investors to use "inside" information they might dig up in the course of research.

On July 1, 1983, the court overturned the SEC's ten-year-old case against the securities analyst who had uncovered the largest stock fraud in U.S. history. The very fact that the sleuthing analyst, Raymond L. Dirks, became a defendant gave the case one irony. But there was another: at least twice, the Securities and Exchange Commission had failed to follow leads to the fraud that Dirks unearthed.

The case sprang out of the collapse in 1973 of Equity Funding Corporation of America, a flamboyant "concept" company that seemed to be making everyone rich. It was a popular stock,

*This could be called the Bidder Protection Rule. It permits a company or individual to buy stock from unsuspecting investors while planning a tender offer (within certain limits under other rules). But an outsider who gets wind of the plan and begins buying is liable to prosecution.

a darling of go-go fund managers and of greedy widows and orphans, all swept along as chairman Stanley Goldblum, a muscular, modishly dressed six-footer, issued dazzling forecasts of sales and earnings growth. Equity Funding had come a long way, blossoming in less than a decade into a half-billion-dollar empire controlling mutual funds, insurance subsidiaries—even an offshore bank. The magic flowed from a unique marketing scheme that combined sales of life-insurance policies and mutual-fund shares. Big Board stalwarts such as Burnham & Co., Hayden Stone, Smith Barney, and Wertheim & Co. churned out bullish recommendations for the stock. It was one of those giddy moments when any investment story finds buyers, a speculative high on the eve of the 1973–74 bear market.

Glamorous companies always have detractors, and disparaging rumors about Equity Funding were dismissed at first as routine carping. But by March 1973, the whispers were loud enough that an analyst at Hayden Stone declared: "Several rumors have been circulating which have affected Equity Funding's stock. We have checked these rumors, and there appears to be no substance to any of them. At 6.0 times estimated 1973 fully diluted earnings, we believe that Equity Funding is considerably undervalued. . . ."[27] The comment's faults extended beyond unconventional grammar; the 1973 earnings projections were flights of Stanley Goldblum's imagination. As a matter of fact, 1972 earnings had been pulled out of thin air as well. But Hayden Stone's man was right that there were rumors. Some of them owed to Ray Dirks, a Bohemian-looking analyst with Delafield Childs Inc., who was making a name for himself in insurance stocks. Intrigued by tales of wrongdoing from a former Equity Funding employee, Dirks had begun privately snooping into the money machine.

What he found, in a few weeks, was that Equity Funding executives had conjured up the company's astounding growth rate by wholesale fraud, fabricating thousands of phony life-insurance policies. The scale of the forgery was massive, requiring the collusion of hundreds of employees. After creating the fake policies, Equity had to peddle them to reinsurers, hiding the conspiracy not only from other insurance companies but also from its own auditors, innocent employees, brokerage-house analysts, and miscellaneous regulators. The last proved relatively easy. More than a year before the scandal broke, the Securities and Exchange Commission's regional office in Los Angeles had heard tales of fraud but failed to pursue the leads. There was more smoke than fire, the agency decided.

By March 1973, however, Dirks was finding evidence that eluded the regulators. Traveling across country, he talked to a number of institutional investors with large holdings of Equity Funding stock. The stench, meanwhile, had attracted the attention of insurance regulatory commissions in at least four states. In early March, only days after Dirks heard the allegations, the California insurance commission advised the SEC of possible fraud at Equity Funding. The federal agency's response: it had a manpower shortage and couldn't do much.[28]

Institutional investors to whom Dirks talked were alarmed. Some dumped Equity Funding shares. Others gained reassurance from chairman Goldblum that all was well. Sizing up the rumors as a bear raid, some well-known institutions bought the stock heavily. Dirks, meanwhile, had passed along his suspicions to *The Wall Street Journal*. On April 2, after the SEC had belatedly halted trading in the shares, the newspaper broke the story of a multimillion-dollar fraud. That was the end of Equity Funding Corporation of America. Goldblum resigned, and the company was soon forced into receivership. Investors lost virtually everything they had in the stock.

Fragments of justice emerged from the affair. Goldblum and nearly a dozen others went to prison. But long before they were so much as indicted, both the New York Stock Exchange and the SEC turned on the man who had exposed the fraud. The Big Board accused Dirks of spreading rumors and violating the securities laws. G. Bradford Cook, chairman of the SEC,* denounced Dirks for having tipped the institutions. The commission

*Cook's tenure as SEC chairman lasted little more than two months. In May 1973 he resigned after being implicated in a Watergate-related scandal. While an SEC staff attorney in November 1972, Cook had altered a complaint against Robert Vesco, looter of another mutual-fund empire, Investors Overseas Services. Under pressure from Maurice Stans, President Nixon's chief fundraiser, Cook deleted any reference to $250,000 in cash Vesco received; $200,000 of the booty found its way secretly into the Nixon reelection campaign.

charged Dirks and the sellers with violating 10b-5 and other rules. The institutions settled the cases. Fund managers that had bought stock didn't have to settle—they weren't charged. That the buyers, too, were acting on inside information seemed to be mitigated, in the Division of Enforcement's view, by the fact that it turned out to be wrong information, from the chief schemer.

At worst, remarked the editor of *Barron's,* Dirks seemed guilty of jaywalking while rushing to report a rape. As the SEC staff saw it, Dirks was guilty of "selective dissemination" in passing on what he had learned to the institutions. "We're not asserting he had an obligation to report [it to the government]," declared an SEC counsel at one hearing. ". . . He had a duty not to selectively disseminate."[29] From the start, there were problems with the SEC case, not least the appearance of vindictiveness against an analyst who had caught a ball the agency dropped. Among substantive hurdles was the fact that Dirks had gotten his "material nonpublic information" about Equity Funding from sources other than the company's top management, which was still lying when the roof caved in. Moreover, Dirks had pressed the story on *The Wall Street Journal*—hardly selective leaking. There was also the issue raised in the Bausch & Lomb affair. What are securities analysts to do if not dig up information for clients and prospective clients?

An SEC administrative law judge recommended that Dirks be barred for sixty days from association with any brokerage firm. But the full commission, perhaps uneasy about hanging a whistle-blower, softened the punishment to a censure—in effect, a slap on the wrist. It would be a black mark on the analyst's record, but a lot of Wall Streeters operate successfully after being branded for graver lapses. But Ray Dirks, unlike so many others who had tangled with the SEC over 10b-5, was willing to fight. When *Dirks* v. *SEC* reached the Supreme Court in 1983, he had an unexpected—and nearly unprecedented—champion in challenging the SEC: the U.S. Solicitor General.

Arguing on Dirks's behalf, the government lawyer told the court:

> The Commission's erroneous imposition of liability in this case has serious consequences for federal law enforcement, which frequently depends on private initiative to uncover criminal conduct. If the antifraud provisions of the federal securities laws,

> backed by administrative, civil, and criminal sanctions, forbid analysts to trade with or transmit evidence of crime obtained through honest investigation, then few analysts will have an incentive to invest the resources needed to investigate corporate frauds like Equity Funding. Few analysts will be willing to devote substantial resources and expose themselves to personal danger to investigate rumors of crime . . . if they are forbidden to utilize the information they obtain until after it is fully revealed to the investing public. . . . The Commission's approach, therefore, is certain to reduce, and may well eliminate, the role of securities professionals in detecting and analyzing major corporate crimes.

The Solicitor General was acknowledging an obvious fact: markets are not arenas where players pursue good citizenship (or bureaucrats' definitions of good citizenship). Actions in the marketplace—including the pursuit of knowledge—are generally motivated by the hope of personal gain.

The justices ruled six-to-three in Dirks's favor. Their decision sharply limited the scope of insider-trading violations. Jettisoning the SEC's broad interpretation that *anyone* in possession of "material nonpublic information" must disclose it or refrain from trading, the court held that for a tipper or tippee to be liable, the tipper had to have breached a fiduciary duty to shareholders for monetary or personal gain. The former insider at Equity Funding had passed information to Dirks in hope of exposing a fraud, and therefore neither the tipper, nor Dirks, nor presumably Dirks's clients had violated the law.

Dirks noted some of the implications: "The good news for market professionals and the general public is that the Supreme Court has removed a 'gag rule' that has hampered 'insiders,' 'outsiders' and the markets in general for some years. . . . [T]housands of people trade every day on what they believe is information that is 'inside' in some way. From the boardroom to the barroom, rumors travel in hushed tones and sidelong glances." No trader could *check* such tips, however, because corporate officers and directors were in effect gagged: if they hadn't told everyone, they couldn't tell anyone. Now, Dirks argued, outsiders could go straight to people who would know:

> So long as the insider, who is the ultimate source, has nothing to gain personally from the answer, he can say what he pleases.

> In fact, a company president, freshly aware of a prospective doubling in earnings, might well instruct his secretary to give that information to anyone who calls and asks for it before it hits the papers. If the president does not know the caller, so much the better, as the likelihood of the president having an "improper" motive for the disclosure is then remote. . . . All of this means that with the *Dirks* case, freedom of information has arrived in the American stock market. . . . And a marketplace where information can flow freely to all will certainly be more "rational"—at least that is how I would describe the philosophy of *Dirks* v. *SEC*, which creates a system that rewards diligent investigation rather than penalizing naive speculation.[30]

It hasn't been quite that easy.

When the Supreme Court frustrates the self-perceived calling of a bureaucracy, it can't count on having the last word. On the heels of the *Dirks* ruling, the SEC pressed successfully for legislation empowering it to seek treble damages in insider cases and a tenfold increase (to $100,000) in fines. Urged again (by Chairman John Shad, among others) to define insider trading, the majority of commissioners instead maintained the agency's sweeping claim, twice rebuffed by the Supreme Court, that a violation need only be based on "material nonpublic information." Declared Stanley Sporkin,* the former director of enforcement at the SEC who pursued Dirks for almost a decade: "The governing rules should not depend on the motive or intent of the insider or his relationship to the person to whom he may pass the information. The law should require an insider either to 'disclose' or abstain from trading."[31] Chimed in his successor, John M. Fedders: "Trading on material nonpublic information is both deception and fraud. Simply put, it is stealing. . . . The . . . *Dirks* case will not impede our enforcement program. The decision reflects the practical equities of Ray Dirks' conduct—

*As SEC counsel, Sporkin was a harsh critic of Wall Street's mores. When he left the agency, he became general counsel at the Central Intelligence Agency under his old mentor William Casey, a former SEC chairman who became Director of Central Intelligence. Casey swung a big line in the securities market, and his timely buying and selling of stocks, combined with his access to top-secret global data, aroused demands that he put his holdings into a blind trust. For two years he resisted. Helping to oversee this ultimate insider's trades for probity was the SEC's former resident moralist, Stanley Sporkin he disclosed an enormous fraud. An angel or a devil? The difference between a halo and Satan's crown is one of perspective—a six-to-three vote."[32] In other words, notwithstanding the Supreme Court's "perspective" and its six-to-three votes, investors could expect business as usual at the SEC.

Yet an investor approaching the market today knows that two substantial Supreme Court decisions support his right to use what information he can find—provided no insider has breached a fiduciary responsibility for personal gain. A case brought by the SEC early in 1984, charging former LTV Corporation chairman Paul Thayer with tipping friends on takeovers (but not profiting himself), promised to put the SEC's position to a further test.

A newer SEC contention, that outsiders can be prosecuted for fraud for "misappropriating" inside information, also was dealt setbacks in court in 1984. Nor has the agency succeeded in stretching the law to encompass nonpublic *market* information, such as leaks about upcoming news articles. Clearly, it would love to gain such a ruling. The agency began probes in 1984 of stock trading before a CBS television program knocking G. D. Searle & Co.'s new low-calorie sweetener and of a series of trades by Wall Streeters preceding articles in *The Wall Street Journal*'s "Heard on the Street" column. Information in the SEC's idealized market needn't be "inside" to be illegal but merely "unfair." The latter is an impossible concept in a competitive market. So far the courts haven't come to the agency's support.

## Reality and Insider Trading

The key question, of course, is whether the SEC's enforcement policies on insider trading serve investors. The underlying theory of insider regulation is that the modern securities markets should be reasonably level playing fields, where no player can act on significant information not available to the rest of the participants. "Insider trading jeopardizes the integrity of our marketplace," says Fedders. "Our capital markets are broad, efficient and liquid largely because of the precept of fairness. Without it, who is to know what savers would seek as alternative investments?"[33]

Well-publicized prosecution of inside tippers and tippees, by contrast, reassures the public. But does it really affect the conditions the public encounters in the market—or merely affect the public's *perception* of the conditions? There's evidence that use of "material nonpublic information" by insiders and other persons is endemic in the marketplace and that the most vigilant regulators could not root it out. A number of academic studies have found that insiders consistently outperform the market in their stock transactions, even when the activity is nominally aboveboard and is routinely reported to the SEC.[34] This cannot be explained by insiders' sophistication alone; it's simply that insiders call on superior information in making buy and sell decisions. Among the myriad details that a president knows about his company, items of scant interest to an outsider may tell the insider a great deal about the outlook for business. A major rise in the order backlog may require a press release, under the "disclose or abstain" rule, but a subtler change—perhaps new orders have stopped declining—can prompt an executive to buy his company's stock in silence, probably within the law. I say "probably" because with the SEC's refusal to define "material nonpublic information," legality or illegality depends upon the zeal of the SEC staff. But federal prosecution in such cases is all but unheard-of; regulation of this gray area would require an SEC agent in every executive suite. As a practical matter, not many press releases get written announcing jumps in backlogs, but no one gets prosecuted for buying on that oversight, either.

The regulatory framework acknowledges that insiders will exploit their knowledge to some extent with impunity. This is implicit in the "short-swing" profit rule, requiring insiders to repatriate trading profits won in less than six months.[35] After six months, insiders' premiums, if not too blatantly a product of specific nonpublic information, are as safe as the key to the executive bathroom. Among reformers, this prompts occasional huffing and puffing, but it's a fact of life that isn't likely to change. The task of inspecting tens of thousands of trades each year for the taint of privileged information is too massive. The Internal Revenue Service could as well set out to examine each corporate lunch chit for martinis drunk over business as opposed to those drunk over ripe jokes.

As for the "hot tip," the leak on a takeover, evidence suggests that this continues unabated. Thirteen years after the landmark Texas Gulf Sulphur ruling, the market gave a verdict of its own. In June 1981, the share price of the company (by then known as Texasgulf Inc.) bounded ahead for days in anticipation of a $2.8 billion takeover proposal by Société Nationale Elf Aquitaine of France.

Two academics, examining price action before takeovers of 194 companies between 1975 and 1978, found leaks were commonplace. Among stocks listed on the New York or American exchanges, 43.3 percent of the price change occurred *before* an offer was announced; for over-the-counter shares, 56.3 percent of the price action was over before any public disclosure occurred. The authors found evidence of "substantial trading upon inside information concerning the prospective merger, beginning approximately one month before the announcement date with uncontrolled abuse of Rule 10b-5 occurring in the five to eleven trading days immediately prior to the announcement date." The authors uncovered little trading by registered insiders, which "combined with the dramatic increase in volume suggests that much insider trading is carried out through third parties so as to escape detection."[36]

Not much has changed since that study. It's still a rare stock that doesn't get a lift in the days preceding a tender offer. Whether the levitator is an obscure American Stock Exchange issue like Altamil Corporation, which jumped on heavy volume the day before a buyout offer, or a Big Board conglomerate like Alleghany Corporation, which surged 8 points before word of a sale to American Express, valuable secrets are the hardest kind to keep. Any tape watcher could have spotted 1,000-share blocks of Metromedia changing hands on upticks on a Friday afternoon in December 1983. On the week, the stock jumped 11 percent on the heaviest trading in months. The following Monday, the company unveiled a going-private plan that lifted the shares another 10 points. When RCA Corporation got ready to sell its CIT Financial unit in September 1983, a bullish development, RCA shares got a jump on the Friday announcement. Said a trader at one brokerage house: "Everybody on the Street was talking about this by late Thursday."[37] For every episode in recent years that has brought the SEC in pursuit, one can point to several that escaped prosecution.

When an economic phenomenon is this widespread, two conclusions are possible. Either crime is rampant, and more cops with bigger clubs are needed; or the phenomenon is a *natural* part of the marketplace, in this case as information commands its price. The Securities and Exchange Commission is animated by the first conclusion. The second is more consistent with a market-driven economy. *Information rushes to markets,* however much regulators might cry for orderly disclosure; the very existence of a supply of material information ensures that the demand will arise to pull it to market. The value of knowledge, however obtained by legal means, is accepted in other markets—for example foreign exchange and commodities, where professionals and the public view "material nonpublic information" as the only kind worth having. In *Dirks,* the Supreme Court seemed to acknowledge the SEC's folly when it chided the agency for going too far in seeking "equal information among all traders."

The SEC's drive to level the playing field stems from an almost platonic view of markets as being sort of egalitarian foot races, in which everyone leaves the starting line at the same moment and has roughly the same chance of finishing first. But this isn't the way markets work. Not only can't all traders enjoy access to the same information, but in most transactions the parties come armed with widely uneven stores of information—uneven in volume, uneven in quality. Inevitably, the part-time investor suffers a disadvantage vis-à-vis both insiders and professional investors. A 100-share trader in Des Moines won't know one-tenth as much about a company as the chief financial officer knows. The Des Moines investor also stands far back on the chain of information and interpretation compared with institutional investors courted by top brokerage-house analysts. He or she lacks even the access to market data enjoyed by traders at brokerage houses. These are not really legal problems; they are parallel to information disadvantages hampering many people in many kinds of transactions outside the securities markets. Buyers and sellers each accept the risk that the other is a better judge of value, is wiser, or is better informed. The losses investors suffer from lacking the best information certainly exceed their losses from missing hot tips.

Given such built-in disadvantages, the SEC's crusade against insider trading can deliver only a marginal impact on public investors' welfare. If any interests are clearly served by high-profile regulation, they're those of the retail securities industry and of the regulators themselves. The business of Wall Street is raising capital, which means selling investment merchandise. It gets a boost in this, as John Fedders acknowledged in commenting on the Dirks affair, from the "precept of fairness," from public confidence that the markets are a fair game. The industry's technical analysts, who know better, watch for indications of public optimism or pessimism and bet against the amateurs. When the brokerage trade calls on enormous resources in fact-gathering and analysis, when its traders monitor markets tick by tick, there's nothing resembling "fairness" in its relationship with the small investor. It's a rare year that the trading or stock-underwriting operations of a major broker lose money. A rarer year still that the professional arbitragers, tuned in to the Street's whispers on takeovers, wind up in the red. Not many small investors can make such a claim for their own adventures in the market.

The campaign against insider trading serves the institutional interest of the Securities and Exchange Commission by making defense of its budget and expansion of its powers more plausible, even as the failures of other kinds of regulation have become better understood. Curtailing insider trading still has gut appeal—who in an administration or Congress could oppose protecting the little guy from the fat cats?—whether or not it really can be done. With last year's law empowering the commission to seek treble damages and $100,000 fines, the agency's empire-building gained a major victory. More cases will have to be litigated, in contrast to past high rates of consent settlements, and that will require more SEC lawyers and administrators.

What's best for the agency isn't necessarily best for the investor. On the contrary. If investors are lulled into complacency, the illusion of safety leaves them vulnerable. No need to watch insiders if the SEC seems to be forcing the rascals to toe the line.

If for fear of violating 10b-5 or 14e-3, an investor hesitates to act on a rumor or information that comes his way—perhaps a friend has heard that a local company expects a big defense subcontract—is he better off for regulation? Or would he be better off if Congress and the SEC permitted the securities markets to function as other markets do, with information being rewarded?

On a subtler level, too, prohibiting use of inside information cripples the market to the disadvantage of all investors. When information comes into a market, it affects prices and is conveyed to other participants. If regulators attempt to control the flow of price information—whether because they deplore the premiums that natural gas producers collect on a useful commodity or because they deplore the premium insiders collect on useful knowledge—they deprive other actors in the market of some of the information required for intelligent decision-making.

Henry Manne, director of the Law and Economics Center at Emory University, has noted another important way in which crimping the information flow can directly injure outsiders. An investor who sells unaware before a tender offer is likely to get a *lower* price if inside tippers and tippees have not been buying in anticipation than if they had been buying and bidding up the price. Insiders' action in the market, Manne observes, reduces the uncertainty—the cost of surprises—for all participants.[38]

That sophisticated view doesn't answer the complaint of the SEC staff and many in Congress that insiders' use of their privileged information is "unfair" or a "fraud." Manne, for one, argues that it's neither, that a seller would be a seller whether or not there's a buyer with inside information on the other side of the trade. Moreover, he argues, stock-trading profits can be viewed as an inexpensive form of executive compensation.[39] Apart from executives' cashing in on takeovers or other earth-shaking news, that's much the case already, as small-scale insider profiteering passes with few challenges.

The argument that buying on inside information is fraud is difficult to support, in any case, in a modern market where buyers and sellers never come together, where one never offers the other a warranty that "I don't know anything important that you don't know.'' In practice, the reverse assumption is more apt to be true of both sides—''I'm buying because I think it's a stock to own and you're a dunce to sell it!''

One thing's certain. The rules on outsiders' use of inside information were far less restrictive at the start of 1985 than two years earlier. Twice the Supreme Court has exonerated defendants who bore no fiduciary duty to other stockholders. Another court has put a narrow reading on Rule 14e-3's ban on buying before a tender offer; to be illegal, the knowledge of the offer seemingly must be pretty definite.[40] None of these rulings erodes the basic investor protection against overt fraud and manipulation that grew out of the New Deal.

But they may encourage investor realism. As they say, it's a jungle out there, and you have to go armed.

For the average investor, the overriding problem is a lack of the first-rate information insiders enjoy. Diligent research can close the gap only part of the way. Insiders still can tap hundreds of details that remain out of reach to the public.

Fortunately you can skip ahead one step in the information chain. You needn't know everything insiders know if you can watch what they *do*.

That's our starting point for finding good stocks. The *whys* behind insider buying can be filled in later.

In the following chapters, we'll look over insiders' shoulders as they make their investment decisions.

# THREE
# *Insiders Share the Wealth*

Between January 1978 and the summer of 1984, the price of Chicago Milwaukee Corporation rose on the New York Stock Exchange from $3 to more than $150. In that time, the company had little in the way of profits. Its chief asset, carried on the books as virtually worthless, was a bankrupt railroad.

But the railroad's track, timberland, and other properties were worth far more than its debts—apparently well over $100 a share more. While public investors gave up on the stock, it came under quiet, persistent accumulation by its officers and directors, along with several groups of professional investors based in New York. What happened at Chicago Milwaukee is a classic example of insiders' sweeping up assets for pennies on the dollar, right under the noses of public investors.

One of the first persons to recognize the value in the holding company was Robert C. Reed, a wealthy Florida businessman and member of the Chicago Milwaukee board of directors. Reed had made a fortune in bankrupt railroads going back to the old Chicago North Shore & Milwaukee Electric Railroad in the 1930s. Capitalizing on the public taint attached to bankruptcies, Reed would buy mortgage bonds selling for a fraction of their claims on the failed line's assets. As the lines were reorganized, the bond prices usually recovered. His investment philosophy was old-school: "You see what appears to you as an undervalued situation, and you have to act on it before others see the value."[1]

By the late 1970s, Reed was semiretired, but he couldn't resist the possibilities he saw in Chicago Milwaukee. The holding company, put together in 1971, controlled a couple of food-service firms and a paving business—products of a diversification move—along with the money-losing rail line, the Milwaukee Road, formally known as the Chicago, Milwaukee, St. Paul & Pacific Railroad. The railroad hadn't yet filed for bankruptcy. But because of its red ink, the parent company had potential access to millions of dollars in tax losses. From an accountant's vantage, old losses are an asset, since they can be used to shelter future income. If the holding company could swing a couple of acquisitions, for example, the earnings from those businesses might not see a tax bill for years. Still another attraction in Chicago Milwaukee was the potential value of the railroad itself, either dismembered and sold piecemeal or restructured into a profitable carrier. At $8 a share in 1976 and 1977, the stock seemed to hold more promise than most outsiders realized. Over those two years, Reed sank almost $1 million into purchases.[2]

For a while, the investment looked foolhardy. At the end of 1977, the railroad's poor cash flow forced it to file suddenly for bankruptcy, jolting investors so badly that trading in Chicago Milwaukee common was frozen for two weeks. When it resumed, the price plunged below $3. More than half Robert Reed's $1 million had evaporated.

Reed's reaction separates the investor from the gambler. Many amateurs faced with a severe loss would sell out and lick their wounds, muttering about the market's unfairness. The difference in Reed's behavior wasn't mere stubbornness but *informed* stubbornness. He returned to a Texas financier, John D. Murchison, whom he had tried to hook on Chicago Milwaukee several months earlier. Now the stock was half its prior price, and Murchison was interested. He began buying the shares and agreed to join the board to offer ideas for rescuing the company. Reed added to his own stock holdings, and by the end of 1980, his family controlled upward of 150,000 shares of the holding company, plus several thousand shares in the bankrupt railroad's common, which traded over the counter.

Reed no longer was alone in appreciating the company's possibilities. Wall Street professionals had begun sniffing a big play. Railroad bankruptcies had rewarded generations of the Street's old-timers, and there were still a few analysts able to make horseback appraisals of values that might lie dormant in a company that had run short of cash. Several investment houses bought stakes in Chicago Milwaukee, as did a handful of individuals. Allen & Co., Drexel Burnham, and Merrill Lynch soaked up some of the bonds, which had fallen to deep discounts as interest payments stopped. If the line was liquidated or reorganized, the bondholders might collect face value. Others speculated on the common stock, with an eye both to the tax losses and to the Milwaukee Road's considerable assets. The rail line owned its rolling stock and thousands of miles of track, plus more than 150,000 acres of timberland.

The heaviest buying came from the private partnership controlling another New York broker, Oppenheimer & Co. The firm's principal partners—Leon Levy, Jack Nash, and Ludwig Bravmann—operated independently on the side (first under the Oppenheimer name, later as Odyssey Partners*) and had earned a reputation as tough, smart deal-makers. In the spring of 1979, Odyssey and Peter Sharp, a New York real estate developer, revealed their control of more than 5 percent of Chicago Milwaukee Corporation's common, which by then was trading in the high teens. The group already held more than $11 million in face value of the railroad's bonds, plus several thousand shares of railroad common.

Despite the group's disclosure, which was available to anyone through the Securities and Exchange Commission, public interest in Chicago Milwaukee proved short-lived. In April the stock shot up to almost $20, but by year end the shares had sunk back to $12. Even if there was value in Chicago Milwaukee, the market seemed to say, the uncertainties accompanying a bankruptcy reorganization were too overwhelming: investors might never reap the rewards. Who could know at what price bondholders' claims would be settled? How much of the Milwaukee Road's track and land would be sold, and at what price? What

*For simplicity, I refer to the group as Odyssey Partners throughout.

would become of the tax losses if the land sales showed a profit? How would claims by labor be settled? Meanwhile, the bankruptcy trustee was being forced to borrow heavily against the assets to keep the railroad running at a loss. His plan to conserve cash by shutting down part of the line had been blocked by Congress at the behest of labor and regional political interests. So the assets were to be bled further. Even an analyst who favored speculation in some of the bonds, Basil Vasiliou of Bear, Stearns & Co., couldn't overlook the risks. Since the Milwaukee Road had filed its bankruptcy petition, operating losses had totaled $118,235,000. However massive the Milwaukee Road's assets might be, they wouldn't last forever. In the circumstances, it was scarcely surprising that the share price melted.

Rail reorganizations ride as much on politics as on economics. The scheme the unions, some shippers, and a couple of state governments had pressed on Congress envisioned a grand new tax-greased rail line linking the Midwest and the Northwest. Good news for regional interests, bad news for anyone hoping to see the Milwaukee Road liquidated. But the Interstate Commerce Commission, which had veto power over the linkup plan, gave speculators another 180-degree turn. The ICC not only rejected the link on grounds it couldn't be self-supporting but also backed the trustee in urging the Milwaukee Road to abandon two-thirds of its system to regain solvency.

Bullish news! Chicago Milwaukee's shares shot toward their old high—then collapsed once again, along with the rest of the market in the spring of 1980, as the Federal Reserve clamped down on credit. By April, the common was fetching little more than $10 a share in lackluster trading. All the talk of assets, tax losses, hidden value—all seemed to be forgotten.

But the investors aligned with Odyssey Partners were buying, and so were corporate officers, including a newly installed president, Charles W. Metter. Over the spring and summer of 1980, the rail company sold off chunks of track to other railroads for a total of $59 million and talked about other sales. One prospect was the Milwaukee Land Company subsidiary. The bankruptcy trustee had chewed the numbers over and thought Milwaukee Land might net more than $110 million. That was the equivalent of $44 for each Chicago Milwaukee Corporation share, though bondholder and other creditor claims stood between stockholders and the cash.

In October, news broke that flung the old estimates of land values out the window and confirmed that the Milwaukee Road sat atop assets worth a bundle. The bankruptcy trustee announced sales of just *part* of Milwaukee Land's timber and mineral holdings for $179.7 million—more than the earlier projection for the entire property. As often happens before extraordinary news, the stock already had been moving for days, jumping on large volume from $13 to $17. When word of the sales' terms crossed the tape, the quote soared. One day it was $20. The next $23—then $29.

In the next six months, details spilled forth. The bankruptcy trustee's investment adviser, Lehman Brothers Kuhn Loeb, now estimated that the Milwaukee Land subsidiary alone might bring in $250 million—more than twice the figure of a year earlier and over six times the assets' stated value on the railroad's books. The trustee, a former Illinois governor named Richard B. Ogilvie, was ebullient. If the shortened Milwaukee Road rail system (dubbed Milwaukee II) could find a buyer to assume federal loans the company owed, Ogilvie declared, that would be another $100 million improvement on the balance sheet. Sales of track, locomotives, rolling stock, and other assets, he said, might total $182 million for 1980–81. "We can't quantify it," Ogilvie said in an interview in early 1981, "but we may be coming out of bankruptcy with a sort of junior Penn Central."[3]

That was a name to reckon with, and investors who hadn't paid attention to Odyssey's interest in Chicago Milwaukee perked up their ears. The firm had been among those profiting as the Penn Central rolled out of bankruptcy. It was difficult to get a fix on the liabilities—they still depended on the price accorded the bonds and old labor contracts—but by the middle of 1981, the Milwaukee Road was showing assets, likely to be converted into cash, of well over $400 million. On the holding company's snug 2.5-million-share capitalization, that was equivalent to $160 a share. There was talk that ultimately the reorganization and partial liquidation of the Milwaukee Road might yield well over $200 a share to the parent company. By the spring of 1981, the stock had topped $70.

Early investors like Robert Reed and the Odyssey group—who had paid $8, $10, and $15 for much of their stock—already had made many times their money. But even with the shares commanding three times the price of a year earlier, members of the

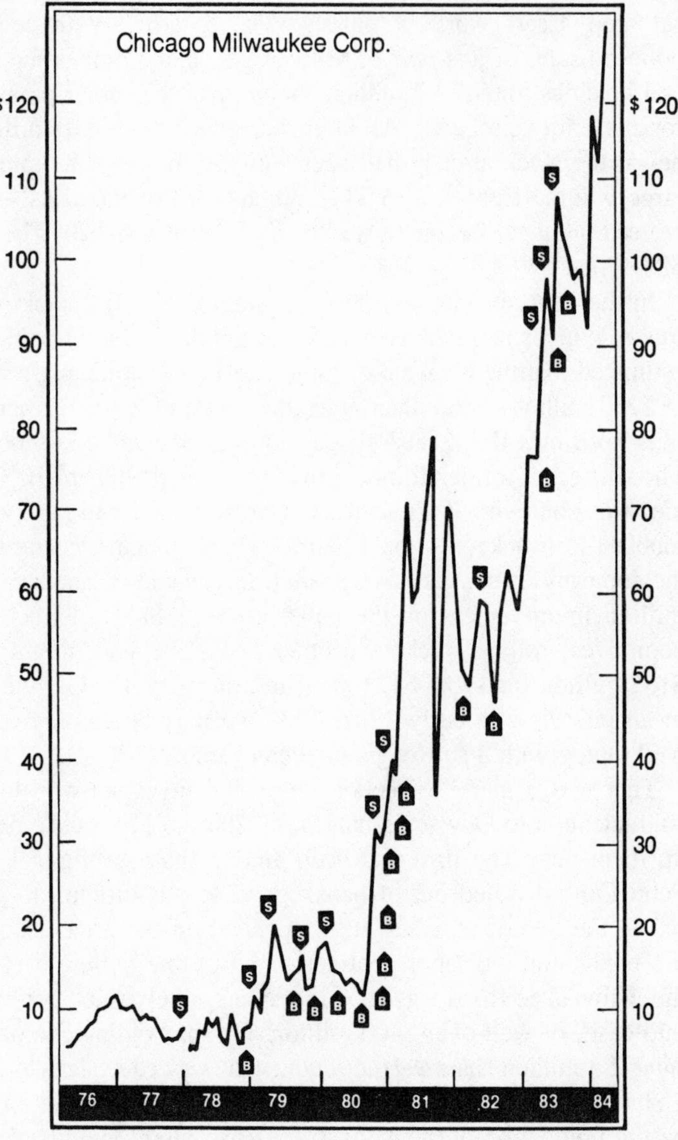


**Figure 1. Officers, directors, and big investors piled into Chicago Milwaukee Corporation, seeking value in a bankrupt railroad.**

Odyssey group continued to buy. By now, the syndicate included an international banking family led by Ezra K. Zilkha, a Swiss investment group,Compagnie de Banque et d'Investissements, and a British player, Electra Investment Trust PLC. At the end of 1981, the Odyssey group owned 35.1 percent of Chicago Milwaukee and had won two seats on the board of directors. Other professionals had taken an interest as well. The Madison Fund Inc., a New York investment company, reported that it had acquired 6.7 percent of Chicago Milwaukee, doing much of the buying as the stock soared into the $60–$70 range.

The market still welcomed any skeptical word, as relayed now and then by *The Wall Street Journal*'s "Heard on the Street" column, with a sell-off in the shares that would shake loose anyone who wasn't a firm believer. There was a plan to revive the carrier rather than liquidate it. In three weeks, the quote collapsed from $68 to $32. Odyssey investors bought more stock. There was a battle by bondholders, including Ohio financier Carl Lindner, to win more compensation for themselves—perhaps, *The Journal* suggested, hacking $50 a share off the breakup value. The stock tumbled from the high 60s to $40. The Odyssey crowd bought.

By 1983, with the group controlling 40 percent of Chicago Milwaukee, events were unfolding much more favorably than skeptics had imagined. The shrunken Milwaukee Road line was drawing heated bids, including provisions to pay off all debt and permit the company to keep its valuable tax losses. And yet another well-regarded New York investor had weighed in, Hungarian-born George Soros, of Soros Fund Management Company, reporting a 7.1 percent holding purchased at $63–$76.

By mid-1984, Chicago Milwaukee common topped $150.

For that canny Floridian Robert Reed, veteran of railroad speculations, a $1 million stake had been parlayed in seven years into $15 million. For Chicago Milwaukee's president, sixty-year-old financial consultant Charles Metter, 4,000 shares purchased three years earlier were worth five times his $82,000 cost. For the Odyssey group, which acquired most of its position under $50, profits exceeded $50 million.

## Making Things Happen

We'll look at some of Odyssey Partners' other successful exploits in a bit. But there are several lessons to be drawn from the Chicago Milwaukee saga. Two key assets set corporate insiders and heavy hitters like the Odyssey group apart from most investors. The first is information; the second is the ability to make things happen. They have the access, the financial talent, the experience, and the "little extras" that lead them to situations where money can be made. In comparison to these professionals, the average investor is bumping around blindfolded in a dark room. Further, the average investor is passive, depending on management to deliver on his expectations. But officers and directors influence their companies' fate directly, and substantial professional investors—the likes of Carl Icahn, Odyssey Partners, and Victor Posner—have the muscle to shake the money tree. They seldom come up losers.

Consider a couple of sidelights to Chicago Milwaukee. One of the big risks facing Odyssey was the fact that the holding company and its shareholders had no direct control over the disposition of the bankrupt Milwaukee Road and its assets. The railroad lay in the custody of the court-appointed trustee, whose obligation was to the bench and to the Milwaukee Road's creditors—not to speculators in the holding company. But as the Odyssey group's stake rose, it flexed its muscle to revamp the board of directors, gaining a vantage from which to fight the trustee on some issues and, when it suited the group's interests, to back him in resisting bondholder claims for a bigger settlement. Another tack was more controversial. In late 1980, some members of the Odyssey group had gained control of another bankrupt, a Florida land developer that was reborn as Avatar Holdings Inc. Odyssey's kingpins invited the Milwaukee Road trustee, Dick Ogilvie, to join Avatar's board of directors. The director's fee was modest, only $6,000 annually,[4] but bondholders cried foul and Ogilvie quickly dropped Avatar. The job had posed such a stark conflict of interest that acquaintances were surprised Ogilvie ever accepted—though not surprised that Odyssey members had made the offer. After all, it never hurts to make friends. No fuss arose over another apparent edge Odyssey enjoys in railroad speculations. Since 1980, an Odyssey executive, Stephen Berger, has been chairman of the board of the United States Railway Association, the federal nonprofit agency that oversaw the Northeast rail bankruptcies. How many small investors can go into a deal with talent like that in the next office?

## Follow the Insiders

The next best thing is watching the smart money at play. This is not especially difficult. Corporate insiders and professional investors both leave their tracks on the market.

As they socked away Chicago Milwaukee shares, officers and directors reported their purchases each month to the Securities and Exchange Commission. Their reports were available for public inspection and were passed along to investors by a number of publications. Odyssey and its hangers-on added a score of amendments to their original 13D, disclosing progressively larger accumulations of stock. Many of the amendments were noted in small stories in *The Wall Street Journal,* and occasional magazine and newspaper articles drew attention to the group's interest.

All that's typical. Major investments by professionals usually become public knowledge fairly quickly, as does routine stock buying by insiders. Sometimes the result of a disclosure is electric. Word that Carl Icahn is accumulating a stock is apt to spur a jump of several points on the strength of his success in forcing takeovers. Word that insiders are buying a down-and-out company may excite speculation on a turnaround. But often the news produces little investor reaction, or excitement soon wanes and prices drift back to the bargain area that attracted the pros. When that happens, investors who have done some homework can lay their bets with the smart money without overpaying. Some of the best private money managers make careers of the game.

Most insider buying isn't done by household-name investors like Carl Icahn but instead by corporate executives and professional investors you've never heard of. The typical motive for their buying differs from Icahn's, or at least the time horizon is longer. Where Icahn the Terrible masterminds fast, rough-and-tumble raids from the outside, the average insider plays a more sedate game. He's like a squirrel picking up nuts for the winter after they've fallen within reach. He abhors going out on a limb. He's hard to panic and is apt to be buying 1,000-share blocks as the stock market slams toward a bottom (just as the public trader or institutional tiger cries for his broker to sell). The insider's eye for low-risk value is admirable.

Stock buying in the open market by insiders commands respect in part because it's relatively rare. What with their stock options and stock-appreciation rights, most corporate officers have more of their companies' shares than they want, and they're traditionally net sellers. When they turn around and *buy*—not at artificial discounts but at the market price—it's an anomaly that deserves notice.

Insiders favor the less efficient corners of the market, the less analyzed, less well-known companies where values are overlooked.

In general they buy under any of three situations:

1. *A development is about to improve the company's fortunes.*
2. *The stock price has fallen so far below intrinsic values that the shares seem irresistibly cheap.*
3. *Stock buying is part of a regular investment program.*

As an outsider, you can make money from any of these situations.

The first is typical of corporate turnarounds. In recent years insider buying has signaled better times at Burroughs Corporation, Firestone Tire & Rubber, Macmillan, Nortek, Occidental Petroleum Corporation, Pier One Imports, Recognition Equipment, Seagull Energy—the list could go on for dozens of other names, some mighty, many obscure. The second situation, insider bargain hunting, often crops up when a company or an industry has fallen out of favor with the majority of investors. Insider bargain grabbing grows intense near market bottoms, when virtually all stocks and industry groups are out of favor. The third category, insider buying as part of a regular investment program, is the broadest. It includes the corporate executive who

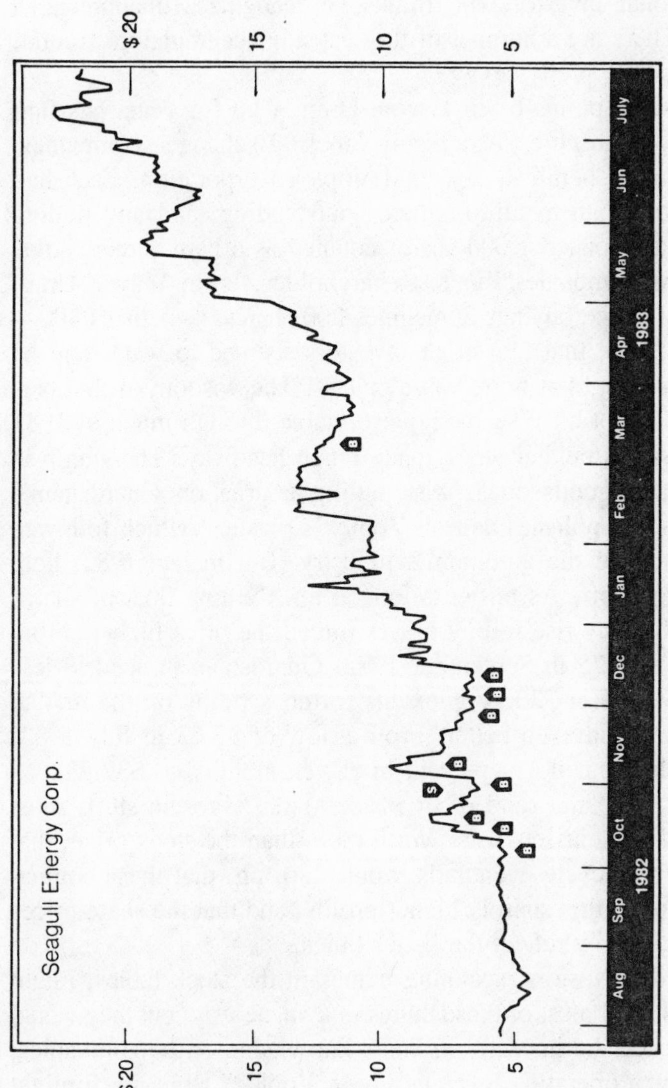


**Figure 2. Inside money poured into Seagull Energy, an oil-gas-pipeline outfit, between October and December 1982. Earnings soared, and the stock tripled.**

buys his firm's stock regularly because he can't think of a better place to put his money (he's a rare bird). It also includes the professional investor who thinks he recognizes unappreciated value. There are a number of these steady accumulators around, and some are pretty savvy.

A case in point: Irwin Wayne Uran, who for years has fancied two obscure American Stock Exchange companies, Guardsman Chemicals Inc. and Voplex Corporation. Each had little more than a million shares outstanding, and any trading session that totaled 1,000 shares counted as a barn-burner. Some days, the companies' biggest shareholder, Irwin Wayne Uran, did most of the buying. Sometimes 200 shares, sometimes 400—he took stock that few other investors seemed to want, and he typically bought at book value or less. The wisdom of that persistence might have seemed questionable through much of 1981 and 1982, as neither stock made much headway. The slump in the durable-goods cycle was putting a drag on Guardsman's coatings and polishes and on Voplex's plastics, which followed the swings of the automobile industry. But in late 1982, both stocks took off. As business looked up, the tiny float of shares meant that any rise in buy orders forced the price higher. From a low of $8.25 in September 1982, Guardsman jumped in less than a year past $20. Voplex, its fortunes riding on the revival of Detroit, did even better. From a low of $7.63 in July 1982, the stock climbed 414 percent in eleven months, to $39.25.

What did Uran (and other insiders) see? Prosaic stuff, most likely: that the assets were worth more than the stock price, that the business cycle eventually would turn up, that these companies would enjoy sharply higher profits, and that the share prices would probably reflect the better times.

Outside investors, scanning names in the stock tables, might have assumed most of those things in a vague way, but they would have lacked the insiders' intimate knowledge of the companies. How much operating leverage lay in Voplex? How much might earnings rise on a rebound in sales? How much were the assets worth? Even a close reading of the companies' annual reports would provide only approximations—management's hopes and promises. Trips to reference sources such as Standard & Poor's would have yielded the statistical histories, which shed little light on the future. But what outsiders *could* observe was a major insider voting consistently with his money. (In fact, Uran's buying was noted in *Barron's* more than a year before the stocks turned.[5])

A long-hoped-for recovery at Burroughs Corporation was telegraphed by officers and directors, including chairman W. Michael Blumenthal. Toward the end of 1981, Blumenthal and five other insiders bought several thousand shares, mostly in the low 30s. One vice-president picked up 400 shares at $29.25, just 2 points off a fourteen-year low.[6]

The speed with which Blumenthal spruced up the hard-pressed computer company caught most of Wall Street napping. He had come to the job after stints as chairman of Bendix Corporation (where he served as mentor to William Agee) and as Treasury Secretary in the Carter Administration. The latter post lasted a shorter time than he had expected ("When the prime rate intersects with the President's popularity rating," Blumenthal explained, "it's time for the Treasury Secretary to go"). Agee didn't want his old boss back at Bendix, but neighboring Burroughs was looking for a new broom. For years, the computer maker had lived off its capital, as management's investment in new technology fell below industry norms. When Blumenthal took over as chairman in 1980, the price of neglect was becoming apparent. Despite tremendous assets, $3 billion in annual sales, and formidable market position, Burroughs products had lost their competitive momentum. Its minicomputers had gained a reputation for unreliability that disgruntled owners celebrated in newspaper ads. Blumenthal's shakeup went so broad and deep within the company—including a temporary sacrificing of sales and profits—that analysts and the financial press expected any recovery to take years. As if Burroughs's own headaches weren't enough, Blumenthal soon paid $102 million to buy loss-plagued, debt-ridden Memorex. While the acquisition's memory technology filled a big hole at Burroughs, the Street's reaction, Blumenthal admitted, was "He must be off his rocker." But by early 1982, it looked as though chairman Blumenthal might have made the right moves. Burroughs wasn't out of the woods, but the improvements were remarkable. Memorex had turned out to be a good buy (its worst problems were behind it), and Burroughs's

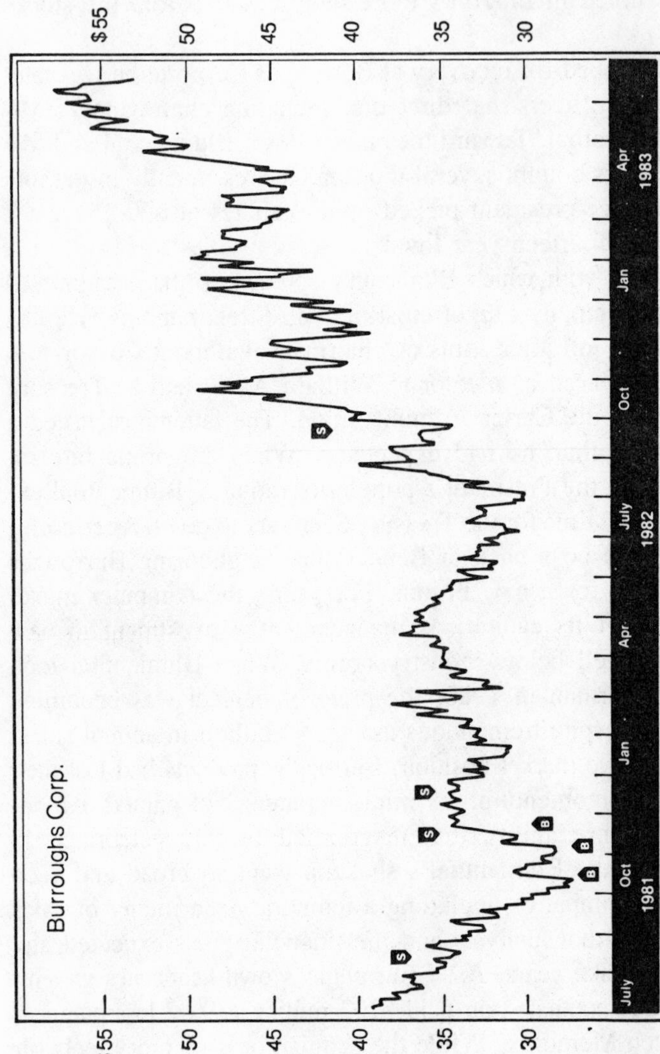


**Figure 3. Michael Blumenthal and his crew turned around Burroughs Corporation and nearly doubled their money.**

own results perked up as well. Within a year the stock was trading above its $52-a-share book value.

No effort was made to conceal the good news from outsiders. Much the contrary. Blumenthal had insisted at the outset that his demolition and rebuilding wouldn't take "too terribly long." But analysts had heard such promises before. There's a clumsy but concise saying about companies in trouble: "Turnarounds don't." Except sometimes they do. Burroughs was one of many rebounds that have demonstrated the benefits of watching insiders. However cheap an executive's promises of better times, the man who buys his company's stock in the market—who wants a bigger stake than his options provide and will pay for it—is putting his money behind his words. When half a dozen insiders vote with their cash, as they did at Burroughs in the last five months of 1981, it's hardly surprising when they turn out to be right. To sense the company's drift, they need only look down the hall and see whether the financial VP is grinning or gulping Maalox.

The depressed stock prices of 1982 were seized as opportunities by hundreds of insiders. In the year after three of them bought 16,000 shares of Thousand Trails Inc.,[7] an over-the-counter operator of campgrounds, the company's profits more than doubled, analysts forecast 30 percent growth, and the stock price climbed 220 percent—from less than $9 to $29.

A few other examples:[8]

Mentor Corporation, an OTC maker of urinary-care products, traded as low as $2.20 a share in the summer of 1982 (prices are adjusted for stock splits). Between May and September, three directors, plus President Christopher J. Conway, bought 30,000 shares, predominately under $2.67. In the next year, the stock rose more than 500 percent.

On the American Stock Exchange, two directors and an officer bought 4,500 shares of Showboat Inc., a casino operator, within a fraction of the $7.33 low. Twelve months later, in July 1983, the shares hit $20.

An executive vice-president of Shopwell Inc., a Curb-listed supermarket chain, bought 26,000 shares in a five-month stretch. A year after the buying began, he had a more than 300 percent profit as the company's earnings soared.

Pier One Imports Inc. lost money for five straight years through

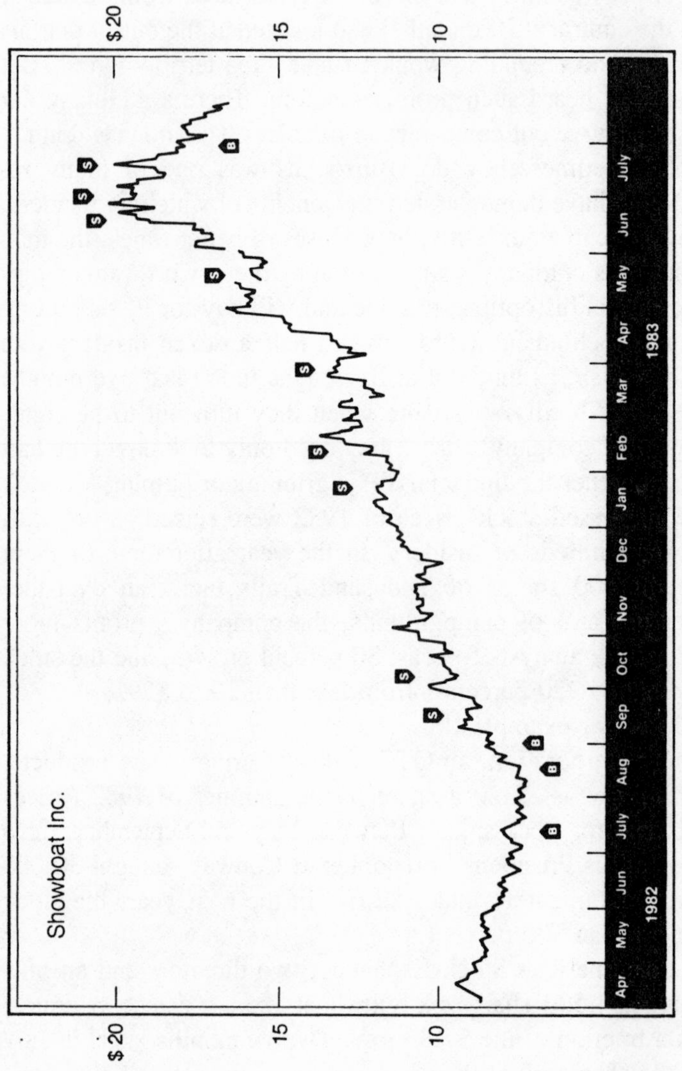


**Figure 4. Insiders bought Showboat, Inc. in 1982 just before the hotel-casino operator's stock climbed from under $8 to $20.**

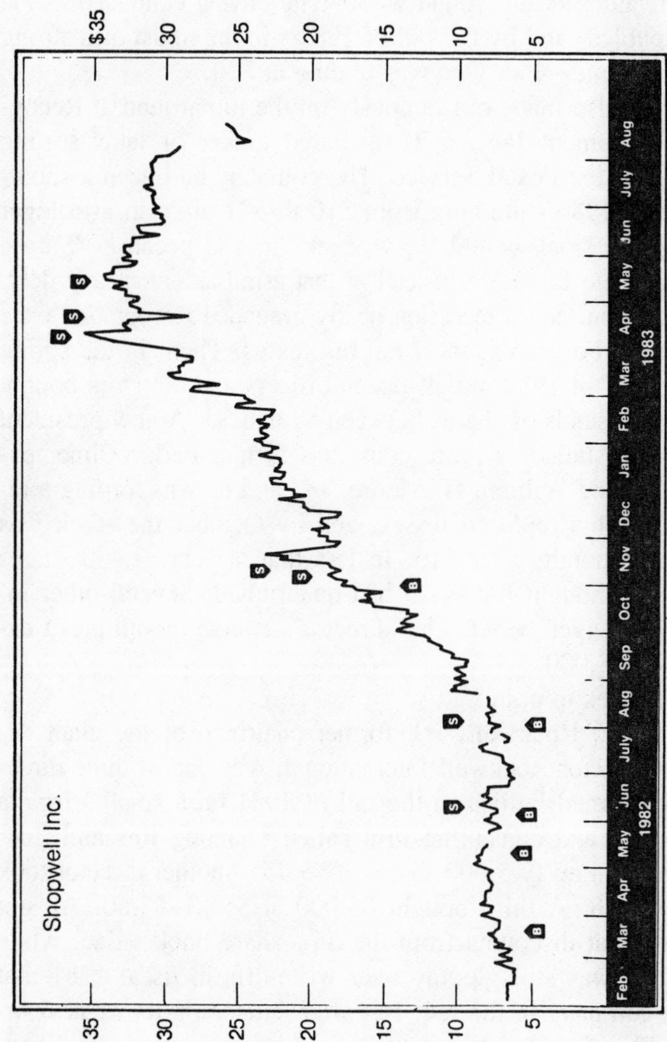


**Figure 5. Shopwell Inc., a supermarket chain on the American Stock Exchange, gave an insider a 300 percent gain in a year.**

1980. Two years later its fortunes still looked rocky as a subsidiary threatened to dive into bankruptcy and earnings fell. But insiders in February 1982 bought several thousand shares of the import-retailing chain around $4.50. The buying continued as the stock doubled, and by the fall of 1983—in the midst of a strong profits rebound—Pier One was trading at $20.

Insiders also made out famously on the turnaround at Recognition Equipment Inc., a Texas-based maker of letter-sorting systems for the Postal Service. The company had been a shooting star in 1980—jumping from $10 to $21 after an astrologer declared the stock would "skyrocket" to $83 because "Saturn is moving into Libra."* Instead of that astral ascent, heavy debt, overexpansion, and a recession nearly grounded Recognition once and for all. For two years it ran big losses. Then, in the spring and summer of 1982, a half-dozen officers and directors bought tens of thousands of shares between $4 and $5. A new president had been installed, a profit-conscious former Perkin-Elmer executive named William G. Moore, Jr., and he was forging a recovery. Profits replaced losses, and by October the stock was $8, seven months later $16. In less than a year, 2,400 shares that Moore bought for $4.25 had quadrupled. Several other insiders fared even better. One director's twelve-month profit exceeded $225,000.

More cases in point:[9]

Willard F. Rockwell, Jr., former chairman of the giant defense contractor Rockwell International, was one of three directors who turned bullish in the fall of 1981 on a small Virginia engineering and consulting firm called Planning Research Inc. Rockwell put away 5,000 shares at $5.75. Another director took 200 at $5.88. A third bought 65,000 at $5.13–$5.50. All got their stock at discounts from the $6-a-share book value, while the public was still gloomy over write-offs in fiscal 1981 that put the company in the red. But after jettisoning its weak operations, Planning Research was in fine shape as new federal contracts began pouring in. In each of the next two years, its earnings topped $1 a share—and by June 1983 the common stock reached $21.50.

Insiders also recognized a good thing in Mediq Inc. After the

*I would like to hear how *that* fits into efficient market theory.

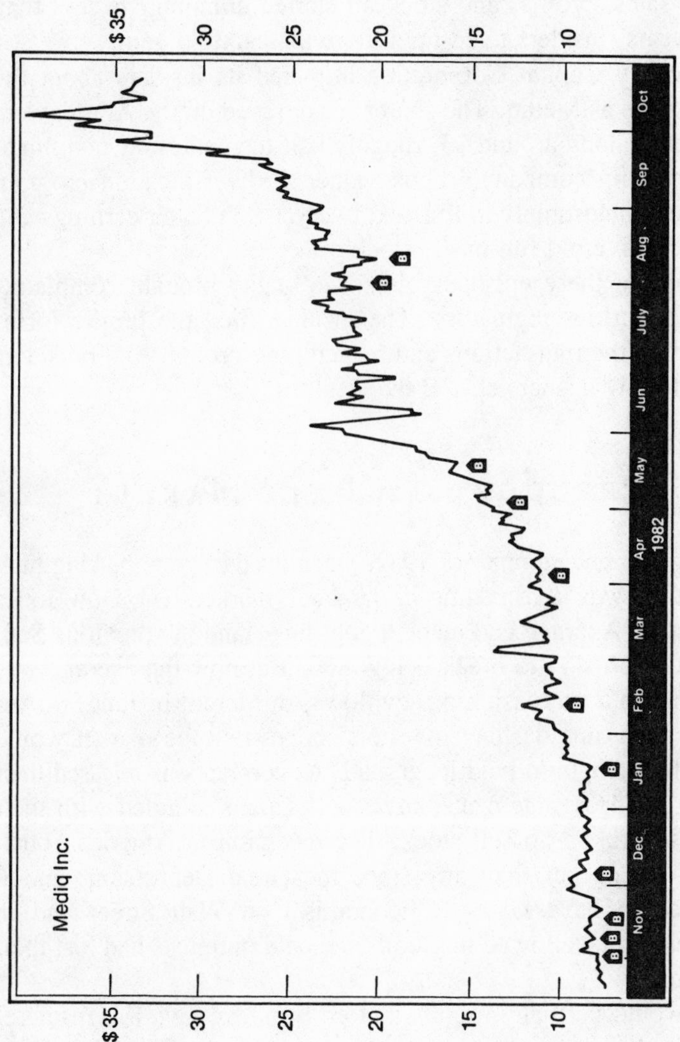


**Figure 6. An obscure issue on the American Stock Exchange. Insiders bought Mediq heavily and made six times their money in two years.**

maker of medical and dental supplies was spun off in its parent's 1981 liquidation, the new shares drifted lower on the American Stock Exchange. Insiders began steady buying. Mediq's sales, profits, and stock all started climbing. In less than two years, insiders toted up a more than sixfold gain.

Security Capital Corporation attracted its insiders about the same time as Mediq. The shares, also traded on the Amex, were bumping along around $3, roughly half the real estate and financial holding company's book value. A diversification program paid off handsomely in the next two years in better earnings and a nearly fivefold run in the stock price.

None of these episodes of insider acuity brought complaints from securities regulators. The insiders filed the proper forms reporting the transactions and reaped their profits. And outsiders who follow insiders shared the wealth.

## Prelude to a Bull Market

The spring and summer of 1982, when insiders were picking their bargains, was a grim time in the stock market. The Dow Jones Industrial Average had made a goal-line stand the previous September, refusing to break below 800. But now the average was sagging to a succession of new lows, in March, in June, in August, each time dashing investors' hopes that the market would find the strength to hold its ground. As corporations released their profit-and-loss statements, investors' groans mingled with their calls to brokers to sell stock. The recession in American business was deeper than any since the Great Depression, and it seemed to have no end. Economists on Wall Street and in Washington wallowed in gloom; the paid optimists had lost their credibility.

It would be many months before business gave a sign of recovery. In most industries, better profits—or any profits at all—lay a year down the road. But through the spring and summer of 1982, while the public and institutional investors sold stock, insiders bought. They bought in literally hundreds of companies, often within a wink of the low. The accompanying chart (Figure 7) tells the story. At three of the stock market's major

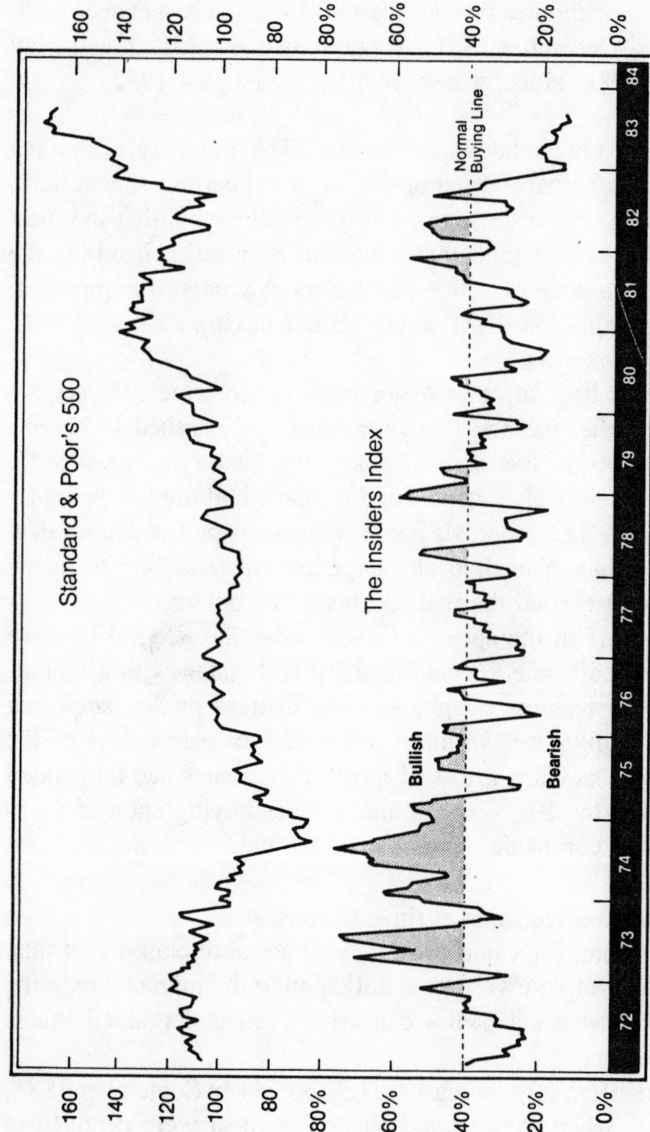


**Figure 7. The Insiders Index charts insider buying as a percentage of total insider transactions. Peaks represent times of heavy net buying, while valleys show times when insiders sold more heavily. (Courtesy of *The Insiders*, Fort Lauderdale, Florida)**

lows in an eleven-month period—in September 1981 and in March and August 1982—insiders were substantial buyers. Rallies followed each of the lows: more than 90 Dow points between September and December 1981; 90 points between March and May 1982; and 500 points (at last count) since August 1982.

These were not isolated phenomena. The intensity of buying varies from company to company—a few hundred shares here, tens of thousands elsewhere—but a reliable signal that the market is undervalued (and that a bottom *may* be at hand) is the sudden appearance of inside purchasers at scores of companies, including giants like IBM where insider buying strikes as often as July snowstorms.

Let's look back at other major bottoms from recent years.

In 1978, after the first "October Massacre" slashed 130 points from the Dow in five weeks, heavy insider buying presaged a rally that lasted twelve months and reclaimed all the lost ground.

After 1979's October Massacre, which swept away more than 100 Dow points, a small insider surge led a three-and-a-half-month upswing that carried the market ahead 120 points.

The sell-off in the spring of 1980, after the Federal Reserve tightened credit, was especially sharp and ended with a vicious freefall. But insiders bought into the distress prices, acquiring shares in many cases within a few points or a few days of the bottom. Weeks later, prices of most of the issues had rebounded smartly. On the Big Board alone, insider buying showed up in roughly 300 companies, one-fifth of the list.

Are insiders perfect market timers? Alas, no.

Insiders look for values, but they're no more clairvoyant than other conservative investors in anticipating the market's extreme swings. Bear-market panics can drive even undervalued shares sharply lower.

Insiders often buy too early. They bought in September 1981, remember, when shares were cheap but most were destined to get a bit cheaper over the next eleven months. In 1973 and 1974, insiders failed to foretell the devastation that lay ahead. As the Dow peaked in January 1973, they were correctly cool toward stocks, but a tumble in prices soon brought them back as net buyers. The next rally ran out of steam in a couple of months. As prices crumbled again, insiders on balance were net buyers through the entire 1974 bear market. The fact that their buying was most intense near the bottom was little consolation for investors who had been lured into shares early in that disastrous year, thinking that insider accumulation (or a dearth of selling, which was a factor) meant the market was safe.

Still, insiders didn't do that badly.

During much of the 1973–74 bear market, stocks *were* historically cheap. Many secondary issues suffering a final washout had been declining for six to eight years and represented once-in-a-lifetime bargains. As the chart illustrates, the result of insiders' early buying was that by the market's bottom in October 1974, they were loaded up with stocks. The public and institutions by then were sold out. Insiders' value judgments were vindicated, as the prices of most shares entered a secular bull market after the 1974 bottom. Many second-tier companies—the smaller concerns that insiders usually favor—have since climbed 1,000 percent or more.

It isn't necessary, in any case, to share insiders' market risk in full to share their profits, J. Michael Reid, who edits a service called *Insider Indicator,* one of several market advisory letters that report on insider trading, has a formula that would have prevented investors from venturing after insiders too soon in 1974. His suggestion: "If insiders are buying on weakness, don't you buy on weakness. You'll reduce your risk if you wait until the stock has bottomed and come back up to where the insiders bought. That's when you buy, at the price the insiders paid but on strength. You'll also have the time value of your money in between." Reid's strategy also lowers an investor's risk of being lured into a bad situation by overoptimistic insiders—for example, a "turnaround" such as Itel, in the early 1980s, that doesn't happen. At both Burroughs and Recognition Equipment, the stocks began showing strength as insider buying persisted, in effect reinforcing the executives' judgment.

Another caveat concerns the use of specific levels of insider buying or selling as a technical indicator for forecasting the market. Figure 7 proves the limited usefulness of such devices. Whether it's time to buy stocks when insider net buying reaches

30 percent, or 40 or 50 percent, varies with the particular market. All that a rise in insider buying can tell an investor is that stocks are probably undervalued. (Even more questionable is the use of specific levels of net selling as evidence that the market is too high. This error caused many insider watchers to turn skeptical of the market far too early in both 1975 and 1982.)

No investment method can remove all risk. Watching insiders simply stacks the odds in favor of success. The assumption is this: that investors inside a company understand its value better than those on the outside; and that if one group is buying while the other is selling, the group armed with the greater amount of specific knowledge—the insiders—is more likely to be right.

The chairman of one NYSE-listed company summed it up this way: "Insiders are making more seasoned, long-range judgments than others. You know what Bernie Baruch said: you should buy when everyone else is selling and sell when they're buying. An insider looks at bad news and says, 'Hey, is this a temporary adversity, or is it something long-term?' " The speaker, CEO David W. Wallace of Bangor Punta Corporation, had been accumulating shares of his general aviation manufacturing company for years, usually paying little more than half its book value. "I watch insider buying in my own investments," Wallace added. "The insider knows the strengths of his company; he has more confidence stepping in when everybody else is stepping out."

He spoke in 1982. Last year Lear Siegler Inc. came along and took over Bangor Punta.

# FOUR

# *How You Can Profit—Legally—from Inside Information*

You've been watching Amalgamated Textiles' stock, and it looks cheap. It's edging higher on the American Stock Exchange, trading around four times earnings, a few points above its fifty-two-week low, 20 points below its high. You've noticed that Amalgamated's price seldom sinks much below four times earnings, and when the textile manufacturers are hot, near the top of their business cycle, the threadbare old company sometimes goes for seven or eight times earnings. If you buy the stock now, while it's down in the dumps, you might get a "double play" in a couple of years: higher earnings and a bigger multiple on the earnings. You're tempted—but, well, textile companies aren't very glamorous, or very predictable.

Still, it would be interesting to know what insiders have been doing.

The Securities and Exchange Commission has attempted to make an investor's job easier in watching the buying and selling by insiders. The agency requires corporate officers, directors, and owners of 10 percent or more of the stock to report details each month when they trade their companies' securities. The insiders file a one-page form entitled "Statement of Changes in Beneficial Ownership of Securities," known as a Form 4 for short. The Form 4 discloses the type of security (common stock, preferred, etc.), date of the transaction, number of shares, kind of

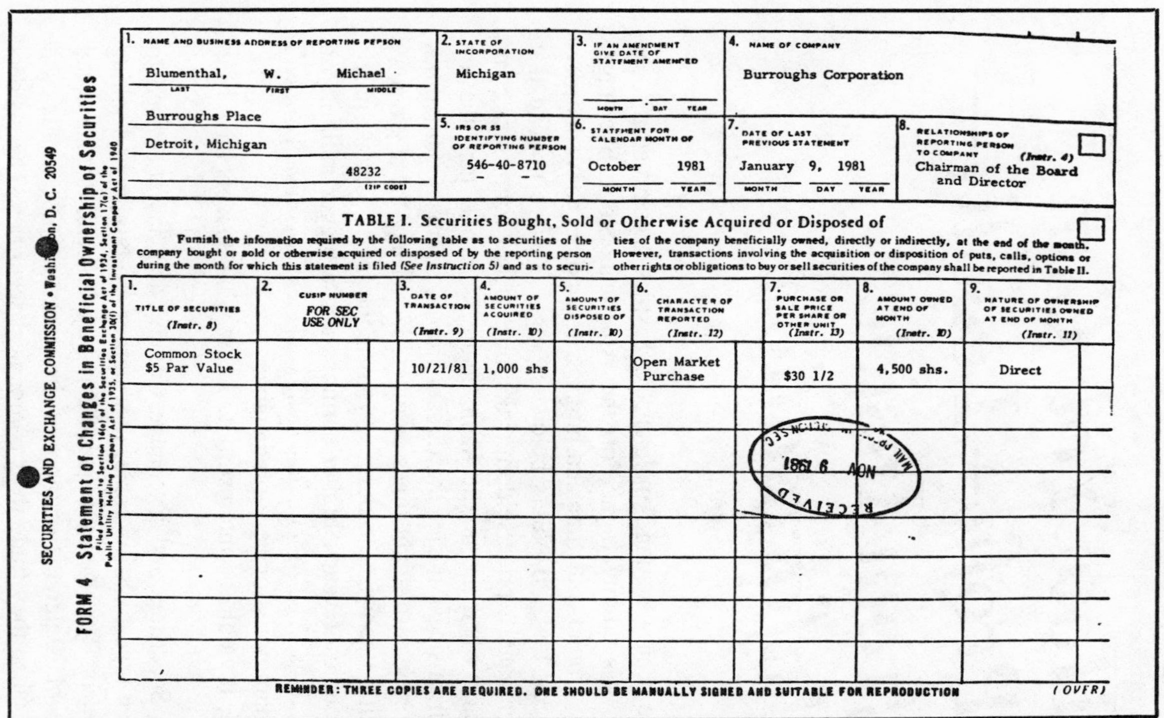

SECURITIES AND EXCHANGE COMMISSION • Washington, D. C. 20549

**FORM 4 Statement of Changes in Beneficial Ownership of Securities**

Filed pursuant to Section 16(a) of the Securities Exchange Act of 1934, Section 17(a) of the Public Utility Holding Company Act of 1935, or Section 30(f) of the Investment Company Act of 1940

| 1. NAME AND BUSINESS ADDRESS OF REPORTING PERSON | 2. STATE OF INCORPORATION | 3. IF AN AMENDMENT GIVE DATE OF STATEMENT AMENDED | 4. NAME OF COMPANY |
|---|---|---|---|
| Blumenthal, (LAST) W. (FIRST) Michael (MIDDLE) | Michigan | (MONTH, DAY, YEAR) | Burroughs Corporation |
| Burroughs Place | 5. IRS OR SS IDENTIFYING NUMBER OF REPORTING PERSON | 6. STATEMENT FOR CALENDAR MONTH OF | 7. DATE OF LAST PREVIOUS STATEMENT |
| Detroit, Michigan 48232 (ZIP CODE) | 546-40-8710 | October (MONTH) 1981 (YEAR) | January (MONTH) 9, (DAY) 1981 (YEAR) |

8. RELATIONSHIPS OF REPORTING PERSON TO COMPANY (Instr. 4): Chairman of the Board and Director

**TABLE I. Securities Bought, Sold or Otherwise Acquired or Disposed of**

Furnish the information required by the following table as to securities of the company bought or sold or otherwise acquired or disposed of by the reporting person during the month for which this statement is filed *(See Instruction 5)* and as to securities of the company beneficially owned, directly or indirectly, at the end of the month. However, transactions involving the acquisition or disposition of puts, calls, options or other rights or obligations to buy or sell securities of the company shall be reported in Table II.

| 1. TITLE OF SECURITIES (Instr. 8) | 2. CUSIP NUMBER FOR SEC USE ONLY | 3. DATE OF TRANSACTION (Instr. 9) | 4. AMOUNT OF SECURITIES ACQUIRED (Instr. 10) | 5. AMOUNT OF SECURITIES DISPOSED OF (Instr. 10) | 6. CHARACTER OF TRANSACTION REPORTED (Instr. 12) | 7. PURCHASE OR SALE PRICE PER SHARE OR OTHER UNIT (Instr. 13) | 8. AMOUNT OWNED AT END OF MONTH (Instr. 10) | 9. NATURE OF OWNERSHIP OF SECURITIES OWNED AT END OF MONTH (Instr. 11) |
|---|---|---|---|---|---|---|---|---|
| Common Stock $5 Par Value | | 10/21/81 | 1,000 shs | | Open Market Purchase | $30 1/2 | 4,500 shs. | Direct |

RECEIVED NOV 9 1981 ... SEC

REMINDER: THREE COPIES ARE REQUIRED. ONE SHOULD BE MANUALLY SIGNED AND SUITABLE FOR REPRODUCTION (OVER)

Figure 1. A Form 4 report filed by the chairman of Burroughs Corporation in 1981. The stock never traded below 27⅛ and twenty months later reached 57⅝.

transaction (open-market purchase or sale, private purchase, gift, etc.), price, and number of shares owned by the insider at the end of the month. A number of services compile and sell this information to investors. Their names and addresses appear later in this chapter.

The SEC also requires outside investors to disclose their buying—and their intentions—via a Form 13D filing within ten days of obtaining control of 5 percent or more of a company's securities. The 13D describes the individual or group acquiring an interest in the company, identifies key individuals behind corporate fronts, and states (usually in very general terms) the investors' objectives. Corporate raiders are masters at turning such innocuous words as "for investment" into bone-chilling threats to management.

The information from a typical Form 4 report might go like this:

| | |
|---:|---|
| COMPANY: | Amalgamated Textiles Inc. |
| BUYER: | Sanford, George K. |
| TITLE: | Vice-president/finance |
| DATE FILED: | June 12, 1984 |
| TYPE SECURITIES: | Common stock ($1 par value) |
| DATE OF TRANSACTION: | 4/27/84 |
| AMOUNT ACQUIRED: | 1,500 shares |
| AMOUNT SOLD: | |
| CHARACTER OF TRANSACTION: | Open-market purchase |
| PRICE: | $45¼ |
| AMOUNT OWNED: | 125,500 shares |
| NATURE OF OWNERSHIP: | Direct |

If the insider has made multiple purchases, you might learn that he paid $45 for 1,000 shares on 4/3/84; $44.50 for 500 shares on 4/16/84, and $45.25 for 1,500 shares on 4/27/84. If all those are open-market purchases, it seems that Amalgamated's financial VP is pretty bullish on the company. Looking further, you might find that he hasn't been alone in buying. In March the president bought 5,000 shares at prices between $42 and $43.75 and in early May 4,000 more between $46.25 and $47. It wouldn't be surprising if Amalgamated Textiles is about to enjoy better earnings or some other favorable development.

## Grading the Bulls

Not all stock buying by insiders is equal. Here are some points to check:

- The nature of the transactions. Purchases made on the open market deserve the greatest respect. Insider buying via company-granted options or discounts is generally disregarded. The rationale is that stock bought at a discount may be attractive largely because of the discount. You want to know what insiders think of the market quote, which is what you're going to have to pay.
- The number of individuals making trades. The larger the number, the more convincing their action. One buyer might be a hopeless optimist, or a true believer, who will pay any price. It's less likely that several insiders are caught up in self-delusion.
- The unanimity, or near unanimity, of insider decisions. Dissenters cloud the picture. Some analysts favor buying a stock only if insider buying has been unanimous—not even 100 shares to the contrary; if a company's outlook is splendid, they reason, executives would rather keep their stock than put the money to other use. I find this too confining. Insider selling is usually less meaningful than buying. Officers acquire stock through options and tend to be net sellers, and there are many reasons for an executive to sell stock—tax planning, a house purchase, etc.—unrelated to the company's prospects. An officer may have been fired and have sold his stock in a huff. Or sold to raise cash to exercise options. Such a rigid rule would have kept investors out of many of the best-performing insider stocks. Instead, look for the balance of activity. How many buyers vs. how many sellers? How big are the purchases vs. the sales? If several insiders are buying thousands of shares while one lets go of a few hundred, odds favor the buyers.
- Who is buying. Decisions by officers with direct access to important corporate numbers—the chairman, the president, a senior vice-president for sales, the treasurer, the chief financial officer—count for more than buying or selling by outside directors.

- ✔ The size of the trades. Large dollar amounts merit attention. So do purchases or sales that represent a significant change in the insider's holding. An officer who bets $50,000 on his company's future is more convincing than one who puts $5,000 into the stock. The latter trade may be window dressing to impress the public.
- ✔ The timing of the trades. Recent ones rate the most respect. Conditions change. A product that looked like a company-maker in January may be obsolete come June. (Have you heard much about Cabbage Patch dolls lately?)
- ✔ Does some special condition make the buying suspect? Insiders aren't indifferent to the impression they create on public investors. The old art of painting the tape—crossing trades to attract attention—is alive and well under more polite names ("We like to show our confidence"). This is difficult to quantify, but I tend to look twice at a series of minor trades by corporate officers if they come as the company is tooting its horn in other ways. I grow more skeptical if the officers have been around for a while and own little stock. If business looks good, there should be some heavy buyers.
- ✔ Is the purchase a "first buy" by a new officer or director? Or a ritual transaction by the president as the stock gains an exchange listing? Companies like their officers and directors to own at least a few hundred shares, if only to quiet the gadflies at annual meetings who ridicule insiders who don't own stock. Small purchases of this sort usually say nothing about a company's prospects.
- ✔ Why are they buying? The most important and most difficult question to answer. Often there isn't a clue. But sometimes good numbers on sales or earnings will have begun surfacing. Or perhaps the footnotes to the financial statements reveal hidden values. Is the backlog rising? Have new contracts been bid? Are margins expanding? If you can understand something of the stock's appeal to insiders, you'll be closer to knowing whether it's for you as well.

Unfortunately, a string of dubious insider buys may set the bells ringing on some advisory services' computers. Several market

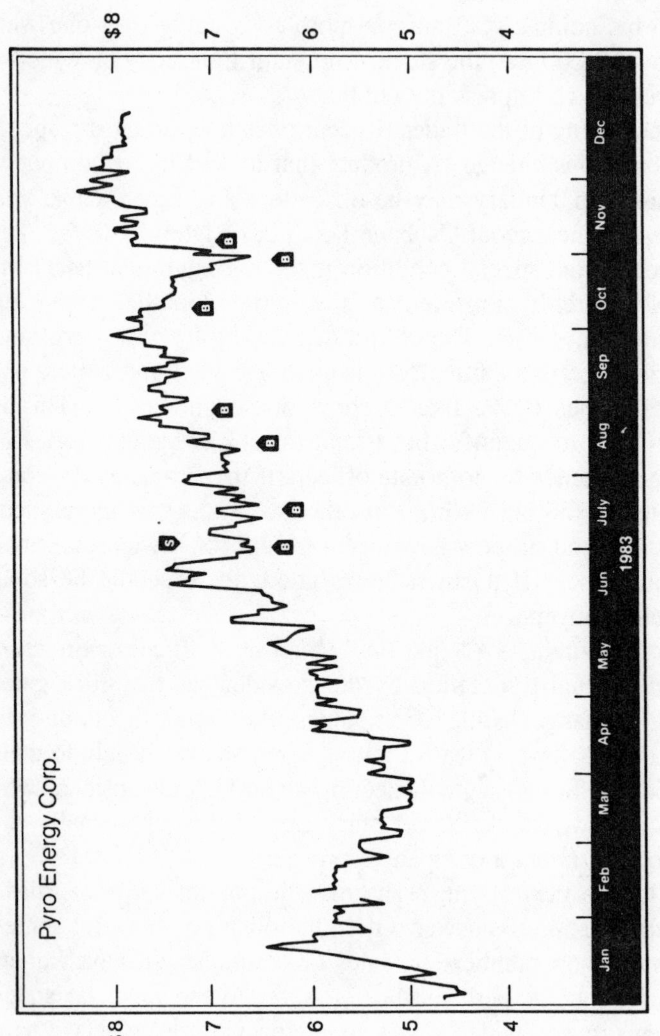


**Figure 2. Steady purchases by two directors accompanied a recovery at Pyro Energy Corporation.**

letters grew bullish on Gulfstream Aerospace, a new issue of 1983 that picked up a little insider buying at its public offering. A better measure of insiders' esteem was the fact that Gulfstream's chairman sold more than half the 7 million shares of the offering[1] at about forty times his cost. At last look, the sellers had done better than the buyers. Insider buying in companies that have just gone public is probably meaningless. Management can award itself all the stock it wants before the offering.

The three best indications that insider buying is for real are the number of similar transactions, the number of insiders involved, and the size of the transactions. Case in point: in the latter half of 1983, two directors of Pyro Energy Corporation bought about 50,000 shares of the coal producer between $6.75 and $7.63. So skeptical was the market of anything concerned with energy that other investors largely ignored the insiders' repeated forays after more stock.

It's important also to study a company's history. Insiders were buying Data Access Systems Inc., a small maker of computer terminals, in the first half of 1981. Yet the company's background was a woeful saga of suspicious stock moves, inflated earnings, and cozy inner-circle transactions.[2] A few weeks after an advisory service touted Data Access as a "High-Tech, Low P/E Growth Situation," the company's president was indicted for hauling fraudulently obtained checks across state lines. Eventually the SEC charged that he and some friends had milked the company for millions. Two years after the bullish article, the chairman faced prison, and Data Access was in Chapter 11. Stocks with fragrant histories sometimes rise, and the companies sometimes prosper. But public shareholders seldom share any bounty.

Here are some other guidelines for buying insider stocks:

### *Diversify by Industry*

Even if insider buying is concentrated in one stock group, you should spread out. Insiders are less likely to be wrong about the outlook in several industries than in one. In 1981 and 1982, inside money poured into oil and oil service companies much too early. (The list of insider stocks from *Barron's* in Appendix I notes some of the buying.) The insiders were undone by *one* development: the bear market in energy was more prolonged than anyone expected. Diversification makes good investment sense in any context, because it reduces risk from any particular event. A portfolio balanced among oils, electric utilities, computers, foods, consumer products, and cyclicals would have fared better in 1981 than a portfolio overloaded with energy issues. In most of those groups, insiders could *act* to improve their companies' fortunes and help make their bullish prophecies self-fulfilling.

### *Diversify in Time*

If you were lucky and bought a selection of insider stocks in August 1982, within a year you would have doubled your money. (See the *Insider Indicator* list in Appendix I.) That was about twice as well as the broad market averages performed. But most of us rarely buy at the bottoms of bear markets. Insiders aren't that astute, either. If you had become fully invested a year earlier, again following insiders, your nest egg would have *shrunk* in the next twelve months by 23 percent. By investing over a period of time, you reduce the risk that you're jumping in just before prices take a spill.

### *Go with the Pros*

When insider buying is especially heavy and broadly based, you can probably step up your own purchases. The market is cheap, if not risk-free. When selling overwhelms buying, it's time to tread gently. That needn't mean ignoring an attractive situation because insiders are selling the rest of the market; a stock being bought by smart money may be shaping up as a leader. But it does mean recognizing that the risks are at least somewhat higher than they were when insiders were grabbing stocks across the board.

### *Buy Close to the Insiders' Price*

Stocks may run up on news of insider buying or a 13D filing. Don't chase them. The excitement probably will wear off, let-

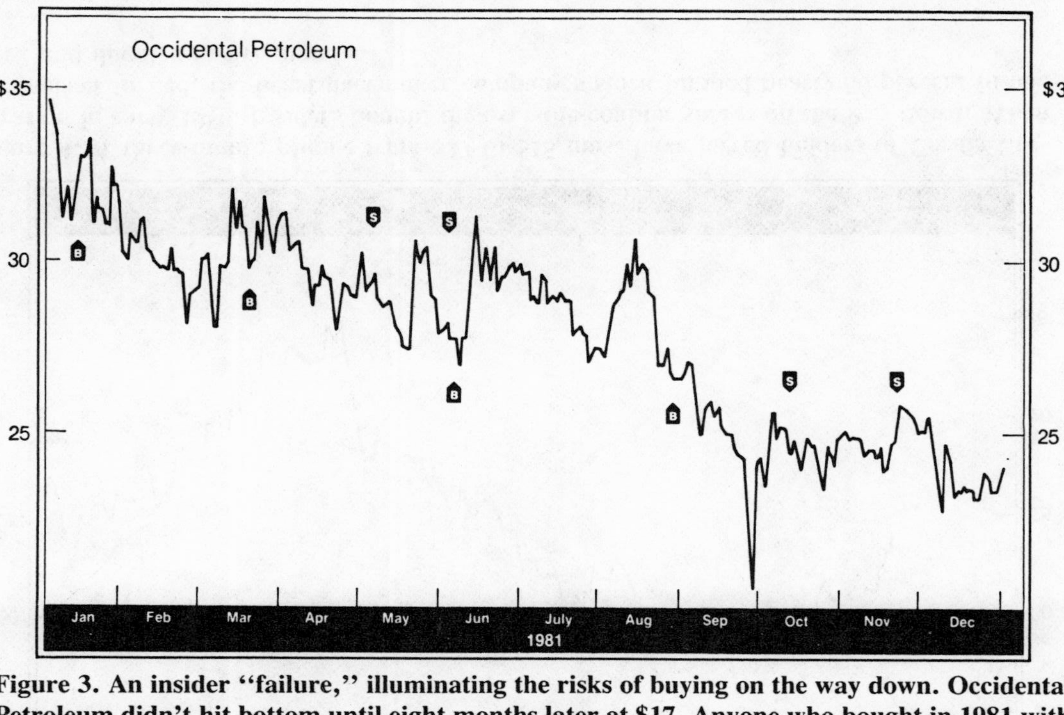


**Figure 3. An insider "failure," illuminating the risks of buying on the way down. Occidental Petroleum didn't hit bottom until eight months later at $17. Anyone who bought in 1981 with the insiders had a long wait. A better strategy was buying into strength in early 1983, along with investor David Murdock.**

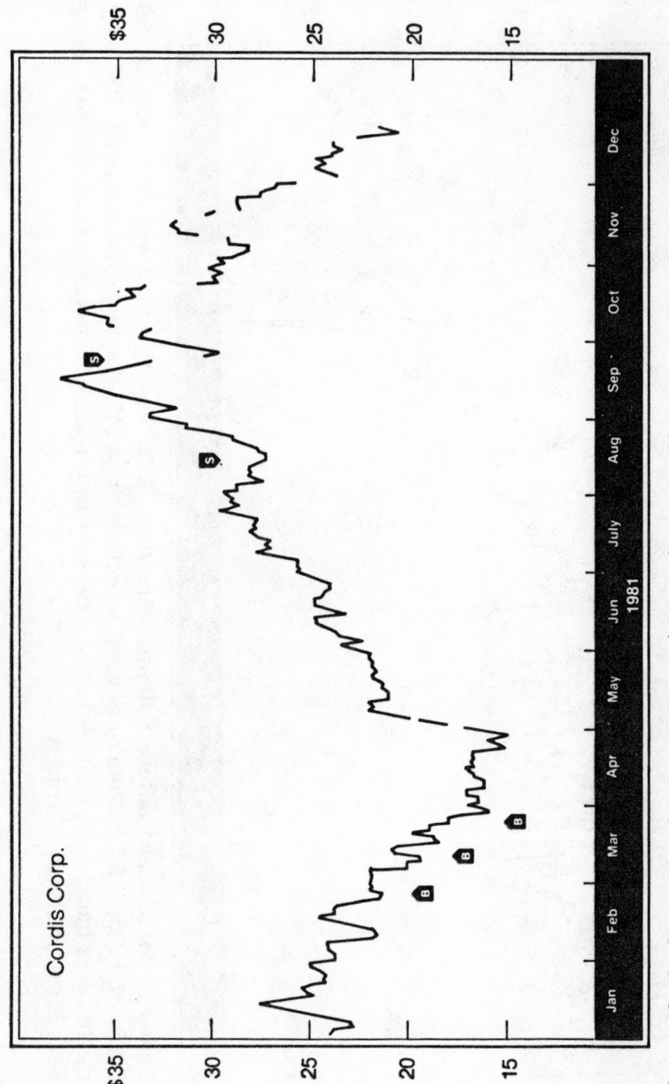


**Figure 4. A three-month plunge from $27 to $15 must have jarred holders of Cordis Corporation in early 1980. Insiders bought the over-the-counter shares on the way down. When the market turned, the heart-pacemaker company's stock jumped nearly 50 percent in one week and doubled in five months.**

ting the shares come back close to the price insiders paid. That's the time to buy. You may learn later that the insiders have returned as buyers with you; if they have deep pockets, the stock may find major support here. Chasing an issue that's flying on takeover speculation after a raider has shown his hand is too rough a game for most of us.

### *Buy After Bottoms (If You Can)*

You can't be certain that a stock won't go lower. But the point is to be wary of issues in solid downtrends. Even if insiders are buying, they may be early—or wrong. Once the shares look as though they've bottomed, you can buy close to the low with a stop-loss in case the sinking spell resumes.

### *Buy Values*

"If it goes up," Will Rogers might have said, "it was a value." They come in all shapes and sizes. To narrow the search, the next chapter reviews some of the canons of security analysis. In the meantime, a general point: The better an investor's understanding of why a stock is undervalued, the less likely he or she will be shaken out of it by some unimportant market fluctuation. If you *know* you've bought assets for 60 cents on the dollar, would you sell merely because the bid drops to a half-buck? A veteran observer of insiders, Rodger W. Bridwell, described the fortunes won by officers and directors who in the 1950s began buying woebegone Crown Cork & Seal. A new president, John Connelly, paid $15–$18 for his first stock and within a few years held more than 100,000 shares—with a $400,000 paper loss. From every appearance, noted Bridwell, "this was certainly a time when insiders seemed to be 'wrong.' " But by 1961, one of the great back-from-the-dead stories in corporate annals had lifted the quote to $120. In 1978, Crown Cork sold above $700 (before stock splits)—forty-seven times the $15 that Connelly had been "wrong" for paying in the mid-1950s.[3]

### *Recognize Insiders' Limits*

Insiders aren't better at foretelling events outside their ken or control than the rest of us. Crowd psychology may drive the market to extremes no one can anticipate. Political disasters may intrude. If insiders are buying stocks across many industries, it's because they see signs that business will improve. This judgment can be usefully tapped; it's a form of real information. But it isn't a guarantee that the Federal Reserve Board won't suddenly tighten credit and stall the recovery. This is a point to consider when deciding how much to risk even in stocks insiders like.

## SILENT INSIDERS

Following insiders is much easier today than it was a quarter century ago. Under SEC rules, insiders must report more detailed data on their trades and, in theory, do so within certain time limits. But there are shortcomings in the disclosure system that leave outside investors at a disadvantage.

SEC enforcement of the filing deadlines on insider trades is lax. (This is in keeping with the agency's emphasis on regulating the *use* of information in the market rather than on demanding prompt corporate and insider disclosure of information.[4]) Hundreds of late insider reports are accepted by the SEC each month without penalty. The agency was unable to estimate the percentage of tardy Form 4s, but a private survey for the month ending August 12, 1983, alleged that 43 percent of 11,818 stock transactions that were disclosed to the SEC had been reported late.[5] The SEC's director of public affairs, Andrew L. Rothman, said the figure was "certainly possible."[6] *The Wall Street Journal,* reporting on the study, commented that "the SEC has never considered strict enforcement of the filing requirement to be among its most important duties,"[7] to which Rothman responded, "I guess I wouldn't argue with [that]." Not only hasn't the agency applied administrative penalties at its disposal—such as censure—to force insiders to deliver their information to the marketplace in the required time, but also for much of 1983 the staff had even stopped sending out warning letters to late filers. In that environment, it's hardly surprising that some insiders ignore the rules and don't bother to report their transactions.

Even as written, the rules allow insiders an inordinate amount of time to provide information to electronic-age markets. In theory, an insider must report a trade no later than the tenth day of the month following the transaction. An officer who buys or sells on October 31, for example, has ten days (until November 10) to file his report; an insider who acts on October 1, however, also has until November 10 to file, or forty days. To quicken the information flow, one market letter, *The Insiders,* has urged the SEC to require insiders to file the simple Form 4s within five days of their trades. Doing so, the editor argued, would impose no new burden on corporate officers or directors and would be of considerable benefit to other investors. The proposal has found little support within the Securities and Exchange Commission.

*The Insiders* also noted a major loophole in insider disclosure, the fact that officers of subsidiaries needn't report transactions. This leaves open a vast area for abuse; the 1982 selling by two executives at the Atari unit of Warner Communications was a rare episode that caught investors' attention. This issue, too, appears to be on the SEC's back burner.

There are loopholes in the rules requiring 13D filings as well. In theory, any investor or group that controls 5 percent or more of a company's securities must disclose the fact within ten days. In practice, brokers and investment advisers can accumulate more than 5 percent in clients' accounts and not disclose; as individuals with nominal control of their own accounts, the clients aren't considered a "group."

Investors socking away major interests in a company's debt instruments needn't tip their hand at all. This loophole has enabled big players like Carl Lindner and Odyssey Partners to take large positions in bankrupts such as GAC and the Milwaukee Road with the public being for a time no wiser. With GAC, the bonds were exchanged for stock as part of a reorganization plan, and Leon Levy, Peter Sharp, and associates emerged in control of a new company, Avatar Holdings, and only then had to file a 13D. About the only way outsiders can follow these intriguing plays is by accumulating bales of court filings on bankrupts.

A number of SEC reforms are in order: speeded-up insider filings, with sterner enforcement; broader reporting requirements, to include officers of subsidiaries; broader and stricter rules on 13D filings. To curb persistent leaks on takeovers and other major developments, the commission could also draft specific guidelines on when corporations should disclose such information.[8]

## THE INSIDE WORDS

Any number of services, from the Government Printing Office to private investment advisers, collect and sell information in various formats on insider transactions. Some get the data out while it's fairly current. Here's a rundown.

### SEC News Digest

Published daily, the *SEC News Digest* reports on 13D filings and amendments, along with routine business of the SEC and the stock exchanges, regulatory enforcement actions, stock registrations, and filings (known as 8Ks) by companies disclosing important developments. Although newsworthy 13D filings often are reported in *The Wall Street Journal* before mail subscribers receive their *Digest,* many other 13Ds and amendments appearing in the *Digest* never make the newspapers. The most glaring deficiency of the service, for our purposes, is that it doesn't cover the Form 4s by which insiders report their buying and selling. But it's still a useful resource for the investor who wants to keep abreast of what the big money is doing. Subscription: $135 (first-class mail) and $110 (second-class mail) annually from Disclosure Inc., 5161 River Road, Bethesda, MD 20816. Telephone (800) 638–8241.

### Official Summary of Security Transactions and Holdings

The *Official Summary* is a monthly compilation of the trading reports filed by insiders with the SEC. A typical edition runs 300 pages and includes entries on several thousand companies. This is an invaluable reference. The information is dated, because the volumes are mailed approximately a month (sometimes much longer) after the closing date for inclusion of reports. As insiders have up to forty days to file on any month's transactions, that means their buying or selling may have occurred two to three months (or more) before you read about it. Some of what the *Official Summary* lacks as a short-term trading tool it makes up in completeness. Browsing these pages, an investor discovers companies lying far off the beaten track. Subscription: $70 annually from Superintendent of Documents, Government

Printing Office, Washington, DC, 20402. Telephone (202) 783–3238.

The titles below are private advisory letters. Some editors massage the statistics and recommend stocks. Each has his own formula for weighing the importance of insider activities. All are professional, in my view, and worth a look.

## The Insiders

This is the largest-circulation (11,000 subscribers) market letter focusing on insider trading. Editor Norman Fosback took his Bachelor of Science degree at Portland (Oregon) State University under Shannon Pratt, co-author of one of the classic academic studies of insider trading. Fosback has evolved a complex formula for grading inside activity. Besides using size, number, and recentness of trades, Fosback weighs an insider's position (top-ranking officers count more than outside directors) and the transaction's value relative both to the company's total capitalization and to the insider's previous holding. He gives less importance to entirely new positions. Insiders' choices gain points with Fosback if the stock's industry group has also attracted strong insider buying. Each issue of *The Insiders* ranks about 2,600 stocks and notes the twenty highest- and lowest-rated issues on each exchange and on the NASDAQ list. Another regular feature, "The Insiders Index," charts aggregate insider activity as a market barometer. In its first several years, the service recommended purchase of about thirty securities, and its success ratio was impressive. (The track record appears in Appendix I.) Fosback is an acerbic critic of insider abuses and occasionally bestows a "Lucky Insider" award on executives or directors whose timing has been too good. Subscription: $49 annually (twenty-four issues), free trial (two issues), from the Institute for Econometric Research, 3471 North Federal Highway, Fort Lauderdale, FL 33306. Telephone (305) 563–9000 or (800) 327–6720.

## Weekly Insider Report

This service's computer base provides raw data to a number of other publications. Editor Edwin A. Buck employs a tighter screen, noting only insider trades of at least 500 shares for listed stocks, 2,000 shares for over-the-counter issues. *Weekly Insider Report* also keeps tabs on companies whose insiders have reported at least five purchases or sales. Other features include a sell-buy ratio, covering overall insider activity, and a tally of companies buying stock for their treasuries. The service's prime strength is its timeliness. Readers receive the tallies days after the SEC. Subscription: $85 annually, $25 three-month trial, from Vickers Stock Research, Box 59, Brookside, NJ 07926. Telephone (201) 539–1336.

## Insider Indicator

The *Indicator* has expanded on the benchmark study of insider trading at Portland State University in the 1960s. Editor J. Michael Reid puts to work a data base that includes ten years of insider history on the two major stock exchanges. This gives him a rare perspective on how individual stocks have performed after previous rounds of insider buying and selling. A buy or sell signal is generated when three or more insiders buy—or sell—within roughly five weeks, with none bucking the trend. That unadorned system has generated 700 NYSE buy signals since 1974, reports Reid, with an average annual return exceeding 20 percent on stocks held one year. The twice-monthly service also monitors corporate investors in a "Who Is Buying Whom" section. (The track record on *Indicator* buy signals appears in Appendix I.) Subscription: $145 annually, $45 three-month trial, from Insider Indicator Inc., 2230 N.E. Brazee Street, Portland, OR 97212. Telephone (503) 224–8072.

## The Insiders' Chronicle

Besides statistics, the weekly *Chronicle* provides lengthy profiles of companies attracting insider buying. Other features include company briefs and lists of 13D filings, "intent to sell" notices under Rule 144, and companies with the largest insider purchases. Subscription: $325 annually, $165 six months, $29 trial (thirteen issues), from Kephart Communications Inc., P.O. Box 9662, Arlington, VA 22209. Telephone (800) 336–5407.

## Street Smart Investing

This service, begun in 1983 by a well-known financial writer, focuses on the so-called "smart money" investors—the likes of Carl Icahn, Odyssey Partners, Victor Posner, Saul Steinberg, along with many who keep lower profiles. Editor Kiril Sokoloff monitors 13D filings by these investors, looking for undervalued, out-of-favor stocks and prospective takeovers. Issues appear at approximately two-week intervals. Subscription: $195 annually, $48 trial (three months), from Street Smart Inc., 2000 Maple Hill Street, P.O. Box 491, Yorktown Heights, NY 10598. Telephone (914) 962–4646.

## Dunn & Hargitt Market Guide

Editor Edwin Hargitt makes buy and sell recommendations based on insiders' filings. The *Market Guide*'s overview is limited to 1,000 of the largest companies, based on Hargitt's belief that insider trades are more significant in big companies. Subscription: $125 annually (fifty issues), $18 trial (eight issues), from Dunn & Hargitt, 22 North Second Street, Lafayette, IN 47902. Telephone (317) 423–2626.

## Consensus of Insiders

Published since 1962, the weekly service monitors industry groups and individual stocks attracting insider buying, forecasts market risk, and reports on options traders' sentiment. *Consensus* boasts that its revolving model portfolio of stocks favored by the most insiders posted a gain of 1,012 percent between December 1962 and September 1983 versus 85.5 percent for the Dow Jones Industrial Average. Subscription: $247 annually, $137 six months, $27 trial (six weeks), from Consensus of Insiders Inc., P.O. Box 10247, Fort Lauderdale, FL 33334. Telephone (305) 563–6827.

## Special Situation Report

Editor Charles M. LaLoggia has put together a solid record of spotting takeover targets and undervalued shares. Twenty-three of his recommendations had drawn takeover bids in the six years through May 1984. Last year he got on a real roll, as City Investing, Cone Mills, Dr. Pepper, Huntington Health, Royal Crown Companies, Southwest Forest Industries, and Superior Oil drew bids in the first five months. Not every pick strikes gold, but many do. LaLoggia puts his own spin on insider trading. In June 1982, when Firestone Tire & Rubber was trading around $10 and the chairman was buying, LaLoggia noted it held $6 a share in cash and had shrunk its capitalization. In eight months, Firestone was at $20. Issues appear every two to three weeks. Subscription: $170 annually, $90 six months, $35 trial (three months), from the CML Market Letter Inc., P.O. Box 167, Rochester, NY 14601. Telephone (716) 232–3020 or 232–1240.

# FIVE

# *Would You Buy This Company?*

How do we go about verifying insiders' judgment that a stock is a bargain?

It's no easy task. The business of investing consists of buying values that aren't fully appreciated by the markets. This means speculating on all sorts of unknowables: on future appetites, opinions, fashions, fears, hopes, creditworthiness—not to mention on the way other investors will price assets, income, and risk tomorrow.

Uncertain business all around.

Economists crank up computer models to forecast levels of prosperity, despite evidence that they have no predictive value. Stock market technicians ponder chart patterns and volume trends for clues to next year's prices. Analysts extrapolate profits as though a business operated like a compound-interest table. One astrologer has piped up with predictions not much worse than several prominent Fed watchers'. The business of fortune-telling, whatever its professional credentials, is the art of describing something that doesn't yet exist. When the next moment arrives, it seldom has the exact texture we expected.

These uncertainties hamper anyone trying to project a future value on a common stock, whether the projection relies on earnings forecasts, macroeconomic models, chart trends, interest-rate guesses, the sequence of planets, or the outcome of elections. If any foolproof method had been developed, two things are certain: the founder would not have shared the secret in return for a newsletter fee, the price of a book, or brokerage commissions; and had he done so, the perfect system would have collapsed as investors adjusted to the information.

Uncertainty, disagreement, and neglect create the inefficiencies in the market, the undervalued and overvalued stocks on which money will be made. An investor's task is to reduce the uncertain and unpredictable elements in judging those situations. Watching insider trading helps, because an investor collects a royalty on better-informed people's information.

Confirming insiders' judgments requires realism, an acquaintance with the basics of securities analysis, and a modest act of faith: a willingness to assume that investors will value assets in the future on somewhat the same principles they've employed in the past. Specific levels of valuation will vary with the business climate, the inflation outlook, and the public's animal spirits. But the underlying premise is that stock market values, while not *absolute,* are nonetheless *real* and produce real returns which will be recognized.

Here's a conservative investor's primer on things to examine in a prospective investment. Most stocks will look good from some angles, questionable from others.

## Book Value

Book value is the nominal net worth of a company, the assets after all liabilities have been paid. A stock selling for substantially less than book value may be a bargain. The discount is evidence that the company or its industry (or the entire equity market) is deeply out of favor. Any number of things could account for this. Perhaps the company (or business in general) is earning a subpar return on assets. Perhaps investor psychology is on the ebb. In any case, a discount from book value represents inefficient pricing of capital, which the market over time tends to try to correct. If the company is doing well, investors' low opinion eventually gives way to a more accurate appraisal—one recognizing the real returns available—and the price rises. If the assets are badly managed, financial scrap dealers may target the company for a takeover or liquidation.

When many companies in many different industries sell at 20–30 percent discounts from book value, the entire stock market is probably a bargain. The discounts mean that investors are anticipating a prolonged bout of low returns on all business assets—a depression—and fortunately such fears are rarely fulfilled. At the market bottoms in 1974 and 1982, shares of hundreds of well-known companies were trading below book. Insider selling of these bargain-basement assets shrank to almost nothing.

Does book value really tell what a company is worth? Well, it's a benchmark, but a number of caveats apply. Book value may overstate or understate the value that can be realized. If the assets consist largely of obsolete inventory, for example, or include inefficient plants that must soon be shut down, book value will prove fluid, some of it destined to go down the drain. Computer companies have proved notorious for writing down inventory that can't be sold at cost; retailers get hit during recessions, when they have to move merchandise at a loss. If a manufacturer has set up more assembly or distribution centers than business will support, a big write-down may loom on the excess capacity. These misfortunes and others can take a hefty bite out of book value.

So can operating losses running out of control. International Harvester, to cite one of the grimmest recent examples, carried a tangible book value of $69.84 per share at the end of 1979. By the end of 1983, it was all gone.

On the other hand, book often understates the value of such assets as real estate and other natural resources, especially after periods of inflation. Likewise, plant and equipment may be worth much more than their value on the books. This is true particularly of assets that have been held a long time and depreciated to a fraction of what it would cost today to replace them.

Book value also includes intangible assets, such as capitalized expenses and goodwill. For years, computer software companies declined to recognize costs for product development and instead put them on the books as assets, to be written off over a period of years. Insurance companies have played similar games with the costs of acquiring policies. Book value of this sort can turn to water in an investor's hands if the computer programs no longer sell or the policyholders don't renew. These are not assets in any real sense but out-of-pocket expenses which accounting conventions permit companies to delay recognizing. Conservative companies take their expenses up front.[1]

Goodwill finds its way onto a balance sheet another way. If a company pays more for an acquisition than the value of the tangible assets, the difference is called goodwill and gets written off over forty years. This recognizes the fact that a going concern has value above the total of its machinery and inventories—brand recognition, a trained sales force, inspired management, divine approval.

For the company as a going concern, these intangible elements often count for more than the value of its plants, desks, and typewriters. A successful company, boasting widespread brand recognition and delivering high profits on its equity, may command a premium in the stock market many times its book value. If the flow of profits is likely to continue, this premium may be reasonable. Such companies, however, lie outside the inefficient part of the market where undervalued capital can be acquired. They're priced according to best expectations, not worse expectations, and thus surprises are more likely to be negative than positive. The periodic bloodletting in technology stocks demonstrates the point. By contrast, it has been a number of years since there was much blood available to spill in basic industry stocks such as steel and coal.

Asset values guide the stock market's scrap dealers and liquidators, who arrive after "worst expectations" have been realized. The net value of property, plant, equipment, cash, receivables, inventories, and the like—even if the number is only a horseback guess—is worth knowing in any investment. It helps measure ultimate risk. If an asset-rich railroad cracks up, there may be a future left in the wreckage. If business curdles for a computer software company whose entire value lies in providing services, there may be nothing except broken dreams to liquidate.

On the positive side, if the market is pricing a profitable company's assets at 50 cents on the dollar, you know that by one historical norm, the stock is undervalued and is likely to attract

**Altamil Corporation**
**Condensed Consolidated Balance Sheet**
**February 28, 1982**

| *Assets* | *Totals* | *Per Share* |
|---|---|---|
| Curent assets | | |
| Cash and short-term investments | $ 4,773,713 | $ 3.49 |
| Accounts receivable | 8,616,467 | 6.29 |
| Inventories | 11,771,270 | 8.60 |
| Other current assets | 1,021,019 | 0.74 |
| Total current assets | 26,182,469 | 19.12 |
| Other assets | 117,484 | 0.09 |
| Property, plant and equipment, less depreciation | 11,419,031 | 8.34 |
| Total assets | 37,718,984 | 27.55 |
| *Liabilities* | | |
| Current liabilities | | |
| Accounts payable | 2,959,739 | 2.16 |
| Accrued expenses | 5,835,172 | 4.26 |
| Other current liabilities | 288,351 | 0.21 |
| Total current liabilities | 9,083,262 | 6.63 |
| Long-term debt | 3,775,247 | 2.76 |
| Deferred federal income taxes | 768,000 | 0.56 |
| Total liabilities | 13,626,509 | 9.95 |
| *Shareholders' equity* | | |
| Convertible preferred, common, and additional paid-in capital | 6,527,779 | 4.77 |
| Retained earnings | 24,683,106 | 18.03 |
| Treasury stock at cost | (7,118,410) | (5.20) |
| Total shareholder's equity | $24,092,475 | $17.60 |

other bargain hunters. In the Altamil Corporation balance sheet you'll see an example of just such a bargain. Book value (shareholders' equity) was $17.60 a share. The stock was selling on the American Stock Exchange one afternoon in February 1982 for $7.75.

## Current Ratio

This ratio measures a company's liquidity. It's obtained by dividing total current assets on the balance sheet by total current liabilities. A ratio of 1.0 means the company has exactly as much in current assets (cash, receivables, inventories, and the like) as it has in current liabilities (accounts payable, debt falling due, taxes, etc.). On the surface, no problem. The company should be able to pay its bills without raising money on the outside.

But suppose inventories and accounts receivable represent much of current assets. If business weakens, it may become impossible to sell inventories without sharp discounts—and difficult to collect payments from customers. In short, the company could be hard put to pay creditors. In general, a current ratio of 2.0 is considered healthy in a manufacturing company. (A service firm without significant inventories or receivables, such as a restaurant chain or broadcaster, may get along quite well with a ratio below 1.0, because of its cash flow.)

In a deteriorating business climate, several of these numbers bear close attention as you review the quarterly financial statements. Is the cash position shrinking significantly? This could mean the company will soon have to borrow (probably at distress terms) or take other untimely steps to raise money. Is the inventory line bulging compared with six months or a year earlier? This could mean the company is getting stuck with finished products. Is the receivables line growing? This could signal trouble collecting bills. On the liabilities side, is the accounts-payable line growing? If the answer is yes, and cash has shrunk, the company may be running short of money and slowing its payments to suppliers. A business recession puts pressure on all these numbers. One test of management is how well it avoids serious swings toward liquidity trouble.

You can find very conservative companies with three, four,

and five times as much in current assets as current liabilities. If debt is modest and the business is sound, it will be hard for such a company to get into trouble. Easy for it to get a takeover bid.

## Working Capital

Subtract current liabilities from current assets and you get working capital. This is another way of looking at the current ratio. Beyond seeing the benefits of liquidity, investors look at working capital in absolute terms. If a stock is trading for less than the working capital per share, it's generally viewed as cheap. Glance back at the working capital of Altamil: $12.49 a share.

## Net Current Assets

Here's an even more rigorous measure of value. Net current assets (also known as net net) consist of a company's current assets minus all current liabilities, long-term debt, and other liabilities. This measures the company's most liquid value. Sometimes, very depressed stocks sell for less than the net current assets. This means that the company's property, plants, and equipment are, in effect, changing hands for free—as is whatever intangible value you might want to assign to the firm as a going concern. This is not a common occurrence. It marks a fire sale of a corporation's assets. If the company is running huge losses and the assets are rapidly eroding, the stock may be no bargain. If the assets are not slipping away, this is the sort of play that shows up on professional bargain hunters' computer screens: a chance to buy industrial property for 30 or 40 cents on the dollar. At Altamil, net current assets were $9.17 a share (current assets of $19.12 minus liabilities of $9.95). You could buy $8.43 a share in plants and equipment for nothing.

## Cash

Undervalued companies may be rich in cash and in short-term investments that could be turned into cash. To find out the cash per share, add together the cash-and-equivalent balance-sheet numbers and divide them by the number of common shares. Near bear-market bottoms, some stocks will sell for less than their cash. They represent prime takeover targets. A key question on the value of a company's cash is how quickly it's being consumed. To get a handle on this, compare the latest numbers with those of three months and a year ago. Looking back at the Altamil numbers, you'll see that the company had cash and equivalents worth $3.49 a share, or 45 percent of the market price. In the middle of 1984, obscure cash-rich companies included City Stores ($3.87 a share cash vs. $7.50 market quote), Dynalectron Corporation ($6.80 vs. $11), Heck's Inc. ($4.63 vs. $11), Reading Company ($7.83 vs. $17), and Salem Corporation ($6.45 vs. $9).

## Cash Flow

Another popular measure of liquidity, cash flow tells you whether the company can meet its bills, pay its dividends, and fund expansion without resort to outside financing. If a company is generating much more cash than it needs, it's becoming more liquid and, all other things being equal, probably more attractive. Cash-flow fans have a variety of ways of computing this number. They all work from a table in the annual report headed Consolidated Statements of Changes in Financial Position, which explains where the funds came from during the year and where they went. In essence, cash flow is calculated this way:

Earnings are added together with the amount recorded for depreciation and amortization. From this is subtracted amounts paid for new property, plants, and equipment (capital spending), payments on debt, and the cost of cash dividends. If the difference is positive, it means the company is generating cash beyond its needs for capital outlays, dividends, and debt payments. That's good. The company won't have to borrow. It can raise dividends, finance expansion, repurchase stock, or do other good things.

This needs refinement, however. More important than last year's cash flow is the future's. Is the company about to embark on a capital-spending spree? Is it weighing a big-ticket acquisition that will balloon debt payments? Either of those events could trigger a large swing for the worse in liquidity in coming years. In a healthy economy, a negative cash flow may cause no problems. But if business softens and earnings drop, a poor cash flow can turn into a disaster.

If cash flow is expected to remain positive, say aficionados of this analysis, then it's worth looking at the stock price in relation to the amount of free cash being generated. One recent investment book suggested that a stock selling for less than four times free cash flow is probably a bargain. The point is debatable.

Benjamin Graham and David Dodd objected years ago to the "vogue" of cash-flow analysis in valuing stocks. Their central complaint was that depreciation and amortization often verge on being out-of-pocket expenses and therefore do not really improve a company's cash position. They cited, for example, oil companies' costs of dry holes, manufacturers' amortization of short-lived tools, and write-offs of automobiles and trucks—all of which typically appear no faster for accounting purposes than the actual cost is felt by the company. Even depreciation of buildings, Graham and Dodd argued, reflects a real need for their eventual replacement. Only in the depreciation of properties by real estate companies did they find the benefit clearly exceeding the cost. Of other companies, they observed:

> If earnings before depreciation were the *true* earnings, then the amounts deducted for amortization would be really added to equity and invested in the business in the same way as undistributed profit. They should then generate a corresponding increase in subsequent cash-flow earnings. There is certainly no evidence over the long-term past that depreciation charges have been equivalent to earnings and equity, and have either been available for distribution to stockholders or have contributed to the growth of earnings.[2]

One of their explanations for analysts' attraction to cash-flow analysis was probably right on the money: "The rise in average stock prices has so greatly outstripped the increase in reported earnings that Wall Street has been constrained to look elsewhere for a justification of the market level." In 1982, the tactic was employed again, as oil-exploration companies' earnings slid and analysts turned to the better-looking ratios on cash flow. Despite their discovery of bargains at every turn, the stocks collapsed. The problem with cash flow is that you can't bank it or distribute it.

Cash-flow analysis may be most useful in pointing out deteriorating situations. If a company's liquidity is eroding even with depreciation figured as a plus, then you've got trouble. A cash-flow survey of forty-four high-P/E companies a few years ago pointed to twenty-six as worrisome; eleven months later, the stock prices of the twenty-six had fallen an average of 15 percent, while the others' prices were up 1.2 percent. The analysis pointed to trouble in seven companies—AM International, McLouth Steel, Nucorp Energy, Sambo's Restaurants, Saxon Industries, Seatrain Lines, and Wickes—all of which within a year were in bankruptcy.[3] So the numbers are worth running, if only for the bargains they steer you away from.

## Debt Ratios

Some industries are notoriously dependent on debt—airlines, real estate, leasing, utilities. In good times, as operating profits swell beyond interest costs, leveraged companies report abrupt and massive gains in earnings. When business sours, they suspend dividends, miss bank payments, and, now and then, land in receivership. There are no handy ratios on "safe" levels of debt that apply across the board. But in the manufacturing sector, a debt load of no more than 30 percent of total capital is generally considered prudent. Pretax profits should amply cover interest payments. Graham and Dodd suggest that earnings from the poorest recessionary year should be at least five times interest payments to assure safety (this from a bond investor's perspective). Today, with debt levels high and interest rates of 12 percent, such a comfortable margin is rare.

Consider an average company with a debt load equal to half its equity. Say it earns 10 percent on equity before taxes:

Pretax income (10% × \$200 million equity) = \$20 million
Interest cost (12% × \$100 million debt) = \$12 million
Income coverage of debt = 1.67

If debt and equity are equal, pretax profits would be less than interest expense:

> Pretax income (10% × $200 million equity) = $20 million
> Interest cost (12% × $200 million debt) = $24 million
> Income coverage of debt = 0.83

And, of course, if debt is two or three times equity, the company's ability to meet interest payments in lean times is doubtful. The weakening of balance sheets under heavy debt loads reached dangerous levels by the 1982 recession and helped account for the surge in corporate bankruptcies. Fortunately, the subsequent business recovery enabled companies to refinance, enlarge their equity bases, and repay some of the debt.

Dangers of leverage duly noted, a company with no debt may be too conservative. It's bypassing the attractive tax treatment of interest costs, and it may be expanding its market presence more slowly than it could. It also may be achieving a lower return on equity than it could with a little leverage, and, as Graham and Dodd note, a lower market valuation than it might otherwise enjoy.[4] Its main attraction to investors may be the hope that someone else will be attracted by the unused leverage and attempt a takeover.

## Dividend Yield

Dividend yield is the annual payment rate divided by the stock price. It's a well-worn bit of wisdom that above-average yields imply above-average risks. If Amalgamated Textiles is yielding 10 percent while most rag companies yield 6, it's a sign investors doubt Amalgamated's ability to earn profits and maintain the dividend. When a company is squeezed for cash, it will slash the payment to shareholders in a wink of an eye.

A company paying out a high proportion of its income in dividends gets a low investment rating for another reason. The payout suggests management can find nothing better to do with cash than distribute it. In other words, opportunities for expansion or acquisitions appear limited, either by business circumstances or by management's lack of vision. This suggests that the company's growth will be unimpressive. Hence "Don't invest for yield" is a financial columnists' standby. It deserves to be amended slightly to "Don't invest *only* for yield."

A high yield can point to the negative investor psychology that creates bargains. At the bear-market bottom in 1982, many good companies were paying 9–10 percent even though their prospects were only temporarily blighted and the dividend rate was safe. The list included American Brands, American Telephone, Avon Products (even allowing for the payment cut), Burroughs, Continental Group, Dow Chemical, Xerox, a cartel's worth of oil companies (Ashland, Exxon, Texaco), and an assortment of banks (BankAmerica, Chase, etc.). These were not usually "yield" stocks. An investor buying them on speculation that business would improve gathered not only capital gains but also the dividend checks to raise the total return.

## Earnings

Reported earnings are a company's most visible grade for performance. They reveal whether fortunes are rising or falling. They disclose the return on sales, on capital, on assets. They rank the company among its peers and against other industries. Is the net profit on sales regularly 2 percent or 15 percent? Either can provide a good investment. There's more glamour in the second, more leverage in the first, as holders of retail stocks have learned.

Earnings get well worked over in the corporate suite before being let out into the world, and that poses a problem. How much faith can investors place in the bottom line? The answer ranges from "some" to "none." Unfortunately, there are no rules of thumb for rating earnings' reliability. In recent years, the accounting practices of companies in oil exploration, equipment leasing, computer services, financial services, and such exotic fields as credit-card protection have come under challenge. At issue usually is how the companies book costs, or rather don't book them. If you believe that dry holes can be a capital asset for an oil company rather than an expense, you have what it takes to be a financial vice-president. On other fronts, analysts of earnings quality have pointed fingers at pharmaceutical and high-tech firms with offshore operations for understating taxes and inflating profits. What's "proper" in corporate accounting is a field of lively debate.

Evidence of accounting games can be found in the annual report in the section called Notes to Consolidated Financial Statements. There's a subheading to look for, Summary of Significant Accounting Policies. Here's a typical disclosure, by a well-regarded oil company: "Costs of acquiring undeveloped leases are capitalized. . . . The costs of drilling development wells and successful exploratory wells, including intangible costs, are capitalized to producing oil and gas properties. All exploratory drilling costs are initially capitalized and the costs of unsuccessful wells are expensed when determined to be nonproductive." That's cricket according to generally accepted accounting standards, but it provides enormous leeway for managements to understate expenses and exaggerate income. It also creates an area of undefined risk. A company may show growing earnings while embarking on a major exploration program, the cost of which is understood by shareholders only after dry holes force massive write-offs. This can wipe out not only paper earnings but an acre of stockholder equity as well.

Similar problems can snare investors in other industries, from real estate to shipbuilding. If a lot of immediate cash outlays are being capitalized—that is, recorded as "assets" to be written off against future income—the failure of that income to materialize may prove disastrous.

Some companies create all their profits at the accounting desk. Since 1980 and 1981, real estate corporations have been permitted to capitalize interest costs and real estate taxes on properties under development. Does this make a difference? Here's how the more liberal standard affected one Big Board firm. In 1982, the company reported a 5-cents-a-share profit; had it recognized interest and real estate taxes, it would have had to report an 18-cents-a-share *loss*. The following year, the company reported a 36-cents-a-share loss, which, without the accounting adjustment, would have been 67 cents.[5] This isn't improper—corporate managers don't set the nation's accounting standards—but it gives investors a rosier picture of operations than they would have if these costs were recognized when incurred.

Earnings may not be all they seem for other reasons. A profit from the sale of an unneeded plant, or a gain from a lawsuit, or a profit from excess insurance coverage on lost equipment (or on a lamented chairman)—these or other nonrecurring items can give the bottom line a one-time lift. American Maize-Products and Insilco Corporation both reported boosts to recent years' income from selling the public stock in subsidiaries for more than book value. In the first quarter of 1984, all of American Maize's net came from such a gain (it would have posted a loss otherwise). The "net income" figure under these circumstances doesn't represent the company's real earning power, its ability to make money in its normal business.

On a similar note, items such as losses carried forward from prior years inflate net earnings by cutting the company's tax payment. Tax-sheltered earnings represent cash in the till, but they don't reflect normal business results. Financial reports routinely note this kind of gain as an extraordinary credit. A company's tax rate can decline for other reasons as well, but disclosure of these details is likely to be tucked away in the footnotes. The company may have invested heavily in equipment and enjoy an abundance of investment tax credits—with which, earnings are higher than last year's; without which, perhaps, they would have been lower. The lower tax rate, a temporary benefit, conceals the deterioration.

The most reliable description of a company's normal profitability is the line on the Income Statement called Operating Income. This is before one-time gains and before taxes. Its trend over recent years defines how well the company has been doing on its normal operations. Here's an example showing that Xerox Corporation's operating profits fell in 1981 even though it reported higher earnings.

**Xerox Corporation**
**(Millions except per-share numbers)**

| | *1981* | *1980* | *Change* |
|---|---|---|---|
| Operating revenues | $8,691 | $8,197 | +6.0% |
| Operating income | 1,229 | 1,276 | −3.7 |
| Income taxes | 454 | 612 | −25.8 |
| Net income | 598 | 565 | +5.8 |
| Income per share | $7.08 | $6.69 | +5.8 |

Notice that although revenues rose from 1980 to 1981, operating income fell 3.7 percent. But because of substantially lower income taxes (thanks to changes in the United Kingdom, higher investment credits, and a lower U.S. corporate rate), Xerox was able to report 5.8 percent higher earnings per share. The erosion in the company's copier business was already showing up in operating profits, but the trouble didn't hit the bottom line until the next year, when earnings plunged. Most investors probably paid little attention to the early warning sounded by declining operating income. The slump in operating income as a percentage of revenues was even more pronounced: to 14.1 percent from 15.6 percent. That's a noteworthy one-year decline in margins.

## Return on Equity

This is a key measure of profitability. It's obtained by dividing net income by shareholder equity. Returns vary widely from industry to industry and among companies within an industry. Generally the market rewards more profitable enterprises with a higher price-earnings multiple, provided the profitability appears to have staying power. Businesses demanding heavy capital investment as a rule have lower returns on equity. Commodity-type businesses have lower returns most of the time than specialty, niche marketers. Xerox again provides an example. In its heyday in the 1960s, dominating the copier market, Xerox sported a return on equity of over 40 percent. In 1982, under fierce competition in copiers, the return had sunk to 11.4 percent.

Debt also helps lift return on equity. A company with both high profit margins and substantial leverage can boast enormous returns on equity. General Defense Corporation, a manufacturer of tank ammunition, reported $9.5 million in net profits in 1983 on a $21 million equity base, a return of 45 percent. If a company can reinvest such profits and earn the same return, in theory it can grow at a 45 percent compounded annual rate.

By itself, however, return on equity offers limited value in selecting investments. For one thing, the market tends to pay up for high-profit ventures, so the return available to investors is commonly more like 5 percent. Moreover, sumptuous returns tend to attract competition; if capital is earning far more in one industry than in others, it will flow toward the best action. Atlantic City casinos and personal computers are examples of what happens: the sight of a lot of money being made eases the financing of competing ventures, and the rivalry drives returns on capital down toward the market average (or, for a time, below the average). Current return on equity, in other words, may be a fleeting bounty. In 1982, Apple Computer earned 24 percent on equity—a return by no means unique in the technology field. The institutional herd chased the stock price up to ten times book value by summer 1983 only to find personal computers a glut on the market and Apple's earnings falling.

Off the beaten track, an investor may find companies with generous returns on equity that aren't fully discounted in the market. They will be small, *neglected* issues—in contrast to the small issues the growth boys have jumped on. Insiders may be buyers.

Bargain hunters are apt to find more targets, however, sporting mediocre returns. A low return on equity will probably be accompanied by a modest price-earnings ratio, a discount from book value, and perhaps a high dividend yield. The news hasn't been good, and there's a lot of room for somebody—management or a raider—to shape things up.

## Price-Earnings Ratio (and Earnings Yield)

A price-earnings ratio is the price of a stock divided by its earnings per share. Earnings of $4 per share and a stock price of $20 mean a price-earnings (P/E) of 5. The earnings yield is the P/E upside down, the earnings divided by the stock price. A $20 stock that earns $4 has an earnings yield of 20 percent. So what, you say?

If you could buy a healthy company paying 20 percent a year tax-free, it would look tempting. You would double your money in less than four years. That's the attraction of a low-P/E, high-earnings-yield stock. The company's net worth, if it retains its profits, is expanding at a pace worthy of a growth company even if earnings are static.

The case for low P/Es is central to bargain hunting. Whatever the other factors, a low P/E is evidence that a stock is out of favor. There are always reasons for this: doubts over the company's ability to maintain or increase its earnings (as with the international oils in 1982), doubts about its financial stability (as with the money-center banks at five times earnings in 1983), memories of past troubles (as with the textile stocks at P/Es under 4 in the late 1970s). The fears may prove well founded—perhaps the signs are clear that earnings are indeed about to collapse. But often a low P/E signifies nothing more dire than that the stock or its group has fallen out of fashion: the portfolio managers are off collecting moonbeams elsewhere.

The key attraction of low-P/E stocks is that they entail less risk. While a P/E is calculated on profits in hand, it's really the market's way of pricing the expected—but uncertain—stream of future earnings. Much can happen to dash expectations. Stocks with low multiples already reflect substantial concessions to uncertainty. If net isn't as high as had been hoped, the price may fall but probably not as far as when a big-P/E company delivers a shocker. One week in 1983, two companies disclosed surprisingly bad earnings. Beaten-down Tiger International fell 13.6 percent. An institutional darling named Digital Equipment plunged 31.3 percent. (Tiger, with a string of huge losses, wasn't technically a low-P/E stock, but it was certainly out of fashion.) The institutional go-go crowd, born again in August 1982, got roughed up repeatedly in 1983 as superstars like Apple, Diasonics, and Digital burned out. The P/Es left no room for disappointing earnings.

Given the failure rate in analysts' efforts to forecast earnings, it seems impossible to justify on a risk-reward basis buying *any* growth stock at forty times earnings. Such a multiple implies a degree of certainty that is simply beyond reach. Insiders, who should be as certain of the outlook as anyone can be, seldom show up as buyers of higher-P/E issues. Much of the time they're heavy sellers.

Not only is risk lower in modestly priced stocks, but also the potential reward is higher. There's the possibility of a double payoff. The company's profits might improve, which would justify a higher price. Then that favorable news might convince investors that improving earnings deserve a higher multiple. If earnings rise just 20 percent, and the P/E goes from 4 to 6, the stock price will rise 80 percent. Shares selling at forty times earnings don't offer much room for multiple expansion, but there's plenty of room for contraction in response to bad news. If earnings fall 20 percent and the P/E drops from 40 to 20, the stock will tumble 60 percent. The higher-PE shares, as I've said, are usually priced according to *best* expectations; upside surprises are difficult.

What price-earnings multiple is suitable? This depends on many factors, including past earnings stability, prevailing interest and inflation rates, and hoped-for growth. As a rule of thumb, a price seven times earnings seems to put a stock into the realm of possible bargains in most market climates. A P/E of 7 means that the earnings yield is 14.3 percent. If the company hangs on to its net, then its net worth is growing at a 14.3 percent annual rate, or doubling every five years.

One benefit of looking at earnings yields is the ease of comparing a stock's return to those available elsewhere. In early 1984, for example, a 14.3 percent earnings yield was about 2 points better than the yield on top-grade bonds, 5½ points better than Treasury bills, and 10 points higher than the inflation rate. It was competitive, in other words, with alternative investments and offered a handsome real return.

The earnings-yield approach also illuminates a reason low-P/E stocks are less risky. With a 14.3 percent earnings yield, profits can grow little, or even decline a bit, and an investor is still getting good appreciation of value. At a P/E of 40, however, the current earnings yield of 2.5 percent takes *twenty-eight years* to double the investment's value. In that situation, earnings growth counts for everything.

One final word on P/Es: sometimes bargain stocks sport enormous multiples. A company posting losses or negligible profits may trade far below its asset value and at a low multiple of both its historic profits and reasonable estimates of profits once business picks up. Yet on current income, the P/E ratio may be 20, 30, or infinite. This is a different situation from the overpriced glamour stock. If the company's problems seem likely to be resolved, either by internal changes or by a cyclical business recovery, the stock may be on the bargain counter despite the lofty P/E.

# SIX

# *Sleuthing for Beginners*

Let's assume that you don't play golf with the treasurer of Amalgamated Textiles. Insiders have been buying the stock and you want to learn more. How to get information?

The company's annual and quarterly reports provide a briefing on operations and finances. Its proxy statement reveals data on major owners of stock, directors' identities, management stock holdings, salaries, and conflicts of interest (tactfully called "related-party transactions"). Reference manuals published by Moody's and Standard & Poor's, available at most libraries, will provide more background, histories of mergers, descriptions of bonds and stocks outstanding, updates on recent financial results, and other announcements. Many large libraries also carry *The Value Line Investment Survey,* a popular advisory service that publishes financial statistics along with analysis and commentary. The library's *Business Periodicals Index* will steer you to articles about the company in financial journals. Is the chairman an old stock promoter trailing a long history of failures? *Barron's* or *Forbes* might have exposed his mischief. *The Wall Street Journal Index* summarizes that daily's news and feature stories, listed by company; major libraries normally have years of back issues available on microfilm. All of these sources can be indispensable to a serious investor weighing a major long-term speculation in an unfamiliar company.

A valuable manual which most investors—or their brokers—should own is the *SEC Corporation Index—Active Companies.* It contains more than 600 pages giving mailing addresses of every firm that files reports with the commission. This provides access to about 9,000 publicly traded companies, including the most obscure. Unaccountably, the SEC doesn't print copies for sale; a private contractor at the SEC headquarters, Disclosure Inc.—telephone (800) 638-8241—will copy the book for 10 cents a page, or about $70 including postage. Since some of the most promising insider stocks are in companies too small for stock exchange or NASDAQ listings, this manual is a convenient way of tracking them down. A postcard or telephone call to the company's Shareholder Relations department will usually bring a packet of the basic information (annual report, quarterlies, press releases, proxy statement); sometimes the company will send copies of brokerage-house reports (if they're gung-ho enough).

When you've dug through this burden of paper, you'll know a lot about Amalgamated Textiles. You may know enough to have decided that you wouldn't buy the stock at half the price. But let's assume the fundamentals are attractive: a low P/E, rising profits, sound balance sheet, discount from book value, positive cash flow, above-average yield—plus insider buying. At this point you might cast caution aside, tap the kids' tuition, and buy this undiscovered gem. Or you might wonder if it isn't too precious to be true. Perhaps it looks like a bargain only because you don't know something that other people know.

The potential pitfalls are beyond number. Maybe the company was sued last month for fraud and swamp pollution. Perhaps competition is heating up and margins are about to shrink. Maybe the chairman died and his son plans to switch from producing T-shirts to video games. It's true that if insiders have been buying the stock, there's probably nothing terrible going on. But suppose the insider is the idiot son? It never hurts to be too careful. This is why I like to call company officers.

Talking to corporate managers—and listening to them—takes practice. You can come away with information that hasn't reached the public (or been understood). Or you can come away with an earful of soap. A money-managing acquaintance of mine is a master at listening to the hum of the telephone line and guessing what management isn't telling him. He bought Preway Inc., a fireplace maker, for his clients early in the energy boom and got to know the management. The president was talkative, upbeat, ready with straight answers. Then one day the tone was different, indecisive. My friend pressed. Just how was business? Well, said the president, we may have a little problem here and there. The money manager sold all his stock the next day. Preway's problem grew, and the stock lost half its value.

At a small to medium-sized company, it's usually possible to get through to a senior executive. This is worth some effort. Shareholder Relations may be a shack in the back pasture where memos on sales and earnings soak up coffee. If anyone knows what's afoot in the company, the chairman, the president, and the treasurer should. The last may be the most accessible, the person who routinely talks to analysts and major investors. The more knowledgeable a caller sounds about the company, the more doors open.

You're a private (implied: substantial) investor who has been following the company. You've noticed that President Wellborn has been buying the stock. Is business improving? If you've done your homework, you'll be a step ahead of Wellborn or his chosen lackey. You'll already know the questions you want to ask. He'll have only a general suspicion of what's coming. While he answers, you can grade his responses. Does he answer fully and precisely, or puff smoke? For example:

*Investor:* Your sales in the last quarter were up 10 percent. Are you still doing that well?

*Officer:* We're doing pretty well. (Mushy. You might prod him.)

*Q:* Are things slowing down?

*A:* No. Actually, they're a bit better than in the last quarter. As I said, we're doing pretty well. (He wasn't being evasive. He just talks in generalities.)

*Investor:* The average analyst seems to expect you to earn $1.50 a share this year. Are you—

*Officer:* We never forecast earnings.

*Q:* Are you comfortable with the Street estimates?

*A:* Yeah, we're comfortable with a $1.45–$1.55 range.

There's a fellow over at Shearson who thinks we may do $1.60. But sales would have to grow faster than the last quarter's for us to make $1.60.

*Q:* They *are* growing a little faster, didn't you say?

*A:* They are this quarter.

*Q:* Is this normally your strong quarter?

*A:* Actually, it's usually weak.

*Q:* Are you maybe getting sales in this three months at the expense of the next three?

*A:* Well, it could be. But orders for the rest of the year look pretty good.

A happy scenario. Not only do things look as good as the investment community expects—they also may come in a bit better. So far, you and the Shearson analyst have information that hasn't spread through the Street. Moreover, you're fairly confident of the quality of your information. Mr. Wellborn wasn't selling hard; he's a conservative fellow who would rather underestimate earnings than have them come in a nickel lower than he said. You've had to coax the facts out of him. If you can buy the stock at a modest price before other investors sense the scope of the company's improvement, you've a good chance of making money.

But suppose the conversation goes differently. President Wellborn is vague on sales momentum.

*Investor:* Are things slowing down?

*Officer:* I didn't say that. We're doing pretty well, and the next quarter looks even more promising.

*Q:* Would you like to put a number on it?

*A:* I really can't do that. I haven't told anyone else, and I don't want trouble with the Securities and Exchange Commission.

*Q:* Me either. But would you say that this quarter's sales and earnings growth will match the last quarter's?

*A:* They'll be in the same ballpark.

*Q:* I see analysts are looking for you to clear $1.50 a share.

*A:* We never forecast earnings.

*Q:* Are you comfortable with the analysts' forecasts?

*Officer* (laughs): Now if I say I'm comfortable, that's no

different from saying sure, we're going to earn such and such an amount. I don't play that game.

*Investor:* Haven't the analysts who say $1.50 been talking to you?

*A:* They're responsible for their own numbers. We haven't had anyone in here for several months.

In short, Wellborn isn't eager to say the estimates are too high. But it sounds as though something is amiss. Even if Wellborn bought stock—a few hundred shares, let's say, two months ago—business more recently may have weakened.

You may not be convinced that the company is in trouble. But without a straight answer from the top, the uncertainty—and risk—in investing in this company are higher than you may want to accept.

You can hope officers will be candid, but you can't count on it. I've been told everything's rosy when the salesmen are cutting their throats. The ear gets better with time.

## Talk to Customers

Sounding out a company's customers is another useful tactic, especially if the concern's product is new, or unfamiliar to you. You won't get far by standing outside McDonald's and asking customers how they like McNuggets or polling teenage girls on their Calvins. Unless you've got a lot of time, your sample will be meaninglessly small. But if you sounded out retailers on demand for Calvins, or Adam computers, or Chrysler vans, the answer could be important. Customers'—or distributors'—responses can prove particularly valuable when a new product stands a chance of being a company-maker.

A small movie-production company, Laurel Entertainment, attracted speculation a couple of years ago on hopes it had a money-making horror film in the can. It was well worth calls to a couple of Rhode Island theaters where the film was tested to find out if the kids were coming back for second and third helpings. They weren't. Before the film opened nationally, Laurel's chairman and its president voted with the kids, selling more than 50,000 shares near the top.

Investors in a small new issue called Insituform East had a happier time of it. The company was headquartered in Landover, Maryland, and had licensed an unusual process for repairing damaged underground pipe. A nearby money manager became interested and began polling the customers, including the Washington Suburban Sanitary Commission. The responses were enthusiastic, and he bought Insituform East as a small company with big growth prospects. He liked something else: insiders hadn't sold stock at the offering; all the money went to finance the company's future rather than insiders' retirement. So far, the judgment has been profitable.

Time spent on diligent sleuthing is well invested. It bears repeating: information doesn't reach the marketplace in equal rations at the same moment. The more an investor learns about a situation before analysts, brokers, and other investors arrive, the better the early operator's chance of turning a profit. This requires forsaking the comfort of the crowd, the assurance from a retail broker that he's putting you (and everybody else) into a winner (which is up just 60 percent in the last couple of weeks but still a steal). But if you've done your homework and discovered authentic value, the crowd will join you sooner or later. (You can speed the process, after you've got your position, by doing a little unpaid press agentry.)

Charles Allmon, president of a Bethesda, Maryland, firm called Growth Stock Outlook Inc., which publishes market advisory letters, knows the value of burning up the phone lines. He put clients several years ago into a virtually unknown company called Sykes Datatronics, a maker of sophisticated telephone equipment that went from $1.75 to $34 in about thirty months. Allmon was a step ahead of most investors who hear about a small company, because he knew a little about it. But the research that followed is the sort that any hard-working investor can do. Allmon recalls:

> We'd had a file on Sykes Datatronics since 1972, but I wasn't paying much attention to it. In March or April 1979, a couple of our readers wrote and said, "You *must* take a look at this company. They're about to sign this contract with AT&T to produce some of their equipment." Now of course signing a deal doesn't mean they're going to see millions of dollars immediately, so we

> had some time before things began to pick up. The revenues at the time were about $4.5 million, but if Bell was putting its name on Sykes products, that would be just the start. The first thing I did was to get in touch with the chairman and the president. I got the names of people at the local Bell company, C&P Telephone in Washington, who had seen their equipment, and I went to people I knew on the board to get access to the top fellows in C&P and on down the ranks. Over three or four days I talked to at least 10 people. Out of these conversations came one key comment. The head marketing man said to me, "I don't think those fellows at Sykes really know what they're doing. We've identified about 50 uses for this machine that those guys didn't know existed." I said, "*What* did you say?" This told me we might really be onto something.

It also satisfied one of Allmon's key tests for a growth company: customer acceptance of the products. Management might give him a snow job, but he figured that if the customers say they love a product, they probably mean it.

> I wanted to see what the equipment looked like and how other customers felt about it. As it turned out, our broker in Washington had the system and showed me how it improved efficiency in an office with a large number of telephones.

He already had checked the backgrounds of Sykes management and was satisfied—a Harvard Business grad and a veteran of one of the big office-equipment companies were running the show. Large blocks of stock were held by pension plans at Xerox Corporation and at the University of Rochester, New York. He talked to a money manager at the university who was hoping for a jackpot from Sykes. Allmon liked the picture. He had a small company on the verge of explosive growth. Over the next months, he bought the stock heavily, paying as little as $1.75, adjusted for splits. In 1980, Sykes's earnings per share more than doubled, and the stock soared sixfold. In 1981, earnings almost doubled again. The stock tripled. Then, in early 1982, after climbing nearly 2,000 percent in little more than two years, the stock began acting weak.

> The thing went up to $34 at the end of 1981 and dropped back. Then it went up again and dropped back. It was gyrating all around, acting wild. We didn't have any hard evidence. But my

> instincts told me the thing wasn't right. Who was selling the big volume?

Allmon sold half his position in the low 20s, for a handsome two-year profit of several hundred percent. The latest reported earnings were up 80 percent compared with a year earlier. Analysts were bullish.

> In March or April 1982, we had a fellow go over to Alex. Brown & Sons in Baltimore for an investment conference, where the president of Sykes was speaking. He painted a very glowing picture of their outlook. But within a matter of days, a subscriber called me and said Sykes was laying off 40 or 50 people. Well, this was in conflict with the optimistic comments at Alex. Brown. I talked to Sykes the following Monday and they said they weren't laying off people across the board—these were production workers. And I said, *"My God, that's twice as bad!"* So we were gone the next day. We sold everything. The lowest we got was about $18.

Allmon warned his newsletter subscribers that if first-quarter earnings were down, Sykes could crash to $10. His fears proved more than justified. Sykes sank below $4.

What's worth noting in this round trip is a professional's determined search for facts. He talked to management, to major investors, to customers. He tapped his broker and acquaintances on the telephone company board to get an appraisal of the products.

Not every research effort is so fruitful. Calls to Sykes, to the pension fund, or to the telephone company might have met resistance. The broker might not have used the system. But the success sprang less from luck than from Allmon's capitalizing on a situation where he could get information that gave him an edge.

These opportunities don't sprout every morning. But most investors come across attractive situations now and then in their work or other pursuits. Perhaps your company has put in a new computer system, or emergency lighting, or furniture. Have you checked out the manufacturer? Maybe a local drugstore chain seems to be on the ball. Or an auto-parts company. Or a specialty-paper manufacturer. Who arranges the guard service at your company? Who makes the materials for your favorite hobby? Any of these questions could lead to a publicly held company, well known or obscure. If the company attracts you as a customer, you already know more than thousands of investors who see only a name in the stock tables.

How much more you can find out depends on your tenacity, ingenuity, and luck. For the persistent investor, serendipity sometimes lends a hand. It may turn out that an officer of your bank serves on the board of directors. Or a local stockbroker may follow the company. Or your dentist may play racquet ball with the president. You don't find out if you don't investigate. Get the annual report. Scan it for leads. Follow them up.

And, of course, check the insiders. When Wackenhut Corporation was still on the American Stock Exchange some years ago, it provided guard service at a local newspaper. It looked like a low-capital business, buying man-hours wholesale and selling them retail. A little checking revealed that the stock was trading at book value, at seven times earnings, and that a couple of insiders had bought. That was too good to pass up. Twenty months later, Wackenhut was on the Big Board and the price had tripled.

In the 1981–82 bear market, when Altamil Corporation was selling for less than net current assets, an officer in New Orleans was as perplexed as his caller. "No sir, I can't account for it selling that far below assets. I bought 100 shares myself today . . . at 7¾." The caller had already bought a couple hundred at the same price and was just checking. The stock never traded under its low that day at $7.63. And eighteen months later, the board accepted a bid by the Pritzker family of Chicago to take the company private at $22.50.

The knowledge that insiders are betting with you can make the difference between an investment you'll hold through a nervous market and one you'll dump the next time the Dow takes a plunge. It's only one of the things you might find out by picking up the phone.

# SEVEN

# *Smart Money, Rough Money*

*If the price is right, we are going to sell. I think that's true of everything you have, except maybe your kids and possibly your wife.*

—Carl C. Icahn, in court, March 1984

Digital Switch Corporation did something few stocks manage even in the bubbly over-the-counter market. In two years, the thinly traded telecommunications shares zoomed from $2 to $144. The latter price was sixty-four times the young company's book value and sixty times its earnings, which were beginning to explode from sales of a new long-distance telephone switching system. A major beneficiary of the market's exuberance was New York's Allen & Co., a freewheeling investment banking house that bought much of its stock in 1981 when Digital Switch was selling for about the value of the cash it had in the bank. Allen's average cost on its 580,000-share stake, according to one account, was $8.[1] At Digital Switch's peak, the Allen investors had a two-year profit of $79 million.

Wall Street reputations have been built on less. But Allen & Co., a low-profile, family-controlled firm, has been an early partner in many such successes, from Syntex to MCI. It's one of a number of smart, aggressive investors whose moves can provide profitable cues to outsiders. We're going to look at more than a dozen of these players. Some are old-school value hunters. Others are value creators. Some are gentlemen, some scrappers. All have track records of making money—even, occasionally, for people riding their coattails.

## ALLEN & CO.

A risky game, betting that a lowball takeover offer will be topped. There are so many possible outcomes. Suppose management is well fortified and beats back the suitor or buys him off? Suppose no "white knight" appears because the target has beauty only in the eyes of the first bidder? Speculating among the possibilities demands sophistication and top-drawer information. But in a frothy takeover market, when assets are cheap and corporate bidders plentiful, speculation can be rewarding.

Even when Allen & Co. lost a takeover prize in 1983, the firm and some camp followers came out winners. The target was Northwest Energy, a natural-gas-transmission company, which an investor group led by Allen tried to capture in a leveraged buyout for $31 a share. Management submitted, but before the pact was sealed, a rival suitor swept in with a better offer. Williams Companies, a fertilizer and energy combine, bid $39 and won Northwest. For its effort, the Allen group netted about $30 million.

Betting that Northwest was worth more than Allen had offered, an unrelated group put together by a veteran takeover speculator, Ivan F. Boesky, had scooped up more than a million shares around $31 only days before Williams Companies appeared. Their profit: probably $8 million. Boesky waltzes on a high wire too risky for most investors. But some other Allen investments have been suitable for outsiders. The ventures were speculative, but the balance of risk and reward was enhanced by the firm's willingness to take a hands-on approach to upgrading the value of its interests.

Allen plunged into Hollywood in the early 1970s, sinking millions into the nearly bankrupt Columbia Pictures and installing its own man at the top. The investment paid off nine years later when Coca-Cola bought Columbia for seventeen times Allen's cost.

Allen's stake in tiny Digital Switch, for years a company without a product, was even more successful. The firm played venture capitalist and put up money before Digital's initial public stock sale. When the shares later sank to $2, or roughly the cash the company held in the bank, Allen bought heavily in the aftermarket and scored a 300 percent gain in about four months.[2] In much the same way, Allen was an early investor in Digital's biggest customer, MCI Communications. The partners acquired stock for $1.25 that hit $57 in 1983. (Near the peak of the 1982–83 technology fever, brokerage houses began flogging the shares, with Hambrecht & Quist putting out its first "buy" recommendation on Digital Switch at $91, ten times its price of a year earlier. Who is the smart money?)

Allen & Co. is loosely structured, a collection of independent entrepreneurs who have a freer hand than they could get at brand-name Wall Street houses. Given the track record, the firm's presence in a publicly traded company demands attention. The old men are founder Charlie Allen, eighty-two, and his brother, Herbert, seventy-seven. The major force these days is Herbert, Jr., forty-five, who put the company into Columbia Pictures. Last year it took only word that old Charlie, who made a fortune on Syntex in the 1960s, was buying Genetic Engineering Inc. to lift the over-the-counter shares 20 percent. Union Corporation, a dowdy hodgepodge with a lot of cash, showed up on the buy list. So did American Phonemeter, Intelligent Business Communications, and Jamaica Water Properties.

## Bass Brothers

This well-heeled Texas family and its patriarch, Sid Bass, have fingers in dozens of corporate pies. In 1984, they had substantial holdings of Alexander's, Charter Company, Consolidated Oil & Gas, Development Corporation of America, Doskocil Companies, Fairchild Industries, Georgia Pacific, Gulf United, Kaufman & Broad, Kentron International, Major Realty, Munford, Punta Gorda Isles, Smith International, Valmac Industries, Zurn Industries, etc. The family was adding to many of the positions. If there are common themes in most Bass investments, they are discounted assets in manufacturing, land, or other natural resources. The strategy has served the family well. The value of its stake in Suburban Propane doubled in less than a year thanks to a takeover by National Distillers & Chemical. Bass bought a tankful of Marathon Oil around $55 during the market's sell-off in the fall of 1981 and sold it a few months later at $125 in U.S. Steel's takeover. A multiyear play in Sperry & Hutchinson ended in another takeover, as Bass interests tendered at $36 the shares they had bought under $15. In 1984, the Basses let themselves be bought off at Blue Bell Inc. for about a 30 percent premium and by Texaco Inc. for 25 percent more than the oil giant was worth once the takeover threat disappeared. That's the risk for other investors: that the big money will leave them holding the bag.

By putting together large blocks of stock, however, the Basses raise the odds that a takeover bid for one of their companies can succeed, if Bass says so. It's almost as good as a For Sale sign on the lawn. The family's main vehicles are Bass Brothers Enterprises Inc., Drew National Corporation, and Texas Partners.

## Bear Stearns

One face of this New York firm is a broker and investment banker. The other belongs to a tough arbitrager and trader. Like Allen & Co., these mavericks run on a loose rein. Besides making money in the Milwaukee Road and other bankrupt railroad bonds, Bear Stearns has played rough-and-tumble ball in league with Irwin Jacobs, backing the Minneapolis investor's futile raid on Pabst Brewing and his grab of Bekins Company. The firm's best-known move was a speculative plunge into New York City paper in the midst of Gotham's 1975 fiscal crisis. That brought it a high profile, thanks from Governor Hugh Carey (now a limited partner), and a handsome trading profit as the obligations recovered. In 1984, it was trying to repeat its glory by taking on the unpopular job of market maker in the battered Washington Public Power Supply bonds.

The opportunities for outside investors have come from Bear's astute reading of bankruptcies and other special situations. The firm reportedly has made money on a string of them: Chrysler, International Harvester, Manville, Penn Central.[3] In 1984, bankrupt Revere Copper & Brass Inc. was trading at three times Bear's $4.50 average cost. Revere's convertible bonds that Bear bought at $370 were fetching $700. Given that an investor need put up only 30 cents on the dollar to buy bonds, the one-year profit exceeded 500 percent. And Revere was reporting a sharp turnaround in operations. More honey for Bear Stearns.

## The Belzbergs

There are three of them, brothers Samuel, Hyman, and William, operating out of Vancouver, Calgary, and California. Samuel leads the pack. When it looked as though the Belzbergs would win control of Bache Group several years ago, Wall Street's gasps of dismay rattled windows. The *Belzbergs?* Ugh, next it would be Victor Posner. Prudential rescued the gentlemen brokers. However scruffy the Belzberg reputation—at least in the eyes of imperiled managers—no one can fault the brothers' financial smarts. They made millions on their Bache shares and set out to play black knight a few more times. In 1982, the Bass Brothers were just about to take Suburban Propane private when the Belzbergs elbowed in, owning 10 percent and waving a higher bid. When a third suitor appeared, National Distillers & Chemical Corporation, the Belzbergs quickly agreed to sell their block to National for a $12 million profit. It worked twice, so why not again? Days later, the Belzbergs revealed a 10 percent stake in another propane distributor, Pargas, and threatened a takeover. Pargas began beating the bushes for a nicer bunch of people to own it but had to settle for Saul Steinberg, whose Reliance Holdings offered $37 for stock that had cost the Belzbergs $26. The family controls Bel-Fran Investments Ltd., First City Financial Corporation, and Far West Financial Corporation, which it uses as war wagons (those are the names to look for on 13Ds). Rough company—when they tried to take Far West private in 1983 their own investment banker judged the $30 bid too stingy—but a proven catalyst. Stakes in 1984 included Intermagnetics General Corporation and Revere Copper.

## WARREN E. BUFFETT

As usual, Warren Buffet's smart moves in 1983 evoked yawns from the financial establishment. "What, General Foods?" (Sigh.) "The company's a dog." Analysts have been sighing at Warren Buffett's dull stock selections for years. That's because the chairman and biggest holder of Berkshire Hathaway Inc., the OTC conglomerate that serves as his main investment vehicle, has been playing pretty much the same game from his Omaha headquarters for a quarter century. He buys fundamental business values at large discounts and sticks with them. He bought American Express in 1964 after the company had gotten smeared in the Tino de Angelis salad-oil scam. The stock quintupled in five years.[4]

In contrast to most investors in this chapter, Buffett assumes a thoughtful, low-keyed gentleman's role. Managements welcome his presence as a shareholder. His relationship with GEICO, the auto and casualty insurer that represents Berkshire Hathaway's second biggest holding, is so cordial that Buffett has reportedly promised not to sell Berkshire's 34 percent stake without the approval of GEICO's chief executive. Buffett has reason to be satisfied with GEICO: the 7.2 million shares in Berkshire's portfolio cost $47 million and at the end of 1983 were worth nearly $400 million.

Many of Buffett's other selections have proved spectacularly successful as well. Crum & Forster, an insurer, was taken over in 1983 by Xerox Corporation. Berkshire's Blue Chip Stamps subsidiary booked a $23.9 million profit in 1982 on selling its interest in Pinkerton's to American Brands. Berkshire Hathaway's other stock investments, culled from the 1983 annual report, tell the tale: Affiliated Publications (cost $3.5 million, market value $26.6 million); General Foods ($163.8 million, $228.7 million); Handy & Harman ($27.3 million, $42.2 million); Interpublic Group of Companies ($4.1 million, $33.1 million); Media General ($3.1 million, $11.2 million); Ogilvy & Mather ($2.6 million, $12.8 million); R. J. Reynolds Industries ($268.9 million, $314.3 million); Time Inc. ($27.7 million, $56.9 million); and the Washington Post Company ($10.6 million, $136.9 million).

The sense of value that produced those gains enabled Buffett to tell Berkshire Hathaway's shareholders: "During the 19-year tenure of present management, book value has grown from $19.46 per share to $975.83, or 22.6 percent compounded annually." A year earlier he had remarked, "You can be certain that this percentage will diminish in the future. Geometric progressions eventually forge their own anchors."[5] It's remarkable that at the bottom of the 1981–82 bear market, Berkshire was selling at a discount from book value, at $420. The price later tripled.

One of Buffett's reasons for taking nonmanagement investment positions in public companies has been the discounts available in stocks compared to other forms of investment. His first rule seems to be not to risk permanent capital loss by overpaying. Thus he told shareholders:

> Our partial-ownership approach can be continued soundly only as long as portions of attractive businesses can be acquired at attractive prices. We need a modestly priced stock market to assist us in this endeavor. The market, like the Lord, helps those who help themselves. But unlike the Lord, the market does not forgive those who know not what they do. For the investor, a too-high purchase price for the stock of an excellent company can undo the effects of a subsequent decade of favorable business developments.
>
> Should the stock market advance to considerably higher levels, our ability to utilize capital effectively in partial-ownership positions will be reduced or eliminated. This will happen periodically: just ten years ago, at the height of the two-tier market mania (with high-return-on-equity businesses bid to the sky by institutional investors), Berkshire's insurance subsidiaries owned only $18 million in market value of equities . . . about 15 percent of our insurance company investments versus the present 80 percent. There were as many good businesses around in 1972 as in 1982, but the prices the stock market placed upon those businesses in 1972 looked absurd. While high stock prices in the future would make our performance look good temporarily, they would hurt our long-term business prospects rather than help them. We currently are seeing early traces of this problem.

Notice the difference between Buffett's approach to the stock market and the average investor's. Rather than asking "What can I buy that will double in a hurry?" Buffett appraises stocks as a long-term, patient, value-conscious investor. If an investor's job is accumulating pieces of good businesses at reasonable prices, then absurdly high stock prices "make our performance look good temporarily" but *hurt the long-term prospects.* This statement is worth recalling when prices are booming—and when they have been beaten down. A successful investor finds his best opportunities when the stock market is unpopular.

Buffett's philosophy has spread to GEICO, which also invests in "dull, large companies" such as General Foods and R. J. Reynolds Industries, besides its stake in a smaller insurer, AVEMCO.

Buffett raised Berkshire's positions in 1983 in General Foods and Reynolds Industries, and a year later all three were rising in the esteem of portfolio managers who wouldn't have touched them twelve months before. Naturally the prices were up.

## Carl Icahn

Well-dressed, trimly barbered, moderate in demeanor—the perfect image of a Wall Street ogre. *Institutional Investor* dubbed Carl Icahn "the man CEOs love to hate." Managers' antipathy is easy to understand. Icahn sits on the doorstep and invites bids on the chairman's desk set. Rumors that he was closing in on ACF Industries Inc., a maker of industrial, automotive, and rail equipment, sent the stock jumping in the fall of 1983. Soon Icahn surfaced holding 13 percent of ACF common, for which he had paid $33–$42 a share. With its earnings on the skids, ACF was vulnerable as its new shareholder threatened to seek control. In no time the stock was trading above $50 as speculators jumped on the raider's coattails.

Over the years, Carl Icahn, forty-eight-year-old chief of the New York brokerage house Icahn & Co., has strongarmed a number of companies with undervalued, undermanaged assets and walked away with profits even when the companies remained independent or found other buyers. Public investors haven't always done as well, but the record—once Icahn's stake passes 10 percent—isn't bad. He turned a $2.7 million profit on a $1.4

million investment in 1979 by badgering Tappan Company into a merger with AB Electrolux. Public investors made out fine, too; the shares went out at more than twice their price of a year earlier. Other forays against American Can, Anchor Hocking, Gulf & Western, Hammermill Paper, Owens-Illinois, Saxon Industries, and Simplicity Pattern gave public investors little chance to profit; managements tapped the cash box to make the bogey man go away (with $60 million in profits). But Icahn proved his usefulness in 1982 and 1983, when ugly battles ended in Marshall Field's sale to Britain's BAT Industries and Dan River's sale to its workers. In both cases, Icahn and the public shareholders made money—about $40 million for Icahn and investors he lined up.

Carl Icahn fancies himself a populist whose sallies against sleepy managers benefit the small shareholder. "With the notable exception of a number of good management teams," he says scornfully, "the men who run corporate America today are the same fellows who used to be the fraternity presidents in college. Likable, somewhat politically astute, but not the brightest or the most capable."[6] He bemoans the decline of the shareholder activist.

Icahn's concern for the public investor hasn't prevented him from being bought off with shareholder cash, of course. Nor did image-building preclude his squeezing out small shareholders in Bayswater Realty & Capital in 1982 at less than half the company's estimated "fair market value" and at a 45 percent discount from book value. Icahn had gained control of Bayswater, then known as Baird & Warner Mortgage and Realty Investors, after a proxy fight in 1979. Later, when he issued a $13 tender offer for the rest of Bayswater, the circular noted that Icahn had "considered" the book and liquidation values but gave them little weight because he had no intention of distributing the company's assets to benefit shareholders. Doing so would have exposed him to a "substantial tax liability."[7] So much for the raider's shareholder activism.

When interests coincide, however—in ousting dug-in managements—Icahn's instinct for combat serves outside investors as well as himself.

## IRWIN JACOBS

"Irv the liquidator" also costs chief executives sleepless nights. His raids on Pabst Brewing Company and his takeover of Bekins Company in 1983 both helped put money into the pockets of other shareholders. The Bekins deal was fast. Tipped by friends at Bear Stearns that the moving and storage company had spurned an offer from the Belzbergs, Jacobs leaped into the market and bought 9.4 percent of Bekins and offered $23 a share for the rest. Bekins accepted. Before the bidding, the shares traded around $15.

The Pabst saga opened in 1980, when Jacobs and associates began buying the brewer's shares, and reached a climax in spring 1983 in a bitter three-way proxy fight, which Jacobs lost, if you don't count an $11.5 million trading profit. From $12 in early 1982 when Jacobs made his first bid, Pabst stock reached $66.50.

For Irwin L. Jacobs, a six-foot-four-inch, forty-three-year-old Minneapolis investor, playing hardball with the grown-ups is a relatively new treat. He started as a low-rent liquidator of distressed merchandise and reached the big time in 1976 by buying the receivables of bankrupt W. T. Grant. With his profits from that deal, Jacobs began playing the game according to Carl Icahn, buying blocks of stock in undervalued companies, crowding managements, and letting himself be bought off. None of those scare-'em ploys was notably productive for public shareholders.

In 1983, Jacobs launched his biggest campaign, a bid for control of Kaiser Steel Corporation, which doubled the market price in three months. Not that "Irv the liquidator" had softened. His group's plan for a leveraged buyout would have risked no more than $8 million of its own money in a $270 million deal. When a higher bidder came along, Jacobs threatened to block a sale until his group was promised better terms than the public got. For Jacobs, the price was $52 a share in cash; for the public, $22 in cash and maybe $18 worth of Chinese paper. Either price looked good against Kaiser's $18 quote before Jacobs showed up.

His operating company, Minstar, an OTC conglomerate that owns Bekins, has done even better for investors, recently trading at several times the price of a year earlier. When last heard from, Jacobs was sitting on big blocks of Tidewater, the offshore-oil-service firm, and Walt Disney Productions and sounding restless.

## Carl Lindner

"Right now we don't have any room [for Lindner]." The speaker was Richard Dicker, chairman of Penn Central Corporation, explaining his refusal to grant Cincinnati investor Carl H. Lindner a seat on Penn's board. It was the end of March 1982. Lindner's privately controlled American Financial Corporation was Penn Central's biggest stockholder. Fourteen months later, Dicker lost his job and Penn Central got a new chairman, Carl Lindner.

In his mid-sixties, this intensely private investor who never attended high school has a half century behind him in business. He's a devout Baptist, a crack judge of stock values, a shrewd corporate mender, and a sometimes relentless adversary. His regard for public shareholders is low. Part of his motive in taking American Financial private in 1981 reportedly was that he was fed up with having to answer shareholder questions at annual meetings. His last annual meeting turned raucous as Carl traded words with an investor who ridiculed the price offered to American Financial's outside holders. It was a case, perhaps, of Carl Lindner's regard for value: the Bear Stearns opinion supporting his family's bid had cost the corporate treasury $750,000. Lindner had dumped his longtime investment banker, Goldman Sachs, after it labeled an earlier offer inadequate.[8]

For all that ugly scene, Lindner has proved a valuable man to watch. His pattern has been to edge into public companies, accumulating both stock (duly reported in 13Ds) and influence. Whether because of innate values or because of improvements suggested by Lindner, many of the companies have prospered.

He was rewarded with a tenfold gain on his 2.6 million shares of Charter Company in 1978 and 1979 as gasoline prices soared. A 9.9 percent stake in clothing manufacturer Hartmarx Corporation, put together at prices of $16 and under, was worth $36 a share eighteen months later. Perhaps his biggest profit came from his 32 percent interest in Combined Communications, the advertising and television company that was sold to Gannett Company in 1979. Add to that Lindner's profits over the years in bankruptcies such as Chicago Milwaukee and Penn Central.

Major investments in 1984 included American Agronomics, American Can, American General, Circle K Corporation (a convenience-store chain where Lindner's longtime chum Karl Eller had taken the helm), Fisher Foods, Gulf Broadcast, Mission Insurance, Orion Capital, Pennzoil, Provident Bancorp, Sunshine-Jr. Stores, and United Brands.

Then there was Gulf & Western Industries. It's interesting how often professional investors not only make a run at the same target but also succumb to the same inducements. Carl Icahn and Carl Lindner both sold large chunks of Gulf & Western in 1983; the conglomerate repurchased Lindner's shares for $210 million after spurning his proposal for a merger with Penn Central.

Besides owning most of American Financial, Lindner controls FMI Financial Corporation, which he also uses as an investment vehicle. And, of course, Penn Central.

## David Murdock

First there's the booming bass voice. Then comes the man, five foot four, wealthy, dictatorial, restless—David H. Murdock. In less than a decade, his financial empire has swept up a handful of formerly public companies—Pacific Holding Company, International Mining, Cannon Mills—and greased an $800 million merger that made Murdock a major owner of Occidental Petroleum Corporation. His real estate holdings stretch from Los Angeles to Baltimore. Over the years his investments in public companies have included Dan River, Flexi-Van (he won control after a bitter struggle), General Steel, Sotheby Parke Bernet (of which he was second-largest holder), Southwest Forest Industries, and other properties a bit off the beaten track. His investment philosophy is essentially Graham and Dodd, much like that of his idol Warren Buffett, except that Murdock is scrappier. "I'm never in anything for a short-term profit," he declared several years ago. "I look at what I'm in all the time. One should never be satisfied. As an investor you've got to keep looking all the time at your investments. You always look for value. The market doesn't necessarily indicate value. Graham is the man who wrote the book about undervalued situations. His theories are quite sound."

A tenth-grade dropout in the Midwest, Murdock pumped gas, bought and sold a diner (at a 200 percent profit), and headed west, where he dug ditches in his first years in the home-building business in Phoenix, which was entering a postwar boom. The real estate fortune that followed was shaken when the boom collapsed (there was a run on a Murdock-controlled S&L), but Murdock survived and within a few years was buying real estate again and raiding companies with undervalued assets. He picked up a taste for the arts and now, besides the stake in Sotheby, owns an antique store on New York's 57th Street and acts as a fundraiser for the Joffrey ballet.

Like other poor kids who made it, the sixty-two-year-old Murdock has drawn criticism for some of his methods. When his Pacific Holding Company took over International Mining in the late 1970s, the deal struck *Barron's* as "something less than arm's length," facilitated by "well-placed allies on the board."[9] Helping to run the Murdock empire have been two characters from the Nixon days, G. Bradford Cook, an SEC chairman who resigned in disgrace, and H. R. Haldeman, who went to jail for the Watergate coverup.

Murdock's operations have benefited public shareholders often enough that he's definitely a man to watch. Outsiders got a windfall in the summer of 1981 when he helped engineer the takeover of Iowa Beef by Occidental Petroleum. Oxy swapped stock worth about $77 for Iowa Beef shares that had been going for $50. The merger reportedly gave Murdock, who owned 19 percent of the meat packer, a $130 million profit, or about six times his investment. Just a few weeks after that pact was sealed, outside investors got a chance to cash in on another Murdock stake, 9 percent of Zapata Corporation, as Occidental offered about $36 a share for the drilling contractor. When Zapata rejected the offer, which was about $10 above the market, Murdock took the rebuff as a signal to exit. Within five months, he resigned from Zapata's board and sold his stock back to the company at $32, which was two to three times his cost and about

7 points higher than the NYSE quote. Even if other investors couldn't get such a friendly price from Zapata's board—no chance of that, of course—they would have done well to follow David Murdock out the door. One year after the Occidental bid, as the drilling boom died, Zapata was changing hands under $12.

Murdock went straight from Zapata to another target. For a couple of years his Pacific Holding Company had carried a 5 percent interest in Cannon Mills, a debt-free textile company selling at about two-thirds of its book value. Now, in January 1982, Murdock bid $44 a share for the rest—about $16 more than the market price—and won control. A year earlier, another group led by former ITT chairman Harold Geneen had made an unsuccessful pass at the company. The value was there; it needed only the right catalyst.

Investors who followed Murdock as he upped his stake in Oxy in the high teens also fared well. Within eighteen months, the stock topped $35. Subsequently, Murdock sold most of his shares back to the company after squabbling with Occidental chairman Armand Hammer.

## Odyssey Partners

It was one of the cheekier assaults in recent business history. With a piddling 1 percent of the stock in hand, Odyssey Partners launched a proxy battle against management at Trans World Corporation. Its proposition: Trans World would be worth twice as much if it were broken up into five separate companies. When the vote was counted, management had won, but the dissidents' 30 percent tally (including a hefty chunk of institutional stock) had sent a message upstairs. Not many months later, management decided to spin off its money-losing Trans World Airlines. This didn't fulfill all of Odyssey's goals—the dissidents wanted the other units, Hilton International hotels, a couple of food companies, and Century 21 Real Estate, flung out on their own as well. But Odyssey had made its point and perhaps signaled a new era in proxy battles, in which the stockholding institutions desert management for the fast buck.

How Odyssey Partners developed an interest in TWA explains much about an approach to business that has led the New York group to a string of financial coups. The partners' style is value-prospecting, but more along the lines of "Irv the liquidator" Jacobs than Warren Buffett. It's value prospecting with a crowbar in hand to pry the fixtures loose. This approach brought the partners to Chicago Milwaukee Corporation, to the bankrupt GAC (now Avatar Holdings), to the bankrupt Penn Central, and to dozens of other profitable investments. Leon Levy, general partner in Odyssey, explained part of the concept, as applied to conglomerates, in a bylined article in *Fortune:* "[Trans World] is one of those companies subject to the 'conglomerate discount.' Businessmen who put together or manage highly diversified companies often assert that diversity itself is a big plus. The stock market tells a different story. Stocks of such companies usually sell at a substantial discount from what the divisions would be worth if they operated as independent businesses."[10]

The parts, in other words, are worth more than the whole. This isn't fresh wisdom—Jimmy Goldsmith doubled his (borrowed) money in Diamond International by hacking it apart, and Parker Montgomery enriched Cooper Laboratories shareholders by peeling off subsidiaries—but in the right hands, this approach could make the dismantling of conglomerates as much the sport of the 1980s as patching together conglomerates was the game of the '60s. There have been hints that this is the direction Odyssey Partners and Irv Jacobs plan to go. If so, there'll be restless nights for slower-moving corporate chiefs.

Levy is a beefy, pipe-smoking man in his late fifties who has worked on Wall Street for more than thirty years. All but the last few years were spent at Oppenheimer & Co., the private partnership that controlled brokerage, investment-banking, and mutual-fund operations. When the partnership sold those units in 1982 to a British company, Levy and colleagues left to set up shop as Odyssey Partners. A smarter band of deal-makers would be hard to find. Besides Levy there are Jack Nash and Lester Pollack, the latter a former Loews executive, plus a cluster of other Oppy veterans. At times they play ball with Peter Sharp, a New York real estate mogul, and Ezra K. Zilkha, a cosmopolitan banker who heads a private family investment company.

In the 1970s, the Oppenheimer-Odyssey group went in for leveraged buyouts (Big Bear, Donnkenny, Havatampa) and bankrupts (Avatar, Chicago Milwaukee, the Erie, Penn Central, among others). Sometimes they acquired deeply discounted bonds that later were exchanged for equity in the reorganized concerns. They demonstrated the truth of a bit of well-rubbed wisdom: some companies are worth more dead than alive. As major creditors, the group was in a position to exert leverage in the outcome of the bankruptcies, and not surprisingly they walked away with millions.

At least once the partners clearly got burned, when they put up $3.5 million in 1978 in a $27.5 million leveraged buyout of Donnkenny, a dress manufacturer that had traded on the American Stock Exchange. Whether they were ignorant of the potential pitfalls in the rag trade or just failed to keep an eye on the old management (which had stayed on), Oppy three years later filed suit charging the company's profits and assets had been siphoned off in "systematic frauds" by management. The loss, according to the suit, topped $7 million.[11]

That the affair is remembered at all suggests how rarely anyone gets the better of Leon Levy and his sidekicks. At Avatar, the revived Florida land company, they bought out Carl Lindner on the cheap, according to one account—no easy task.[12] In 1982–83, Avatar shares doubled in over-the-counter trading.

Other Odyssey interests include Thackeray Corporation, a mortgage finance company traded on the Big Board. When the names Levy and Odyssey pop up on a 13D, they excite interest.

## Victor Posner

For years his name was anathema. If Victor Posner, the plump Miami Beach takeover artist, appeared on the horizon, managements dived under the bed and called their lawyers. He made money by scaring executives into buying back stock, and he made it by selling on the open market or to other big investors. "Everything I have has a price," Posner has said. "I buy to sell and make a profit on it."[13] That philosophy has guided him from the time he dropped out of school at age thirteen to manage the family food stores in Baltimore. Before he was twenty, Posner had sold the stores and begun buying and selling houses. He was a millionaire at twenty-five. In the late 1960s, he began amassing control of a series of generally small, publicly held companies that could be used for further investment forays. The raids have proved astoundingly successful.

Consider the stock sales. In 1981, Posner-controlled companies sold blocks of Interlake Inc. to Madison Fund for a $7.4 million profit; Simplicity Pattern Company to NCC Energy Ltd. for an $8 million profit; National Gypsum back to the company for a $9.3 million profit; Foremost-McKesson Inc. back to the company for a $35 million profit; Heinicke Instruments Company to Tyco Laboratories for a $2.7 million profit. In 1982, Posner companies sold interests in Ipco Corporation and Ranco Inc. (results weren't reported), while a third company, Signode Corporation, voted to go private to avoid a Posner takeover. In 1983, Posner traded High Voltage Engineering at a profit—word that he had sold sent the stock plunging—and wrung a premium out of Rexham management for surrendering a 5.4 percent stake.

What's one to make of this? Lucrative trading, to be sure; a smart man capitalizing on his reputation as a relentless raider who had best be bought off. But that is little more than a sideshow to Victor Posner's main business. In the past few years, he has doggedly extended his empire of control to company after company, buying 30 or 40 percent of the stock, then aiming at the next target. A probably incomplete list of Posner-controlled companies included, at last look, APL Corporation, Birdsboro Corporation, Chesapeake Insurance Company, DWG Corporation, Evans Products, Graniteville, Modern Interests, National Can, National Propane, NVF Company, Pennsylvania Engineering, Sharon Steel, Southeastern Public Service, and Wilson Brothers. Most of the companies are publicly traded. In addition, Posner held substantial positions in 1984 in Axia Inc., Burnup & Sims, Chicago Pneumatic Tool, City Investing, Dayton Malleable, Fischbach, Johnson Controls, Peabody International, and Royal Crown Companies, among others. Share prices of many of those companies have benefited as Posner's buying excited speculation of takeovers. Not without reason. In one week in early 1984, two of those firms—National Can and Royal

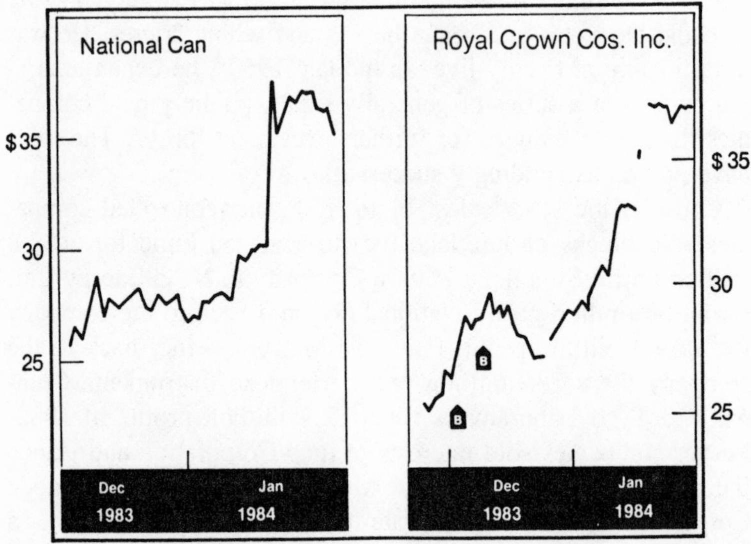


**Figure 1. Victor Posner's touch. Within a week, both National Can and Royal Crown drew going-private proposals.**

Crown—drew buyout proposals. Within a few months, Posner was bidding for three others as well, Axia, City Investing, and Peabody International.

In many cases, however, Posner has seemed content with having *control* of corporations, stopping well short of full ownership. And the stock market history of companies dominated by Posner—the likes of DWG, NVF, Pennsylvania Engineering, Sharon Steel, and Wilson Brothers—wouldn't encourage most investors. Operating results run from mediocre to poor, dividends are scarce or nonexistent, and DWG, for one, typically sells for half its book value. What does that say of the Posner empire?

It says that it isn't designed to serve shareholders. Rather, it serves empire-building. The prizes that are seized, like new vessels in a privateer's fleet, are sent to capture more targets. A former banker, John Brimelow, grasped Posner's insight into the value of corporate control:

> The Posner battle fleet demonstrates that an industrial company, if soundly constructed financially and reasonably success-

> ful commercially, can be converted into a formidable weapon for stock market war. There are technical reasons for this. Dividends in the hands of a corporation are 85 percent tax-exempt, while interest is fully deductible as a business expense. The net cost to a company of financing dividend-paying shares with borrowed money is therefore much less than to an individual. . . .
>
> An operating company with a base of profitable industrial assets holds a further advantage: its access to credit. . . . [This] facilitates stock market operations with cheaper, more stable financing. . . . Perceiving the financing potential in what is essentially a collection of rather staid enterprises is Posner's most impressive achievement. . . . [The Posners] have gained massive stock market power at the expense of sharing some of the proceeds with the public while risking only a fairly small amount themselves.[14]

Actually, the sharing has been hardly noticeable. The market, seeing no way to transfer Posner's stock profits to investors' hands, puts a low value on most of the fleet. The perks of control, moreover, have become a sore point now and then, as in 1977 when Posner and two of his children settled an SEC complaint by agreeing to reimburse their companies for personal expenses (such as $39,000 worth of a daughter's telephone expenses, plus apartments and deli bills); an internal audit committee later demanded another $1 million. Posner's other exploits have aroused more serious allegations. In 1982, a federal grand jury in New York indicted the financier on charges of evading $1,250,000 in income taxes. But that may be beside the point. As Posner closes in on a company, he frequently draws a crowd that produces higher stock prices.

## The Pritzkers

In 1982, the Chicago-based family bought out public investors in its Hyatt International hotel chain, paying $25 a share, spurning an outsider's bid of $30. In 1983, they took Altamil Corporation private, initially offering less than the understated book value and maybe four times the small manufacturing company's earning power. "Shrewd" is one word that crops up. "Grossly unfair'' was another opinion, hurled in a suit by a minority shareholder in Hyatt.

Both views have merit, for the Pritzker clan, overseen by brothers Robert and Jay, has a reputation for buying smart and buying cheap, usually under book value. Typically, the family accumulates major positions in its targets, what a critic of Victor Posner once labeled ''creeping acquisition.'' Then comes a bid for total ownership. With the Pritzkers already in *de facto* control, no rival will bid for a minority position. One of the few occasions when the family had to pay top dollar was the 1981 hostile acquisition of Trans Union, a financial and manufacturing conglomerate, which went for double book value after management tried to counter with a leveraged buyout of its own. The boards at Hyatt and Altamil put up no such resistance. Other takeovers have included Cerro Corporation in 1976, Hammond Organ in 1977, and American Safety Equipment in 1978.

The Pritzker technique is to buy mundane manufacturing assets, refurbish management, tighten controls, and beef up the bottom line. In part because of their drab nature, companies in which the Pritzkers own large stakes may trade at considerable discounts from asset values. If the shares are cheap enough, outside investors can speculate on eventual takeovers even supposing they won't get top dollar. The family operates through a network of corporate entities, including the Marmon Group, Great Lakes Corporation (formerly GL Corporation), Hyatt Corporation, and HCC Corporation. Public companies in which the Pritzkers held interests in 1984 included Elsinore Corporation, General Host, Levitz Furniture, and Salem Corporation. Jay Pritzker's riskiest coup was winning control in 1983 of bankrupt Braniff International by paying $20 million for 80 percent of the airline. That gave the family Braniff's enormous tax-loss credits—$300 million—for a song.

## Saul Steinberg

Babyfat still rounding him, a bankroll from Papa staking him, Saul Steinberg burst onto the scene in the early '60s with a brilliant scheme. Saul would buy IBM computers on credit and lease them for less than the big chip itself charged. There was a lot of buzz-buzz, "depreciation," "cash flow," "genius." The market sopped it all up, and Steinberg's Leasco became a hot stock. Only problem: used computers weren't worth much, not nearly as much as they were being carried for on the books, and when business ran out of zip in a recession, Leasco took to writing off megabytes worth of equity. But the company survived and, thanks to an insurance acquisition, got a new name, Reliance Group. On to the next game. A lot of hungry young men were making money jump through hoops in the '60s, but Saul Steinberg got a reputation for audacity that won't wear off.

The insurance takeover, for example. Three years later, a federal judge ruled that Steinberg's Leasco hadn't told the target company's shareholders just how much value the old-line insurance company might hold. The year after the takeover, Steinberg launched a brash—no, *impudent*—bid for control of a little New York moneylender. Steinberg was twenty-nine. The moneylender was Chemical Bank, the nation's seventh-largest. Some of the gentry thought it reflected badly on them that a crass young fellow from Brooklyn could come so close, and they were probably right. Steinberg's campaign failed. Sigh of relief.

Then there was the Pulte caper, which had a dash of Hollywood glamour. The SEC charged Steinberg with spreading rumors that Pulte Home Corporation was about to be taken over and then unloading some of his own debt-encumbered stock as his friends bought (the perfect answer to "What are friends for?"). One of the eager buyers was a movie actor named George Hamilton (who in turn was accused of doing some tipping and selling himself in another stock, IPM Technology, the president of which was Steinberg's Uncle Seymour). Steinberg, Hamilton, and other defendants settled the government complaints without admitting or denying guilt.[15] Then came a bus-shelter scandal in New York City, with talk of political payoffs, and a messy divorce which had at least one unusual twist: the estranged wife filed a stockholders' suit (later dismissed) charging Steinberg had misappropriated corporate assets to buy cocaine.[16]

The gossip distracted people from the numbers. Buying up stock, Steinberg shrank the float of Reliance Group, which had traded as low as $4 in 1974. By 1981 he controlled enough shares to make his move and took the company private for about $100. Reliance Group swallowed itself. (Carl Lindner's American Financial sold out at a large profit.)

As an investor, Steinberg's performance outside Reliance has been spotty. He took a beating in recent years on Tiger International, buying 23 percent of the company too early in its tailspin. By late 1983, Steinberg's loss was about $58 million. He made lesser profits from investments in MCO Holdings, the New York Times Company, and Paine Webber, and got bought off in 1984 at fat premiums by managements at Disney and Quaker State Oil. Steinberg's other plays, at last report, included large blocks of Champion Products, Imperial Corporation of America, and White Consolidated. The bet on Steinberg is that he's smart enough to come out ahead in the long run.

## Other Players

The heavy hitters combine two traits: the ability to recognize opportunity and the means to make things happen. Their very presence can act as a catalyst. Dozens of other operators play similar games. There's Mario Gabelli, "just a boy from the Bronx" who heads Gabelli & Co., a New York investment boutique. Gabelli's schtick is comparing the stock market price of a company with what it might be worth if it went private. This led him into profitable plays in the broadcasters and other cash-fat businesses. There's Marty Sosnoff, who goes Gabelli one better—"the *barefoot* boy from the Bronx"—and understood better than the Street's pundits the savvy behind Saul Steinberg's maneuverings at Reliance Group. Sosnoff wrote the best column in *Forbes* for a number of years, along with a sassy book, *Humble on Wall Street,* that affords a glimpse of the money game from the inside. With Atlanta Capital, he has made big money in Digital Switch—right in there with the Allens—and the New York Times Company.

There's Alan Gaines, barely thirty and president of Gaines, Berland, Shaffer & Silversheim Inc., New York money managers. He made out shorting Tiger International during a speculative run and, via a partnership called G.S.S. Holding

Corporation, in 1983 bought into Shaer Shoe Corporation. In 1981, Gaines drew notice by picking a hat trick's worth of takeover targets: Marathon, Medcom, and Texasgulf. By August 1983, he could report that seventeen stocks bought and sold in the previous two years had shown average gains of 117 percent.

And TBK Partners, a private New York group based at Tweedy Brown Inc. In 1984, TBK was picking up stakes in such obscure companies as Syracuse Supply, Westwood Inc., and World Wide Ltd. ADRs. Some of the partners operate also as Viridian Investments.

And Milwaukee-based De Rance Inc., a charitable foundation with a portfolio managed by First Wilshire Securities of Los Angeles. De Rance was buying shares of Channel Industries, CHB Food, Compo Industries, Dataram, Diamond Crystal Salt, Florofax International, Kratos, Lion Country Safari, Nature's Sunshine Products, Old Stone, Polymeric Resources, Sunergistic Communications, Thermal Industries, and Universal Telephone. Kratos was having big trouble. Diamond Crystal Salt more than doubled after winning a damage claim.

There are businessmen like Clyde William Engle, of Chicago, who though barely past forty controls a junior Posner-like empire with interests (generally dominant) in Alba-Waldensian, Hickory Furniture, Indiana Financial Investors, Opelika, Publicker Industries, Sunstates Corporation, Technical Equipment Leasing, Treco, Wellco Enterprises, and Wisconsin REIT. From Dallas, there's Harold Simmons, putting together another Posneresque fleet of controlled companies including Amalgamated Sugar, Contran, and National City Lines. Simmons bought Interpace in 1983, along with pieces of Cyclops, GAF Corporation, National Standard, and Kerr Glass (jittery management shelled out a 51 percent premium to reclaim the Kerr shares).

In New York, there's a securities arbitrager, Asher B. Edelman, who won a 1983 proxy fight that gave him control of Canal-Randolph Corporation, a real estate company, and a year later repeated the game at Management Assistance, a depressed computer-systems maker. Edelman operates through Plaza Securities Company.

How well will public investors make out by following these pros? Certainly not all their operations end in takeovers at premium prices. As with Posner's empire, the small freeholder on some of these estates may be the forgotten man or woman. If the insider is seeking another base from which to launch new campaigns, his interests may be at cross-purposes with the small investor's. While the insider expands his stake, he benefits if the stock price remains low. He has no incentive to bring values to the surface. This doesn't make an undervalued situation a poor investment for an outsider, but it makes it more speculative. I can think of several obscure companies today that are sitting on massive assets, such as real estate or tax losses, with no sign that the controlling investors are ready to begin cashing them in.

On the other hand, when a heavy hitter plans to force a profit, the wait may be short. Canal-Randolph common nearly doubled in 1983 in anticipation of lucrative asset sales.

Looking at the stock tables won't reveal what somebody's plans might be. But these are questions that must be asked as you contemplate following a big-money investor into a stock. The bonus for the patient little fellow is this: if a stock is undervalued, the market will try to correct the inefficiency. The odds are on your side.

# EIGHT

# *Bargain Hunters at the Corporate Helm*

For years they talked about Henry Singleton, the chairman of Teledyne Inc., and how adroitly he had deployed the corporation's spare cash. The investments included a million shares of Colt Industries (later target of a failed takeover bid by Penn Central), half a million shares of Conoco (good for a $20 million profit on the takeover by Du Pont), plus blocks of Dart Industries (which merged with Kraft) and Studebaker-Worthington (acquired by McGraw-Edison). Henry Singleton bought below book, at low P/Es, and put away big enough chunks of stock that he could fold some of his investments' earnings into Teledyne's bottom line. That boost plus adept management of the conglomerate's industrial, aviation, insurance, and other businesses produced one of the '70s' more remarkable stock-price ascents, as Teledyne climbed from a 1974 low of about $4 to more than $270 in 1984.

Singleton fans ate cake *and* ice cream. They could opt for Henry's well-run company, with the investments as a kicker, and they could bet with him on companies that Ben Graham would have blessed.

Like—International Harvester? Singleton began buying in 1980, while the farm-equipment and truck manufacturer's shares were around $30. The quote was less than half book value, coming off year-earlier earnings of $12 a share. A bargain, it seemed, even though a strike had hurt results. In 1981, Singleton bought more, and the stock was even more of a bargain: $9 a share. The earnings problem was proving tenacious. In fact, Harvester had suffered a $24-a-share swing in net and had just *lost* $12 a share. In the next three years, International Harvester's losses totaled about $78 a share, wiping out its net worth. Singleton's investment, eventually 16 percent of Harvester's common, turned into a nightmare for Teledyne and cost it a $49 million write-down at the end of 1982. Adding to Singleton's embarrassment, he sold about a sixth of the stake within a couple points of the stock's low. By the end of 1983, although still spouting red ink, Harvester seemed to have survived its brush with bankruptcy and the stock had climbed into the teens, giving Teledyne a profit on about 25 percent of its position. A patient man, Henry Singleton may yet come out a winner on Harvester, but it'll be a while before the abracadabra "Singleton's buying" is again proof of a surefire bargain. It never was, of course.

Nor is it proof of bargains—or even solid investments—that International Business Machines took major positions in 1983 in two technology companies, Intel and Rolm. IBM's investment outlook might differ a bit from that of a hundred-share trader who wants to make money this year, or next. But caveats duly noted—that corporate investors now and then act dumb, and that their perspective may be many years long—these investors run on the inside track. Whether they buy for growth or prowl for bargains, they call on information outside the average investor's reach.

Charlie Bluhdorn of Gulf & Western Industries was a bargain hunter. When he died in 1983, his successor began emptying the corporate strongbox of stakes of up to 30 percent in more than a dozen unspectacular stocks: Amfac, Amoskeag, Bank of New York, Brunswick, Central Soya, General Tire, Hammermill Paper, Hayes-Albion, Hollywood Park, Mohasco, Munsingwear, J. P. Stevens, and United Brands, plus smaller positions in a dozen or so more. It's no coincidence that most of the names have shown up in recent years in the portfolios of other value-conscious investors—no coincidence, either, that some of them rose faster than the averages from the market bottom of August

1982. The stock sales in 1983 netted the conglomerate millions.

At the least, corporate investors alert outsiders to possible values that bear investigating. Many outcomes are possible—from a long, futile wait, to an upturn in earnings, to a takeover offer (one bite leading to another). Nortek, a NYSE-listed maker of building products, set its eye on Monogram Industries and bought 30 percent in early 1983. Within months, it had cut a deal for the rest. Sometimes a third company may appear with a bid, lured by the concentrated block of shares.

While investors can't count on takeovers, they can study the investment judgments made by corporations and see if their own objectives would be served by following the big money. An investor intrigued by technology but confused by its abundance might narrow his focus to companies with major outside investors. A number of the biotechnology companies have one or more corporate shareholders that came aboard as venture capitalists. In the computer field, IBM gave a lift in 1983 to Intel and Rolm by agreeing to buy up to 30 percent of their stock. Both companies are in businesses important to IBM—Intel makes semiconductors, Rolm produces telecommunications switching equipment—and the computer giant's interest was bullish news. By fall, Intel's shares had more than doubled from IBM's initial price in February 1983. But Rolm, after a short-lived run-up, was trading well below IBM's entry price.

The spurt that carried Rolm from $60 to $80 buttresses the case against chasing insider stocks. IBM had paid $59. After the excitement wore off and Rolm encountered problems, investors had ample chance to buy the stock at half that price. On a similar note, American General's purchase of 5.1 percent of Continental Corporation excited speculation that one insurer planned to swallow the other. But less than three weeks elapsed before American General got the cold shoulder and dumped its block. Continental shares lost a fast 5 points.

Corporate investments are well known on the Street, though seldom at the front of anyone's attention. Murphy Oil's longtime romance with Ocean Drilling & Exploration, for example, has fueled takeover talk for years, but ODECO's stock often trades as if that possibility didn't exist. The following list contains a small sample of corporate investments, current as of the fall of

1984. The common thread is that the investors in each have increased their positions in the last year or so.

| *Company* | *Investor* |
|---|---|
| Academy Insurance | American Can |
| Addison-Wesley | Macmillan |
| AIC Photo | Pioneer International |
| Alba-Waldensian | Hickory Furniture |
| American District Telegraph | Guardian Industries |
| | Penn Central |
| American Realty Trust | Southmark |
| American West Airlines | International Lease |
| APL | NVF |
| Arlington Realty Investors | Southmark |
| AVEMCO | GEICO |
| Axia | Pennsylvania Engineering |
| | Guardian Industries |
| Banctec | Control Data |
| BankAmerica | Orion Capital |
| Baruch-Foster | Helmerich & Payne |
| W. R. Berkley | Charter Co. |
| Beverly Enterprises | Hospital Corp. of America |
| Bitco | Charter Co. |
| Bucyrus-Erie | InterNorth |
| California Leisure | Aero Systems |
| Capital Holding | CIGNA |
| Cellu-Craft | Salem |
| Centronics Data Computer | Control Data |
| Chicago Pneumatic Tool | DWG |
| City Investing | Sharon Steel |
| CNA Financial | Loews |
| Compact Video | Technicolor |
| Conwed | Nortek |
| C3 | Penn Central |
| CTS Corp. | Dynamics Corp. of America |
| Cue Industries | Guardian Industries |
| Dayton Malleable | Sharon Steel |
| Diagnostek | Thompson Medical |

| | |
|---|---|
| Dominion Mortgage | Southmark |
| Dual-Lite | U.S. Industries |
| Du Pont | Seagram |
| Duriron | Transamerica |
| Engelhard | Minerals & Resources |
| Ensource | MCO Resources |
| Enzo Biochem | Johnson & Johnson |
| Ferro | Crane |
| First Michigan Capital | DST Systems |
| Flight Dynamics | Pacific Telecom |
| Florida Cos. | Fairfield Communities |
| Foundation Financial | American Plan |
| Galveston Houston | Masco |
| Gearhart Industries | Smith International |
| GEICO | Berkshire Hathaway |
| Harbest Industries | Altair |
| Hershey Oil | Transamerica |
| Hickory Furniture | Technical Equipment Leasing |
| HMG Property | Transco Realty |
| Horizon Corp. | MCO Holdings |
| Indiana Financial | Hickory Furniture |
| Intel | IBM |
| ISSC Industrial Solid State | Honeywell |
| James River | American Can |
| | Zenith National |
| Johnson Controls | Sharon Steel |
| Kidde | Teledyne |
| LLC Corp. | Contran |
| Lloyd's Electronics | Bacardi |
| Lynch Corp. | Curtiss-Wright |
| Major Realty | MCA |
| MCA | Chris-Craft |
| McDowell Enterprises | Charter Co. |
| McRae Consolidated Oil | Lear Petroleum |
| Mid-Continent Telephone | Cincinnati Financial |
| Millipore | Dow Chemical |
| Mine Safety Appliances | Halliburton |
| Morton Thiokol | Dow Chemical |
| National Health | National Medical Enterprises |

| | |
|---|---|
| Newmont Mining | Gold Fields American |
| Norlin | Piezo Electric |
| North American National | Southmark |
| North East Insurance | American Plan |
| Novus Property | Southmark |
| Ocean Drilling | Murphy Oil |
| Offshore Logistics | Atwood Oceanics |
| Peabody International | DWG |
| Pier One Imports | Intermark |
| Ply-Gem | Barris Industries |
| Pogo Producing | Pennzoil, Sedco |
| Porex Technologies | APL |
| Pratt & Lambert | Unicorp Canada |
| Ranchers Exploration | Hecla, Sunshine Mining |
| Richmond Tank Car | Koppers Co. |
| Robertshaw Controls | Reynolds Metals |
| Rolm | IBM |
| Rorer Group | Dow Chemical |
| Scientific Leasing | Hospital Corp. of America |
| Seiscom Delta | Veta Grande |
| South Atlantic Financial | Independence Holdings |
| Southland Corp. | Occidental Petroleum |
| Statewide Bancorp | Midlantic Banks |
| Storer Communications | Loews |
| Sunstates | Hickory Furniture |
| Tesoro Petroleum | Charter Co. |
| Texon Energy | Oxoco |
| Toys R Us | Petrie Stores |
| United Home Life | Southmark |
| Wellco Enterprises | Hickory Furniture |
| Western States Life | Southmark |
| Western Union | Curtiss-Wright |
| Winkelman Stores | Petrie Stores |
| Wolverine Aluminum | Synalloy |

This roster isn't intended as a buy list. Whether any of the companies would make a good investment depends on price, business prospects, and other volatile factors. But if the past is a guideline, a fair number of these companies eventually will be taken over. An early draft of the list included Bangor Punta, Binney & Smith, Core Labs, Esquire, Florida Coast Banks, Gulf Oil, National Can, Royal Crown, and Trane, all of which were taken over between November 1983 and mid-1984.

## "We Like Ourselves So Much!"

Buying the target is only one speculative play. Another is to buy the buyer. As the histories of Berkshire Hathaway and Teledyne attest, sound investments do wonders for the investor's bottom line and stock price.

That's sometimes true, too, when a company invests in its own stock. While critics say such buying may reveal weak management that can't put cash to work in expanding the business, the complaint isn't always fair. Particularly in times of depressed stock prices, the best available return on investment may lie in buying back shares at less than book value and at a low P/E. The repurchases shrink the float and put a lever under future earnings per share. They also sometimes prove a prelude to a move to take the entire company private, witness the fate of conglomerate Norton Simon. Investing in such companies may not be a road to fast and certain riches, since only a fraction of them go private in any year, but it can be part of a sound, value-oriented strategy. For one thing, if the price is cheap in terms of earnings or assets, it's a sign the company is held in low esteem by the financial mainstream—a precondition for successful bargain hunting. When a corporation decides the market's disdain is unjustified and buys its own stock, it's responding much as executives and directors do in their private investing when they purchase inefficiently priced assets. There is no more "inside" buyer than a corporation itself. In the bear market of 1982, corporations stepped up their share repurchases dramatically, reflecting "the generally depressed conditions of stock-market prices," according to Francis A. Lees, a consultant who conducted a study for the Conference Board research institute. In the first ten months, 297 companies with New York Stock Exchange listings had bought 218.9 million shares of their common stock, up 47.5 percent from share repurchases in all of 1981. The 1982 buying was up 116 percent from 1980's activity. Lees said the buying "demonstrates the determination of many repurchasing companies to exploit favorable buying opportunities."[1]

Smart investing wasn't the only thing on some management's minds. As I've noted, buying back stock is a prime defensive ploy when a takeover looms, and takeover threats have been popping up at every turn in the last few years. For most of the buying, however, corporations undoubtedly were driven by the same impulse that pushes individual insiders into the market: the sight of their stock trading at fire-sale prices.

# NINE

# *When Insiders Sell*

There are two faces to investing like an insider. The first is accumulating out-of-favor assets at discounts. The second is peddling them at the highest possible markup. If you can consistently buy values at 50 cents on the dollar and sell them at 200 cents on the dollar, you stand a fair chance of dying rich. Ask Leon Levy.

In 1976, Odyssey Partners and some other investors bought the assets of Big Bear Stores for about $41 million and took the Ohio supermarket chain private. It was a leveraged buyout, so they put up at most $10 million, borrowing the rest from Prudential Insurance Company and other lenders. Seven years later, with giddy popular demand for new stock issues, Odyssey and friends let the public back in on Big Bear. They sold about a fifth of their stake for $18 million. The deal put a total value on the company of more than $95 million—about $70 million of which was still owned by Odyssey and other insiders. Buying under book value, using other people's money, and selling at two and a half times book, the Odyssey group apparently made about nine times its money.*

*Perhaps much more, if some of the $10 million was borrowed and the deal was, like many of Odyssey's, leveraged to the hilt. Curiously, the prospectus for the offering, which was managed by First Boston Corporation and Odyssey's former firm, Oppenheimer & Co. Inc., omitted the boilerplate disclosure on how much selling shareholders paid for their stock.

William Simon turned an even better profit. The former Treasury Secretary got together with some buddies and swung a leveraged buyout of Gibson Greeting Cards Inc. from RCA. The price tag was $80 million. Eighteen months later, they took Gibson public and, with the magic of 1983's bull market, Gibson was valued at $280 million. Three and a half times their money in eighteen months? Perish the thought. The Simon gang put up only $1 million in cash for Gibson. The rest they borrowed. For his part, Bill Simon ponied up about $330,000 for a stake that after the public offering was worth $70 million. Shares he sold at the offering brought him more than $10 million.[1]

With variations, that theme rings through the stock market year after year. The recycling of assets, from wise hands to foolish hands and back around, is one of the forces driving markets. It's a tradition that rewards professionals for their labor and insight, and it leaves amateurs with the recurrent feeling of having been hoodwinked if not mugged. The general rule is this: *Insiders buy when values are cheap and sell when they've been bid up.* Just as they resist the panics that drive public and institutional investors to give stocks away at market bottoms, they also resist the publicists who coax the public to buy at inflated prices near market tops. Insiders tend to be on the opposite side of those trades.

## BEARISH INSIDERS?

The question is, how important is insider selling to other investors? It helps to understand a couple of points. Much of insiders' stock comes to them through option plans and other low-cost devices, and they tend on balance to be net sellers most of the time. This is a normal, unalarming state of affairs. It's when their selling becomes intense that other investors should grow wary and *prepare* to grow alarmed.

Signs of insider selling whisper a suspicion. Is there trouble? Has the stock had its day? Insider sales provide notice that investors with the best information are content with current prices and are taking profits. Most statistical work has found that stocks being sold by insiders fare less well afterward than the average issue, and signs of widespread insider selling are generally taken as being, to some degree, bearish for the stock market. Not necessarily a death knell, but a warning bell.

That's true regardless of the form of the selling. Insiders may unload shares a few thousand at a clip in the open market, or in 500,000-share slugs with the help of underwriters. They may be major sellers at initial public offerings, when companies go public, as the Odyssey group was with Big Bear, or later through secondary distributions, as Apple Computer insiders were shortly before the stock's 1981–82 slide. A booming market in new issues and secondary offerings will be ballyhooed by brokers as evidence of the sunny future awaiting technology and the economy. But it's also evidence of massive insider selling. There may be money left on the table for the public in these deals, because underwriters know that a customer who makes a profit will buy the next issue. Often, however, the best money has been made. In effect, the new-issues market is the retailing of assets acquired at wholesale cost. Despite anything else that might be said of this market, for speculators that's its essence.* If in doubt on the point, ask yourself how many of the "smart money" investors described in the preceding chapters made their fortunes by buying new issues. They were, if anything, like Odyssey Partners and Bill Simon, *sellers*.

This perspective differs slightly from market technicians' views on new and secondary stock offerings. To the technician, booms in such deals are bearish because they reveal the excessive public enthusiasm for stocks that accompanies market tops. There's a long history supporting this perception, but public euphoria isn't a *direct* comment on the market's values; in theory, if public investors grew more sophisticated, they might turn bullish at market bottoms (there would still be the institutions to buy from).

*One thing that can be said is that the new-issues market serves a useful social function, raising capital to finance industry. This is true. But a socially useful function needn't be profitable for its milch cows. Another thing that can be said is that many fine companies, boasting proprietary products, sell new stock issues ("After all, Federal Express was once a new issue!"). This is true, too. But the majority, including some pretty good companies, don't live up to the great expectations implicit in the offering prices. A couple of months after going public, both Big Bear and Gibson Greeting Cards were trading at hefty discounts from the prices public investors paid.

What's significant about new-issues booms is that they're a symptom of insider unloading. These are the investors who pay attention to values.

## FALLIBLE TIMING

One problem in watching insider selling as an indicator of the market or individual stocks is that insiders often act too early. When they're dumping stock, it may be a sign that the best values are gone, but it's not a reliable warning that the best *prices* have been seen. On the heels of particularly vicious bear markets, it may be a sign of neither. Insider selling reached bearish levels, according to the parameters of a popular market letter, in the first half of 1975 (Figure 1). The new bull market had lifted prices sharply, but it still had many years to run during which investors who sold at the sight of insider liquidation may have been out of the market. Even if these investors bought stock again in the second half of 1975, when insiders turned bullish, individual issues had climbed out of reach. At best, these investors settled for short-term profits—and paid taxes on them—when shares could have been kept for the long pull.

Following insider selling would have been just as frustrating in 1982. The selling reached bearish territory only weeks after the bull market took off in August 1982. This prompted *The Insiders,* the market letter, to declare on September 9, 1982, that the "selling intensity throws up a yellow flag: Slow down! Defer new buying!" The Dow Jones Industrial Average closed that day at 912.53. The yellow flag was still flapping a year later, as the Dow stood at 1239.74. No advice was given to sell along with the insiders, but the warning not to buy, in a bull market that had more than a year's life left, repudiated the usefulness of *specific levels* of insider selling in forecasting the stock market. By summer 1983, net selling by insiders was at record levels, and now they were right. The market was on the verge of a yearlong decline.

A high rate of insider liquidation seems only to advise investors to inspect other measures of the market's health. By itself, on the evidence of the past decade, it's not bearish.

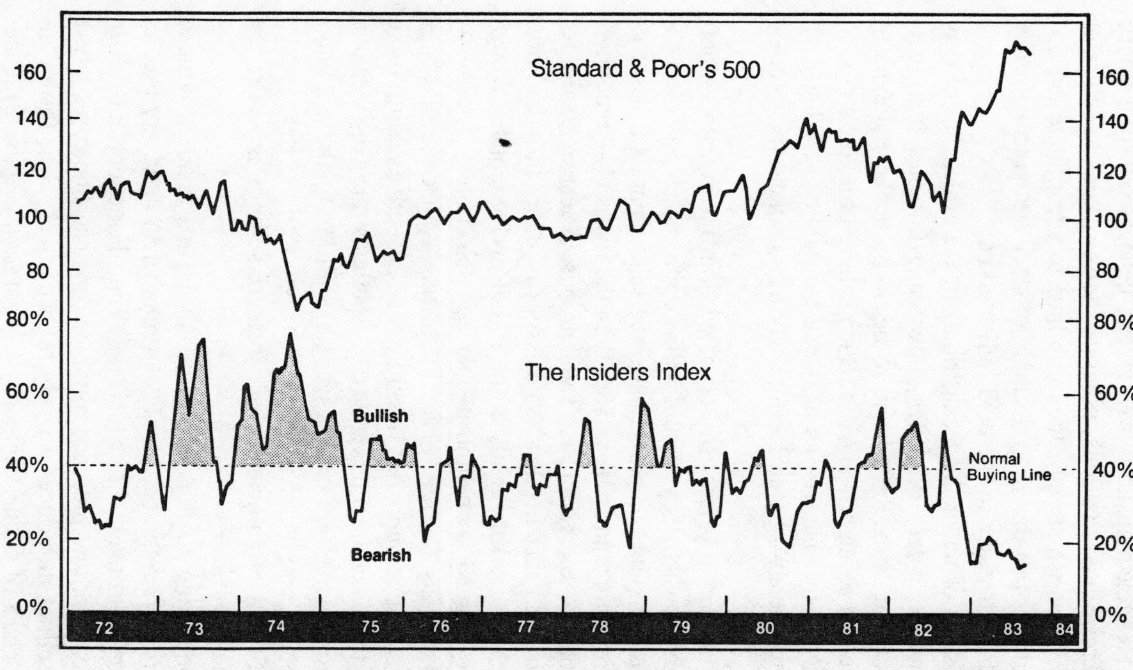


**Figure 1. Insiders became heavy sellers early in bull markets in both 1975 and 1982. As a market-timing indicator, insider selling has little value. (Courtesy of *The Insiders*, Fort Lauderdale, Florida)**

One explanation of this may be that insiders are a source of pent-up supply of common stock at the end of a bear market. When prices reach absurdly low levels, insiders sell little stock. They exercise fewer options, obtaining fewer shares to sell. But during this bearish stretch, they continue to accumulate the options, and thus they build up a supply of stock and potential stock that spills forth early in the next bull market.

Other signs of major insider distribution, the avalanches of new issues and secondary offerings, have rung out past bull markets.[2] But here, too, there seem to be no particular numbers to announce that enough is enough. Such selling provides a clue to the quality of the market—an alert that the public is buying from the smarter money—but it doesn't serve as a market-timing tool.

Nor are insiders a perfect source of wisdom for investors wanting to know when they should sell specific issues. While academicians pumping computers have generally reported that stocks sold by insiders tend to be weaker than the market[3]—sometimes much weaker—the verdict isn't unanimous. A research team reported in 1983 that insiders' sale issues in their study had *outperformed* the market slightly at the end of twelve months, though the shares lagged far behind insider buy selections.[4] The possible explanations for this make interesting conjecture. Perhaps faster-growing companies reward their executives with more options than mature enterprises; or perhaps growth-company executives own more stock to begin with, from the entrepreneurial stage, and therefore produce heavier selling. In any case, the statistical significance of insider selling is more in doubt than ever.

It's one thing to look back and know that insiders jumped overboard before the boat sank, but another to draw any predictive value from the sight of insider selling. For every episode in which heavy selling preceded a plunge, one can find cases where insider selling introduced sharply higher prices. See, for example, the chart of Stone Container Corporation (Figure 2). Sales by insiders have forecast a dozen disasters for every half-dozen that have come to pass.

This makes it harder to nail insiders who unload before bad news. Were they staring at bleak financial forecasts—not yet

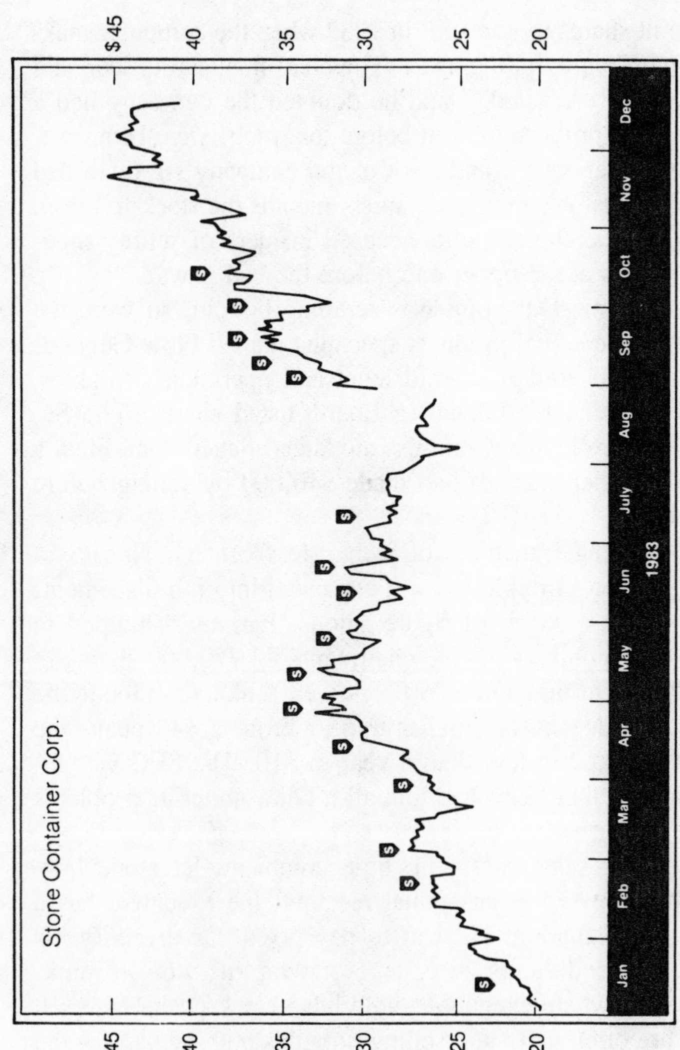


**Figure 2. The controlling family sold tens of thousands of shares of Stone Container Corporation during the stock's steep rise in 1983. The company's prospects were improving all the time. Insider selling doesn't always signal doom.**

public—as they called their broker? Or were they just evening out the portfolio, raising cash for the IRS, or planning their estates?

Datapoint shares took a spill in 1982 when the computer maker's earnings began falling apart. The chief financial officer said the market "overreacted," and he doubted the company had a "really serious problem."[5] But before long, jobs were being cut, red ink was seeping in, and a lot of the company's growth had been revealed as phantom sales. In six months the stock fell from $50 to $11. Shareholder suits accused insiders of selling thousands of shares at the upper end before the bad news.

About the time Datapoint was scraping bottom, so were the shares of a biomedical-products specialist named Flow General. An eight-month collapse, amid legal and operational troubles, knocked 75 percent off the Big Board–listed shares. The Securities and Exchange Commission later alleged that Flow's president (by then ousted) had made $40,000 by selling before the rain.

A fast-growing franchiser of weight-loss centers, Nutri/System Inc., ran into trouble when it expanded into job placement, cosmetics, and a string of figure salons. Earnings slumped in 1983—a few months after the chairman sold 770,000 shares in a secondary offering. Other officers were unloading about the same time in dozens of smaller trades. From a $48 peak, the shares plummeted in less than a year to $10. The SEC was investigating whether Nutri had told all it knew about its problems when the executives sold.

Most insider sales pass with little comment, let alone lawsuits. When pressed at an annual meeting, the executive has a reasonable explanation. He had to pay taxes. Or diversify his holdings. Or send Junior to college or wrap his wife in mink. At companies where executives hold huge stock positions, such accounts are often valid and selling portends nothing bad for the company or its stock. Despite heavy sales in 1982 in most of the hospital management companies—American Medical International, Hospital Corporation of America, Humana, National Medical Enterprises—the companies wheeled in double-digit earnings growth, and the stock prices climbed 100 to 200 percent in the next year (Figure 3).

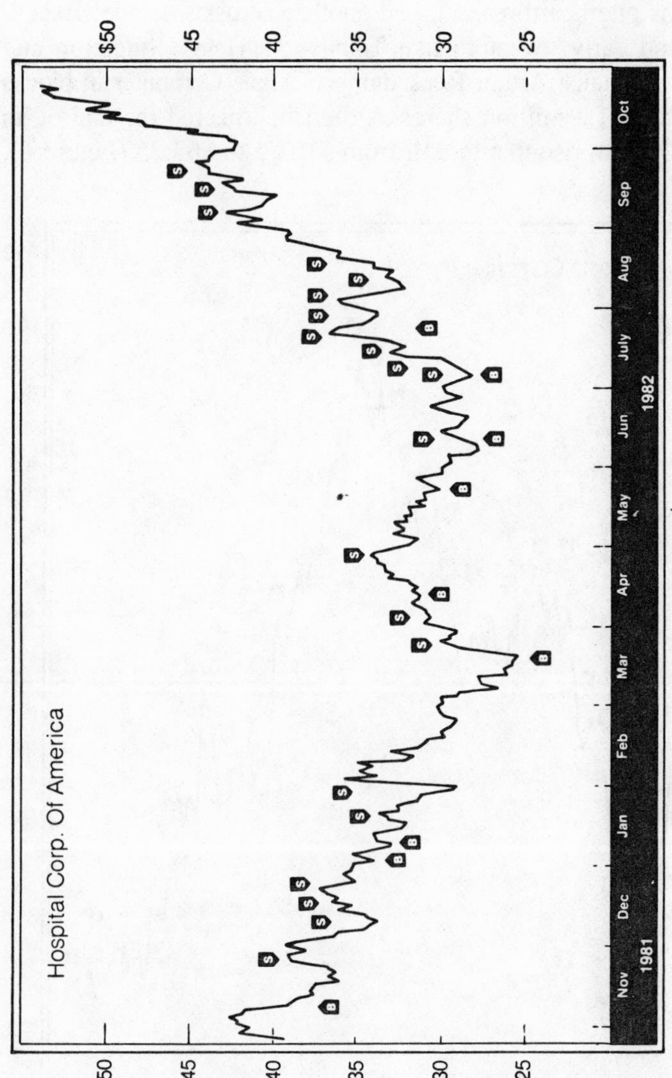


**Figure 3. Fairly typical of its group, Hospital Corporation of America was sold by insiders when it was down as well as up. Growth has remained brisk.**

Yet insiders who sold the technology stocks relentlessly in 1983 as prices reached 40, 50, and 60 times earnings soon looked pretty smart as one heartbreak chased another across the tape. Executives and early investors like Teledyne's Henry Singleton and venture capitalist Arthur Rock dumped Apple Computer in blocks of up to half a million shares as the stock neared the end of an eleven-month rise that took it from $10.75 to $63.25 (Figure 4).

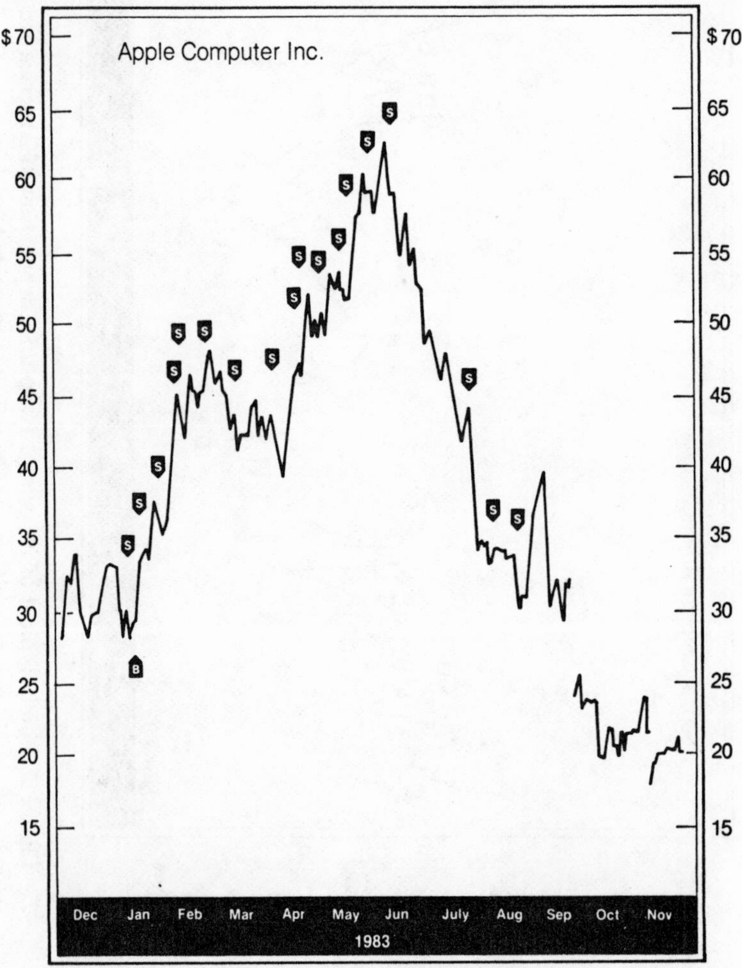


**Figure 4. Apple Computer insiders dumped hundreds of thousands of shares before the company ran into trouble.**

**Insider Selling at Apple Computer**

| *Shares Sold* | *Date* | *Price* | *Insider (Position)* |
|---|---|---|---|
| 10,000 | 1/20/83 | 36⅜ | Arthur Rock (D) |
| 55,000 | 1/20–27 | 36¼–40¼ | Gene Carter (VP) |
| 50,000 | 1/31 | 40⅝ | Henry Singleton (D) |
| 20,000 | 1/21–27 | 38–39 | John Couch (VP) |
| 20,000 | 1/26–27 | 37⅝–40 | Michael Muller (VP) |
| 10,000 | 2/2 | 41½ | John Couch (VP) |
| 100,000 | 2/2–23 | 42½–46½ | Henry Singleton (D) |
| 22,000 | 2/10 | 45 | Gene Carter (VP) |
| 40,000 | 2/10 | 44 | John Vennard (VP) |
| 50,000 | 2/14 | 45¾ | Wilfred Houde (VP) |
| 75,000 | 2/23 | 47 | Armas Markkula (P) |
| 20,000 | 3/9–11 | 41⅜–42⅞ | John Couch (VP) |
| 5,000 | 4/5 | 41⅛ | Arthur Rock (D) |
| 20,000 | 4/27 | 50⅜ | Gene Carter (VP) |
| 500,000 | 4/29 | 50⅜ | Steven Jobs (CB) |
| 30,000 | 5/3 | 47⅞–48 | Armas Markkula (VC) |
| 20,000 | 5/5 | 55 | Wilfred Houde (VP) |
| 100,000 | 5/17–18 | 51⅜–52⅛ | Kenneth Zerbe (SVP) |
| 25,000 | 5/25 | 59⅜–⅞ | Delbert Yocam (VP) |
| 20,000 | 5/25 | 60⅛ | Gene Carter (VP) |
| 5,000 | 6/3 | 60⅜ | Michael Muller (VP) |
| 25,000 | 6/6 | 62 | Henry Singleton (D) |
| 25,000 | 6/7–8 | 60¼–61⅞ | Armas Markkula (VC) |
| 5,000 | 7/25 | 43¼ | Arthur Rock (D) |
| 100,000 | 8/2–18 | 33½–35 | Armas Markkula (VC) |

Symbols: CB: chairman of board; D-director; VC-vice chairman; VP-vice-president; P-president; SVP-senior vice-president
SOURCE: *Official Summary of Security Transactions and Holdings*

That autumn, in the midst of an institutional panic out of technology issues, Apple crashed below $20. Did the insiders know that trouble loomed for the personal-computer maker as IBM weighed in? There's no evidence to suggest it—nor any way to read the thoughts of insiders who were bailing out of dozens of other high-tech stocks in the months before the panic.

What's certain is that insiders who had seen the value of their shares climb as much as sixfold in less than a year were eager to cash in. Stocks do get overpriced—even if analysts and institutional portfolio managers don't believe it.

The moral is that insider selling isn't a trusty enough sign of trouble to rule investment decisions. It's one consideration among many that investors should weigh. Are prices historically high—or have they been beaten down by months of public and institutional selling? Does the P/E reflect pessimism—or does it discount prosperity into the next decade? Insiders sold the hospital companies at ten times earnings, a low multiple by the group's history. Henry Singleton sold Apple Computer at forty times earnings, a P/E that allowed no disappointments.

If you own a reliable company trading at a modest valuation, it makes no sense to abandon the stock solely because of modest insider sales. Examine the nature of the selling. Are numerous insiders unloading large percentages of their holdings? Or are a few executives, perhaps founders of the company, selling modest amounts from caches of hundreds of thousands of shares? If they seem to be stampeding for the door, you may want to join them. Just as a precaution. After all, you can shift your money into a good stock that insiders are buying. But if they're just cashing in a little of their reward for building a company, the stock may still be a sound value.

If insiders are selling a rising stock, an investor can protect profits, suggests J. Michael Reid of *Insider Indicator,* by placing stop-loss orders at the point where insiders sold. If the stock keeps rising, they enjoy the ride, raising the stops on the way up.

# TEN

# *Sell Them Down the River*

Professional investors are not sentimental. They buy stocks and sell them the way they would buy or sell an orange-juice contract. The horizon may be longer; the expected profit may lie two, three, or five years down the road. But the objective is never in doubt. Their goal in investing is to add to their wealth.

But what motivates some part-time investors? I mean the ones who stick with losing companies for years, who vote their stock at every meeting as management advises and wait vainly for profits. Corporate officers love these docile souls. They salute them as "Our Loyal Shareholders"—as if the officers owned the company and the shareholders were trusty retainers.

Dutifully the loyal shareholders elect directors who hand mediocre managers well-stuffed pay envelopes and princely retirement plans. They back proposals to make takeovers next to impossible. They sit silent while management rigs "golden parachutes" to enrich itself should a raider somehow get past the moat. They applaud the chief executive who announces that last year's earnings were disappointing (because of currency-exchange rates, of course) and this year's won't be much better (because of higher research outlays, you know) but next year's look promising (subject to change). Not many feudal lords had it so good.

Insider abuse takes many forms, none of them easily remedied by public moralists. But the most costly abuse of the shareholder—the corporate owner—is the nest-feathering and barricade-building by salaried managers.

Professional bargain hunters like Carl Icahn and David Murdock aren't white knights bent on rescuing small shareholders from bondage. They're self-serving fortune hunters. But sometimes they're the shareholder's best friend. They add efficiency to the market by bidding for assets that are being ill-used by their current owners. The measures of effective use are the traditional numbers: return on assets, return on equity, profit or loss. In general, the market values those performances rationally. A well-run corporation with a bright future usually is priced to reflect its merits. A bear market may make all stocks undervalued, but the assets that have been poorly managed will be the cheapest, after legions of "loyal shareholders" have sold out in despair. Those are the stocks that attract opportunistic predators. The most successful companies seldom offer takeover artists such bargains.

What loyalty do shareholders owe to managers of less successful companies that become targets? The short, sensible, professional investor's answer is: none. Consider how loyally managers behave toward investors. A tender offer yields investors immediate, clear-cut, bottom-line benefits. If it's fair, they can accept. If it seems inadequate, they can say no. That is, they can make those decisions if they get a chance.

## Devil Take the Shareholder

But when officers and directors fear being deposed, their abuse of the public shareholder's interests knows few limits. In recent years, nervous managements at hundreds of companies have thrown up barricades before any takeover threat loomed. With advice from investment bankers and top-dollar legal talent, the insiders have concocted imaginatively named defenses: "Pac-Man" (swallow your enemy), "shark repellent" (require an 80 percent vote to sell), "scorched earth" (sell off your prize assets), and even the "poison pill" (force any buyer to swallow an expensive slug of preferred stock). *Forbes* estimated in 1983 that 15 to 20 percent of the nation's top corporations were asking stockholders to approve measures to discourage takeovers,[1] often by requiring "supermajority" votes of as much as 80 percent of the shares to oust a board of directors. For a couple of years I kept a casual list of companies proposing antitakeover schemes. When I gave up it looked like this:

AAR Corp.
Accuray
American Natural Resources
Amrep Corp.
Atlantic Bancorp
Atlantic Research
Avco Corp.
Axia
BDM International
Binks Manufacturing
Black & Decker
Boatmen's Bankshares
Bowne & Co.
Burlington Industries
Burroughs Corp.
California REIT
Carlisle Corp.
Castle & Cooke
Centerre Bancorp
Champion Spark Plug
Chartercorp
Chubb Corp.
Cincinnati Bell
Citizens Fidelity
Coastal Corp.
Combustion Engineering
Comerica
Connecticut Energy
Cooper Industries
Consolidated Natural Gas
Corning Glass
Data General
Decision Data Computer
Dinner Bell Foods
Dow Jones
Dun & Bradstreet
Economics Laboratory
Empire District Tel.
Enstar Corp.
Federated Stores
Figgie International
Galaxy Carpet Mills
General Datacomm Ind.
Golden West Financial
Greyhound Corp.
Harsco Corp.
Hechinger Co.
G. Heileman Brewing
Hughes Tool
Illinois Tool Works
International Paper
InterNorth
KDI Corp.
Koppers Co.
Lancaster Colony
Leisure & Technology
Louisiana Pacific
Malone & Hyde
Marriott Corp.
Marshall & Ilsley
Maytag Co.
Meredith Corp.

Missouri Public Service
Moog
Morse Shoe
Mosinee Paper
National Gypsum
Network Systems
NL Industries
Nordson Corp.
Norton Co.
Penril Corp.
Phillips Petroleum
Pioneer Corp.
Pitney Bowes
Pogo Producing
PPG Industries
Progressive Corp.
Purolator Services
Quanex Corp.
Ransburg Corp.
RCA Corp.
Realist
R. G. Barry
Riblet Products
R. P. Scherer
Ryder System
Schwab Safe
A. Schulman
Snap-On Tools
Spectro Industries
Sperry Corp.
Stauffer Chemical
Sun Co.
Tenney Engineering
Texaco
Texas Eastern
Textron
Trans-Lux Corp.
United Energy Resources
United Medical
United Technologies
Univar Corp.
U.S. Shoe
Vulcan Materials
Warnaco
Wayne-Gossard
Westvaco Corp.
Wrather Corp.

Like sheep handing out clippers, the stockholders at all but a few of these companies have given management everything it sought. In extreme cases, holders of Figgie International and A. O. Smith backed plans surrendering so much control—in fact, virtually disenfranchising themselves in favor of the controlling families—that the companies lost their listings on the New York Stock Exchange. The shares of Dow Jones fell more than 25 percent in the months after a two-tier voting system was proposed, jeopardizing DJ's listing.

These defenses have risen in a period of economic expansion and buoyant stock quotes. The price for them will be paid in a future recession, as the market knocks down the value of underperforming assets and shareholders find that Carl Icahn isn't pounding on the door. Well-fortified managers will have little to fear from either Icahn *or* unhappy shareholders.

Far from challenging these abuses, state lawmakers by and large have rallied to management's side, erecting new barriers to takeovers in Maryland, Ohio, Pennsylvania, and other jurisdictions. At the federal level, regulators have tinkered with tender-offer rules but imposed no major reforms. For managements, the most reliable tactic when a takeover threatens remains the old one: tap the corporate treasury either to buy off the raider ("greenmail" in the current jargon) or to pay attorneys to sue every s.o.b. in sight.

Warner Communications, where artful management lost $6.35 a share in 1983, found itself a takeover target and ponied up $180.6 million to ransom stock from Australian publisher Rupert Murdoch. Warner paid Murdoch $31 a share—$8 more than the market quote. Managements at Disney, Quaker State Oil, St. Regis, and Texaco also paid massive premiums to buy back unfriendly stock.

The rationales for resisting takeovers naturally include ritual bows to shareholder interests. The price is too stingy. The deal is too hasty. This solemn nonsense prompted a friend of mine to propose adding "It isn't in shareholder interests" to the list of the English language's big lies. He has a point.

Jesse Werner, for two decades chairman of GAF Corporation, even persuaded a federal court in 1983 to throw out a dissident's victory in a proxy battle. GAF, a miniconglomerate with roofing materials, chemicals, and other lines, had compiled such a dismal history under Werner that *Forbes* declared it "one of the worst corporate performance records in American industry."[2] Among the black marks: two-year operating losses totaling $46 million, a score of disappointing acquisitions or expansions, cartwheeling changes in the president's office. As the company posted a $22 million operating loss in 1981, Werner and other executives collected $635,000 in bonuses. The awards gave new meaning to the phrase "a job well done." When dissident investor Samuel Heyman proposed to liquidate the company and distribute the proceeds to stockholders, restive institutional holders flocked to his cause. It was a classic case of a turkey seeming to be worth more carved than whole. As the proxy battle gained steam, GAF common shares climbed on the New York Stock Exchange from $9 to $19.75. Besieged, Werner tried to head off his ouster by embracing much of the dissidents' agenda. Buyers for the roofing and chemicals divisions were lined up, and days before the annual meeting, Werner unveiled plans to liquidate the company. Perhaps remembering an earlier liquidation pledge by the chairman that fell through, shareholders cast their lots for Heyman. After the vote, Werner—still financing his battles from the corporate purse—blocked the insurgents from taking control for more than six months, until an appeals court showed him the door. By then, plans to sell the roofing and chemicals units had broken down. Surprise?

Yet Werner's abuses were, in a way, small ante. Directors of Amax Inc. set the standard. In March 1981, Standard Oil of California offered to buy the metals producer for $78.50 a share. The stock was trading at $37.50. Responding to a 100 percent premium, chairman Pierre Gousseland sniffed: "Amax does not need to combine with any other company in order to achieve its goals."[3] Some shareholders suspected the "goals" were really management's, mundane things like hanging onto their jobs. They sued the board for breach of its fiduciary duty, and a director was quoted anonymously as conceding: "It's going to be hard to prove that the company didn't make a mistake. . . ."[4] By that time, the spring of 1982, the minerals boom that had enticed SoCal was a bust, and Amax was suffering severe financial strain. The company lost $390 million in 1982. For public shareholders, however, the bath was even colder. By the summer of 1982, Amax common stock had plummeted to $17.50. Compared with SoCal's offer seventeen months earlier, that figure represented a loss in value of $3.2 billion. Given the time value of money, it's unlikely that Amax owners will ever be as well off as they could have been in 1981 had Gousseland counted financial interest of shareholders high among the corporate "goals."

After such disasters, stockholders can't be blamed for wondering whose interests boards of directors truly serve. Are directors beholden to owners of stock—or to the corporate insiders who nominate them to sometimes lucrative posts? At Amax, outside directors (those not holding office in the company) received $16,000 a year, plus $800 for each meeting attended. A moderate sum in the circles from which prominent directors are tapped, but at Amax it was only the retainer. Among the outside directors, according to the 1982 proxy statement, former President Gerald R. Ford and former Defense Secretary Harold Brown both held substantial consulting contracts with the company; Ford's brought him $99,996 a year, Brown's $75,000.[5] When it comes time to ponder the merits of a takeover proposal, what's on the minds of these "independent" directors? The benefits to shareholders? Or the potential loss of consulting income? A clue to how their financial incentives are weighted: typically a prominent outside director owns no more than a couple hundred shares of common stock; many own none.

RCA Corporation roared with indignation in 1982 when it learned that Bendix Corporation had acquired more than 5 percent of its stock. RCA hadn't been doing so well, with several years of virtually flat earnings leading into a $54 million loss for 1981. The stock was trading under $20, well below estimates of the corporation's liquidation value. The discount offered an opportunity. Suppose you sold off the NBC subsidiary, or CIT Financial, or Hertz? Maybe Bendix's William Agee was thinking along those lines as he bought RCA stock in the high teens. But RCA Chairman Thornton Bradshaw wasn't interested in chopping up his domain. Greeting word of Bendix's stake, an RCA press release stormed that Bendix was "not welcome" and that Agee by "secretly accumulating a block of RCA stock shows his only purpose is to further his own ambitions and not the interests of RCA." Then, in a remarkable breach of etiquette even in the rough-mannered takeover world, RCA hurled a gibe at Agee's relationship with his former protégé Mary Cunningham: "Mr. Agee has not demonstrated the ability to manage his own affairs, let alone someone else's." RCA vowed to "take all actions necessary to protect the company and its shareholders."[6] Analysts were estimating that RCA could be dismembered for upward of $30 a share, a 50 percent premium over the market price, a prospect from which few investors would want to be protected. But management and the stockholders had different stakes in RCA. In a takeover or liquidation, chairman Bradshaw didn't stand to profit greatly from his stock holdings (6,000 shares), but he was collecting an annual paycheck, bonuses, and other incentives totaling $938,500.[7]

Bradshaw had good reason, moreover, to expect the board of directors to back him in chasing off Agee. None of the corporation's key outside directors owned more than 500 RCA shares, but some of them were raking it in as board members. Especially noteworthy were the rewards of two influential directors, Donald B. Smiley, former chairman of R. H. Macy & Co., and Peter G. Peterson, onetime U.S. Secretary of Commerce and then chairman of Lehman Brothers Kuhn Loeb. When RCA's previous chairman had been ousted, Smiley was paid $250,000 to negotiate the termination package (it came to $1.25 million) and to head a search for a new RCA chief executive. He discovered a candidate right at his elbow, fellow board member Bradshaw, who signed a five-year contract at nearly $1 million annually. Notes the 1982 proxy statement: ". . . and on August 5, 1981, the Corporation entered into an agreement with Mr. Smiley providing for his services from August 6, 1981, to August 5, 1982, to conduct studies and make recommendations on management organization and development matters at a rate of $150,000 a year." Smiley owned 100 RCA shares, worth about $2,000. To help resist takeovers, the board hired Peterson's firm, Lehman Brothers, which collected nearly $2 million in fees from RCA in 1981. Peterson owned 400 RCA shares, an $8,000 stake. Remarked a former RCA director: ". . . [A]ll they do is pass around the goodies among themselves."[8]

At times, directors' income has been found to be so bountiful that their status as "outsiders" has been overturned. Employees in fact become employees in name. Whether more stringent regulatory limits should be imposed on payments to outside directors is debatable; knowledgeable and sophisticated businessmen such as Smiley and Peterson are probably worth at least part of their keep. But their conflict of interest is undeniable.

## Suit and Parachute

In case defensive ploys fail, executives at hundreds of public companies can fall back on "golden parachutes" guaranteeing them millions of dollars in a takeover. After William Agee blundered into the loss of Bendix Corporation, he donned a $4.1 million backpack and bailed out of Bendix's new owner, Allied Corporation. Three Northwest Energy Company executives made that look like peanuts. After Northwest was acquired by Williams Companies in 1983, the three collected $29.8 million.

A 1982 review of proxy statements from 665 major companies found 15 percent of the outfits offered golden parachutes. A year later, the number had jumped to 24.5 percent.[9] The nest-feathering turned up at such giants as Allied Corporation (which later withdrew the packages because of negative publicity), American Can, Anchor Hocking, Ashland Oil, Celanese, City Investing, Firestone Tire & Rubber, International Paper, National Steel, Pennzoil, Phillips Petroleum, Sun Company, and United Technologies. One group had fast-opening parachutes letting top executives bail out if control of 20 percent of the stock changed.

The boilerplate apology for these sweetheart deals is that "employment guarantees" provide the job security needed to retain top executive talent. The timing of many of the packages betrays last-chance raids on the corporate cash box. When Diamond Shamrock Corporation made a pass at Natomas Company in 1983, four top Natomas executives quickly signed golden parachutes worth $10.2 million if they decided to leave the company. Then Natomas surrendered to a merger.[10]

The last couple of years' scuffles at Rorer Group, the pharmaceutical house known for Maalox antacid, sum up the attitudes of defensive managements. Dissatisfied investors holding 13 percent of Rorer hired an investment banker, Oppenheimer & Co., to seek a buyer for the company. Management reacted with a two-pronged defense. First a half-dozen executives (down to the corporate counsel) shouldered golden parachutes. Then the company slapped the dissidents and their adviser with a damage suit asking $50 million.

Rorer's gray-haired, smooth-spoken chairman, John W. Eckman, Jr., admitted that he had been turning away potential suitors for decades, usually before talks passed the preliminaries. The suit was pending when Rorer Group held its 1983 annual meeting. The topic of the dissidents and Oppenheimer produced this exchange:

*First Shareholder:* I wonder if you could comment what types of propositions they [Oppenheimer] have brought you, what you like, what you dislike, and what might be acceptable to management.

*Eckman:* I've never met anyone from Oppenheimer in my life. They have not brought us anything. They have not approached us in any way, shape or form. . . . Oppenheimer, I understand, has been active in trying to shop our company around this country and around the world, . . . and no one has brought us a proposition. . . .

*Second Shareholder:** Are you inviting them to bring you a proposition, in the interests of shareholders?

*Eckman:* I've been with this company for 20 years—uh, I've got my 20-year award here last September. There has not been a year of those 20 years that we have not been the object of acquisition affection and propositions. I have developed over those years a more or less standardized response to those overtures, which is, yes, if we were offered something that represented a major improvement in the prospects of the company under new control—a major improvement over the company's own record of progress under present control—we would certainly give it very serious thought. . . . If someone were to come along and say here's a 100 percent premium over the current market value of your stock, there's no question but what the board of directors would know about it within 24 hours and it would be given serious thought. That's a lot more than the current management's offering to shareholders. On the other hand, if somebody's looking for a bargain and says, well your stock is selling at 25 and we'll offer you 27½, I just say, "Why do you want to put us on the auction block? Because we'll surely be worth a lot more than 27½ or $30 to someone. You'll be outbid, and somebody else will get us. And so why

*The author.

do you want to start something like that?'' It's a very simple but open sort of a proposition.

*First Shareholder:* During the past couple of years, have you had any offers that you have considered at the board of directors meeting?

*Eckman:* No. . . . Offers, we've had none. Overtures we have had quite regularly—overtures ''Would we be interested in sitting down and talking about joining forces with the XYZ Company?'' Well, frankly, no, the XYZ Company is, let's say, in the wholesale tobacco business or something like that. We're not interested in joining forces with you. . . . In terms of our interest in joining this or that company, usually a company pretty far out in terms of synergy, we normally say no. We're not looking for a buyer for this company. The company is not on the auction block. As the president, or the chairman, I guess, of McCormick down in Baltimore said, it's about time people got to realize that this company is not a commodity like pork bellies to be bought and sold at the drop of a hat.*

By no means all of the companies making ''overtures'' were in the wholesale tobacco business. A few months after Eckman offered that description, a generally sympathetic article in *Forbes* cited Eckman in reporting that ''every major pharmaceutical and chemical company in the U.S. and a good many in Europe have coveted Rorer.''[11] So lack of synergy wasn't the problem. And given that talks seldom progressed beyond ''overtures,'' price wasn't the stumbling block. Rather, as Eckman said on another occasion, pharmaceutical companies and other potential suitors had been given the word: ''We've decided to go it alone. . . .

*An unfortunate choice. A year after McCormick & Co., the spice marketer, rejected a $37-a-share offer from Sandoz Ltd. of Switzerland, internal trouble surfaced. Because of accounting games in the grocery-products division, McCormick was forced to restate three years' profits. Its common stock, traded over the counter, sank as low as $16. Owners of most of those shares had no say in the merger proposal; McCormick's voting stock is closely held, a manager's dream come true.

We've made it pretty clear that we're not interested [in being acquired]."[12]

There's room for disagreement on whether corporations should be sold "like pork bellies." Which side one takes depends on where one's financial incentives lie. Rorer's dissidents were discouraged by a stretch of static earnings—$1.67 a share in 1979, $1.82 three years later—and a stock that had run into a ceiling in the low 20s. Having been spurned in efforts to get management to set up guidelines for considering "overtures," the dissidents' ringleader took a more direct approach.

Here was his assumption: that the decision whether or not to sell a company, at any given price and time, belongs to the owners, the shareholders, not to salaried managers. Not only do managers face a financial conflict of interest in knowing they might be jettisoned, but also they have nonmaterial reasons for wanting to remain at the helm, such as psychological gratification. While those reasons serve investors well in the early, growth stages of a company, they can prompt even well-meaning executives to betray their trust later, when a buy-out could make good business sense.

For stockholders, a buy-out *more often than not* makes good business sense. Current dollars simply are worth more than future dollars. An offer that provides a significant premium over today's market price compresses time for an investor, removing uncertainty and risk from future values by delivering them *now*. Obviously a takeover price must reflect not only the target company's current situation but also its reasonable expectations. But the key is that expectations must be discounted, both for the time value of money and for uncertainty. It's one thing to reject a merger price that puts no premium on a two-year backlog of noncancelable orders for a proprietary product; confidence in the company's future growth is reasonable. It's another to spurn an offer that doesn't pay up for *hopes* for the future—particularly when the record shows a string of dashed hopes.

When a professional investor buys for the long term, it's neither a pledge of fealty nor an act of blind faith: it's a commercial judgment. If management performs, it will probably enjoy the professional investor's support. If it fails, the professional investor will liquidate something: either management or his stock position. No owner of a private company would permit hired managers to tell him he couldn't, at any time and for any reason, sell the business for the best price offered. Owners of public companies needn't stand for it either.

# APPENDIX I
# *Three Portfolios*

How would a portfolio of insider stocks perform? Here are three tallies that suggest the answer is at least "pretty well." The first list is of stocks that were pointed out as insider buys in a series of articles the author wrote for *Barron's*. The second and third lists are portfolios recommended by two advisory services. None of these selections represents a controlled, scientific study. But investors don't make their decisions in the laboratory, least of all working backward from historical material. These three portfolios were subject to the variables that would affect investors following insiders—missed chances, poor judgment, blind luck. All outperformed the market. More scientific results, from academic studies of insider activity, are presented in Appendix II.

## STOCKS FROM THE *BARRON'S* ARTICLES

The following table lists all the companies mentioned as targets of recent insider buying in articles in *Barron's* between January 1981 and December 1982. The table describes the prices at which insiders were buying, the prices as each article appeared at which investors could have bought, and the quotes on September 30, 1983.

| Stock | Insiders' Price | Readers' Price | 9/30/83 Price | Gain (Loss) |
|---|---|---|---|---|
| *January 26, 1981* | | | | |
| Chicago Milwaukee | $11–$31 | $35.50 | $95.50 | 169.0% |
| Clorox | 10–11 | 10.75 | 25.00 | 132.6 |
| Consolidated Foods | 21–26 | 24.25 | 47.00 | 93.8 |
| Collins Foods | 3–4 | 4.03 | 17.63 | 337.5 |
| | Average annual return (1/26/81–9/30/83) = 68.7% | | | |
| *March 30, 1981* | | | | |
| Occidental Pete | 28–38 | 30.38 | 23.88 | (21.4) |
| Flowers Industries | 6–7 | 6.61 | 17.38 | 162.9 |
| Campbell Taggart | 14–15 | 18.00 | 36.00* | 100.0 |
| Tenneco | 35–51 | 48.75 | 41.50 | (14.9) |
| Valero Energy | 30–39 | 34.50 | 29.25 | (15.2) |
| Inter-City Gas | 14–17 | 16.38 | 9.25 | (43.5) |
| Macmillan | 10–14 | 14.29 | 32.00 | 123.9 |
| Mission West Prp. | 5 | 5.75 | 7.88 | 37.0 |
| Tucson Electric | 14 | 15.38 | 32.75 | 112.9 |
| St. Joseph L&P | 10 | 9.63 | 15.00 | 55.8 |
| Rochester G&E | 12 | 12.62 | 17.63 | 39.7 |
| Interstate Power | 12 | 11.75 | 16.25 | 38.3 |
| Equimark | 8–9 | 10.00 | 5.13 | (48.7) |
| Hudson General | 6–8 | 9.00 | 17.50 | 94.4 |
| | Average annual return (3/30/81–9/30/83) = 17.7% | | | |
| *June 22, 1981* | | | | |
| Zapata | 8–32 | 24.00 | 19.75 | (17.7) |
| Phillips Pete | 46–52 | 36.75 | 34.13 | (7.1) |
| Juniper Pete | 15–17 | 12.63 | 12.00* | (5.0) |
| Guardsman Chems. | 11–14 | 11.00 | 13.88 | 26.2 |
| Voplex | 11–13 | 6.06 | 17.13 | 182.7 |
| | Average annual return (6/22/81–9/30/83) = 15.9% | | | |
| *September 28, 1981* | | | | |
| Bangor Punta | 20–27 | 17.13 | 19.25 | 12.4 |
| Firestone | 12 | 9.75 | 20.63 | 111.6 |
| Engelhard | 19–29 | 17.38 | 42.38 | 143.8 |
| Beatrice Foods | 21–23 | 18.50 | 30.13 | 62.9 |
| Brunswick | 17–21 | 16.13 | 47.38 | 193.7 |

| *Stock* | *Insiders' Price* | *Readers' Price* | *9/30/83 Price* | *Gain (Loss)* |
|---|---|---|---|---|
| *September 28, 1981* | | | | |
| General Tire | 23–28 | 22.83 | 34.75 | 52.2 |
| Mohasco | 10–15 | 10.13 | 22.50 | 122.1 |
| Munsingwear | 15–17 | 15.00 | 13.38 | (10.8) |
| Nortek | 8–12 | 8.13 | 14.75 | 81.4 |
| Commercial Metals | 11–14 | 10.67 | 24.00 | 124.9 |
| Moran Energy | 21–23 | 14.54 | 16.50 | 13.4 |
| | Average annual return (9/28/81–9/30/83)=41.3% | | | |
| *February 8, 1982* | | | | |
| Burroughs | 29–35 | 33.25 | 53.75 | 61.7 |
| Quaker State Oil | 12–14 | 11.75 | 17.75 | 51.1 |
| Bank of Virginia | 13–15 | 15.50 | 29.00 | 87.1 |
| Planning Research | 5–6 | 7.63 | 15.50 | 110.6 |
| ABA Industries | 8–11 | 13.63 | 13.00* | (4.6) |
| Mediq | 3–4 | 4.39 | 19.00 | 332.8 |
| Nexus Industries | 5–6 | 5.75 | 2.75 | (52.2) |
| Security Capital | 3–4 | 4.25 | 10.63 | 150.1 |
| Weatherford Int'l | 15–18 | 22.50 | 9.88 | (56.1) |
| | Average annual return (2/8/82–9/30/83)=45.9% | | | |
| *June 28, 1982* | | | | |
| Quanex | 12–13 | 8.38 | 9.00 | 7.4 |
| Rowan | 10–14 | 9.88 | 13.00 | 31.6 |
| Apache Corp. | 14–15 | 11.88 | 13.38 | 12.6 |
| Baker Int'l | 27–31 | 23.50 | 21.50 | (8.5) |
| Compucorp | 8–12 | 11.50 | 10.25 | (10.9) |
| Ransburg | 15–21 | 15.25 | 17.00 | 11.5 |
| Pier One Imports | 5 | 6.25 | 20.00 | 220.0 |
| | Average annual return (6/28/82–9/30/83)=30.1% | | | |
| *December 27, 1982* | | | | |
| Recognition Equip. | 4–7 | 8.88 | 17.00 | 91.4 |
| | Average annual return (12/27/82–9/30/83)=121.9% | | | |
| | Portfolio's average annual return=48.8% | | | |

*Price of buyout.
Prices are adjusted for splits. Insider prices, rounded to the nearest dollar, are those reported in the periods covered in each article; insiders may have bought at other prices and other times as well. The average annual returns are simple arithmetic averages, which do not reflect compounding.

# *THE INSIDERS* PORTFOLIO

Stocks were selected by *The Insiders*, an advisory service based in Fort Lauderdale, Florida, from its scan of insider activity in all issues on the New York and American stock exchanges and in many over-the-counter stocks. The portfolio is an actual account.

| Stock | Initial Date | Recommendation Price | May 1984 Price | Gain (Loss) |
|---|---|---|---|---|
| Bay Financial | 8/26/80 | $ 6.50 | $19.50 | 200.0% |
| CalFed | 4/6/84 | 14.75 | 15.00 | 0.2 |
| Conquest Explor. | 12/5/83 | 7.87 | 10.75 | 36.6 |
| Delta Air Lines | 2/13/84 | 34.86 | 33.87 | (2.9) |
| Dixico | 2/26/82 | 3.50 | 6.37 | 82.0 |
| Florida Comm'l Bks. | 5/22/81 | 13.33 | 27.00 | 102.6 |
| GF Corp. | 2/24/84 | 9.37 | 12.12 | 29.3 |
| Gulf Res. & Chems. | 3/4/83 | 15.00 | 23.00 | 53.3 |
| Hasbro Industries | 2/28/84 | 23.87 | 36.00 | 50.8 |
| Helm Resources | 5/28/82 | 2.25 | 2.00 | (11.1) |
| Kay Corp. | 4/17/81 | 20.00 | 11.50 | (42.5) |
| Lowenstein, M. | 1/29/82 | 25.25 | 60.50 | 139.6 |
| Mediq | 12/18/81 | 4.01 | 14.25 | 255.4 |
| Pacific Lumber | 8/6/82 | 16.00 | 23.37 | 46.1 |
| Piccadilly Cafs. | 4/6/84 | 18.00 | 20.00 | 11.1 |
| PSA | 2/15/84 | 19.87 | 23.62 | 18.9 |
| Quanex | 3/12/82 | 11.87 | 11.00 | (7.3) |
| Ransburg | 6/18/82 | 15.50 | 14.87 | (4.1) |
| Seagull Energy | 12/17/82 | 7.37 | 16.12 | 118.7 |
| Spencer Cos. | 11/6/81 | 14.25 | 11.62 | (18.5) |
| Emery Air Freight | 8/11/82 | 8.50 | 22.00* | 158.8 |
| Handy & Harman | 3/19/82 | 13.50 | 19.75* | 46.3 |
| Pacific Rlty. Tr. | 8/26/80 | 25.75 | 38.50* | 49.5 |
| Planning Research | 1/22/82 | 6.00 | 19.87* | 231.2 |
| Rowan Cos. | 4/2/82 | 11.50 | 12.75* | 10.9 |

*Price at which stock was sold.
Prices are adjusted for splits.

# *INSIDER INDICATOR* TRACK RECORD

The table covers all buy signals given by *Insider Indicator,* a service based in Portland, Oregon, in a twelve-month period. The August 1982 "buys" included three NYSE stocks, which gained an average of 140 percent through August 31, 1983. By comparison, in the same period the New York Stock Exchange Index rose approximately 49 percent. The total August 1982 buy signals included eight stocks (three NYSE, three Amex, two OTC), which gained an average of 100 percent. In the same period, the Wilshire 5000 Equity Index, measuring the value of all NYSE, Amex, and actively traded OTC stocks, rose 41 percent. In sum, the Big Board insider buy signals outperformed the average NYSE stock 2.85 to 1. The combined (NYSE, Amex, OTC) buy signals outperformed the broadly based Wilshire Index 2.44 to 1.

| *Stock* | *Month of Buy Signal* | *Signal Price* | *8/31/83 Price* | *Gain (Loss)* |
|---|---|---|---|---|
| AAR Corp. | 11/82 | $ 8.25 | $14.75 | 78.8% |
| AEICOR | 5/83 | 1.50 | 1.88 | 25.0 |
| Aileen | 9/82 | 2.88 | 6.25 | 117.4 |
| American Standard | 9/82 | 27.25 | 32.13 | 17.9 |
| Anglo Energy | 10/82 | 4.75 | 4.50 | (5.3) |
| Apache Corp. | 3/83 | 9.50 | 15.00 | 57.9 |
| Argonaut Energy | 5/83 | 2.00 | 2.88 | 43.8 |
| Aydin | 9/82 | 30.63 | 45.75 | 49.4 |
| Ballys Park Place | 4/83 | 9.50 | 16.50 | 73.7 |
| Bangor Punta | 11/82 | 16.25 | 19.88 | 22.3 |
| Bankers Trust NY | 3/83 | 40.75 | 44.00 | 8.0 |
| Banks of Iowa | 10/82 | 41.50 | 47.00 | 13.3 |
| Beard Oil | 8/82 | 4.38 | 12.88 | 182.9 |
| Bell Pete Svcs. | 8/83 | 4.63 | 4.63 | 0.0 |
| Beltran | 8/82 | 4.63 | 3.00 | (35.1) |
| Branch Corp. | 7/83 | 24.50 | 23.50 | (4.1) |
| Brown-Forman | 6/83 | 34.75 | 28.00 | (19.4) |

| Stock | Month of Buy Signal | Signal Price | 8/31/83 Price | Gain (Loss) |
|---|---|---|---|---|
| CACI | 11/82 | 10.72 | 14.00 | 30.6 |
| Canandaigua Wine | 3/83 | 19.50 | 34.50 | 76.9 |
| Carter Hawley Hale | 10/82 | 15.75 | 20.75 | 31.7 |
| Charles River Breed. | 1/83 | 35.50 | 43.00 | 21.1 |
| Chesapeake Utils. | 4/83 | 19.75 | 23.25 | 17.7 |
| Cincinnati Fin'l | 11/82 | 45.00 | 68.25 | 51.7 |
| Coors | 7/83 | 20.50 | 25.00 | 22.0 |
| Daniel Industries | 9/82 | 11.25 | 11.00 | (2.2) |
| Dauphin Deposit | 3/83 | 29.75 | 31.50 | 5.9 |
| Dayton Hudson | 7/83 | 38.32 | 33.38 | (12.9) |
| Dental World | 5/83 | 3.25 | 3.63 | 11.5 |
| Eaton Vance | 11/82 | 20.00 | 44.50 | 122.5 |
| EIP Microwave | 3/83 | 10.25 | 15.00 | 46.3 |
| Emery Air Freight | 8/82 | 9.00 | 21.50 | 138.9 |
| Exxon | 2/83 | 29.50 | 38.00 | 28.8 |
| First Capital | 1/83 | 30.50 | 38.50 | 26.2 |
| First Chicago | 9/82 | 17.00 | 24.63 | 44.9 |
| First Florida | 11/82 | 11.50 | 16.50 | 43.5 |
| First Wisconsin | 10/82 | 14.88 | 20.88 | 40.3 |
| General Binding | 8/83 | 10.75 | 11.25 | 4.3 |
| Gulf Res. & Chem. | 11/82 | 13.63 | 18.00 | 32.1 |
| Gulfstream Aero. | 6/83 | 21.38 | 16.63 | (22.2) |
| Health-Chem. | 9/82 | 7.88 | 9.75 | 23.8 |
| HMG Property Invst. | 3/83 | 18.88 | 22.88 | 21.2 |
| Huntington Banc. | 3/83 | 24.45 | 27.50 | 13.4 |
| Husky Oil | 9/82 | 5.25 | 9.38 | 78.6 |
| Indiana National | 9/82 | 16.63 | 22.00 | 32.2 |
| InterFirst | 5/83 | 21.38 | 20.50 | (4.1) |
| Int'l King's Table | 9/82 | 4.63 | 18.50 | 566.7 |
| Jacobson Stores | 12/82 | 13.38 | 34.50 | 157.9 |
| Jewelcor | 8/82 | 4.50 | 8.50 | 88.9 |
| Kay Corp. | 12/82 | 13.25 | 15.13 | 14.2 |
| Kearney National | 8/83 | 29.00 | 24.00 | (17.2) |

| *Stock* | *Month of Buy Signal* | *Signal Price* | *8/31/83 Price* | *Gain (Loss)* |
|---|---|---|---|---|
| Kratos | 11/82 | 10.00 | 10.25 | 2.5 |
| Kroehler Mfg. | 2/82 | 11.13 | 21.25 | 91.0 |
| L&N Housing | 4/83 | 29.88 | 26.38 | (11.7) |
| Lehman | 11/82 | 15.76 | 16.75 | 6.3 |
| MGM/UA Ent. | 2/83 | 9.50 | 15.50 | 63.2 |
| Macmillan | 9/82 | 16.50 | 29.63 | 79.5 |
| Mayflower | 8/82 | 7.00 | 14.25 | 103.6 |
| Mediq | 10/82 | 14.50 | 17.88 | 146.6 |
| Michigan General | 1/83 | 2.75 | 9.63 | 250.0 |
| Mission West Prp. | 8/82 | 4.88 | 8.00 | 64.1 |
| Moore Financial | 9/82 | 19.75 | 27.25 | 40.5 |
| Norris Oil | 9/82 | 5.50 | 4.50 | (18.2) |
| North Fork Banc. | 1/83 | 21.25 | 32.00 | 50.6 |
| Overnight Trans. | 6/83 | 29.00 | 27.88 | (3.9) |
| Oxoco | 7/83 | 11.88 | 12.00 | 1.1 |
| Pacific Lumber | 8/82 | 17.50 | 23.25 | 32.9 |
| Paul Harris Stores | 5/83 | 9.19 | 12.50 | 36.1 |
| Penn Central | 7/83 | 39.25 | 38.13 | (2.9) |
| Petrie Stores | 7/83 | 37.00 | 33.00 | (10.8) |
| Pier One Imports | 3/83 | 12.25 | 18.63 | 52.0 |
| Pizza Inn | 10/82 | 5.13 | 13.63 | 165.9 |
| Planning Research | 8/82 | 6.25 | 18.38 | 194.0 |
| Recognition Equip. | 9/82 | 6.63 | 13.00 | 96.2 |
| Repco | 1/83 | 9.75 | 4.75 | (51.3) |
| Rocky Mtn. Natrl. Gas | 3/83 | 9.25 | 10.25 | 10.8 |
| RSC Industries | 1/83 | 5.00 | 5.88 | 17.5 |
| Seafirst | 9/82 | 15.50 | a | a |
| Seagull Energy | 1/83 | 12.13 | 18.88 | 55.1 |
| Showboat | 10/82 | 15.38 | 19.63 | 27.6 |
| Spencer Cos. | 4/83 | 9.88 | 10.38 | 5.1 |
| Stanadyne | 10/82 | 29.25 | 41.00 | 40.2 |
| Sterling Capital | 4/83 | 6.75 | 9.00 | 33.3 |
| Stewart Sandwiches | 4/83 | 4.88 | 4.63 | (5.1) |

| *Stock* | *Month of Buy Signal* | *Signal Price* | *8/31/83 Price* | *Gain (Loss)* |
|---|---|---|---|---|
| Total Petroleum | 11/82 | 10.00 | 12.00 | 20.0 |
| U.S. Bancorp | 8/82 | 14.75 | 24.13 | 63.6 |
| Vicon Industries | 10/82 | 5.17 | 9.13 | 76.6 |
| Warner-Lambert | 3/83 | 31.75 | 29.13 | (8.3) |
| Wichita Industries | 1/83 | 4.50 | 5.38 | 19.4 |
| Howard B. Wolf | 12/82 | 2.88 | 4.63 | 60.9 |

a-Tendered to BankAmerica for $7.70 cash, 0.3 share preferred.
Prices are adjusted for splits. Repeat buy signals are omitted.

The *Indicator* portfolio assumes stocks are held one year, then sold. Thus, the portfolio changes month by month. Results for the August 1981–August 1982 portfolio were dramatically different from the August 1982–August 1983 performance. The four NYSE "buys" in August 1981 had lost 8.8 percent a year later, little better than the NYSE Index's 9.7 percent decline. The broader August 1981 buy list of nine stocks (four NYSE and five Amex) had fallen 23.3 percent a year later, at the market's low, versus approximately an 8.1 percent slump in the Wilshire 5000 Index; insider "buys" did more than twice as poorly as the market. That showing was sharply reversed in the next twelve months.

While results vary widely for insider stocks bought in any particular month, the insiders' selections over a full year display remarkable consistency not only in outperforming the market but also in returning profits, even in down markets. The following table gives results of *Insider Indicator* buy signals published for the NYSE only, from 1974 to 1981. The insiders' performance is measured against that of the NYSE Index. A note "NM" in column five indicates that no percentage can be arrived at, because insiders posted gains while the NYSE as a whole declined. The insider signals were profitable in each of the eight years. They underperformed the NYSE Index only in 1979.

| *Year* | *Net Signals* | *NYSE Index* | *Insider Performance* | *Insiders as % of Market* |
|---|---|---|---|---|
| 1974 | 266 | +8.2% | +18.5% | 225% |
| 1975 | 97 | +19.3 | +39.9 | 207 |

| *Year* | *Net Signals* | *NYSE Index* | *Insider Performance* | *Insiders as % of Market* |
|---|---|---|---|---|
| 1976 | 62 | −2.7 | +20.3 | NM |
| 1977 | 69 | −1.2 | +17.2 | NM |
| 1978 | 64 | +9.6 | +25.4 | 265 |
| 1979 | 66 | +17.4 | +15.2 | 87 |
| 1980 | 69 | +9.6 | +17.9 | 186 |
| 1981 | 44 | −6.0 | +8.2 | NM |

# APPENDIX II

# *Academic Studies of Insider Activity*

Following are the results of several important academic studies of insider activity. The researchers used varying formulas for obtaining insider signals, but all found that insiders outperformed the stock market.

| *Researcher* | *Market Performance* | *Insider Performance* | *Insiders As % of Market* |
|---|---|---|---|
| Rogoff | +29.7% | +49.6% | 167% |
| Glass | +6.1 | +24.3 | 398 |
| Pratt & DeVere | +9.5 | +21.2 | 223 |
| Jaffe | +7.3 | +14.7 | 201 |

Courtesy of *Insider Indicator*.

The full titles of the above studies are:

Donald L. Rogoff, "The Forecasting Properties of Insiders' Transactions." Unpublished D.B.A. dissertation, Michigan State University, 1964.

Gary A. Glass, "Extensive Insider Accumulation as an Indicator of Near-Term Stock Price Performance." Unpublished Ph.D. dissertation, Ohio State University, 1966.

Shannon P. Pratt and Charles W. DeVere, "Relationship Between Insider Trading and Rates of Return for NYSE Common Stocks, 1960–1966,'' Portland (Oregon) State University, 1968. In *Modern Developments in Investment Management,* edited by James H. Lorie and Richard Brealey, Praeger, 1970.

Jeffrey J. Jaffe, ''The Effect of Regulation Changes on Insider Trading,'' *Bell Journal of Economics and Management Science,* Spring 1974.

Other interesting studies include:

Joseph E. Finnerty, ''Insiders and Market Efficiency,'' *The Journal of Finance,* September 1966.

James H. Lorie and Victor Niederhoffer, ''Predictive and Statistical Properties of Insider Trading,'' *The Journal of Law and Economics,* April 1968.

Halbert S. Kerr, ''The Battle of Insider Trading vs. Market Efficiency,'' *The Journal of Portfolio Management,* Summer 1980.

Kenneth Nunn, Gerald Madden, and Michael Gombola, ''Are Some Insiders More 'Inside' Than Others?'' *The Journal of Portfolio Management,* Spring 1983.

## SUMMARIES

Pratt and DeVere covered 52,000 insider transactions in 800 Big Board stocks between 1960 and 1966. A buy signal was defined as purchases by three company officials within one month, with no insider sales in the period. A sell signal was defined as sales by three insiders within a month, with no purchases. In the six and a half years examined, the system generated 211 insider buy signals and 272 sell signals. From the first month after the signals, insiders outperformed the market. Within about fourteen months, insider ''buys'' had brought returns of 24.0 percent and ''sells'' had done less than half as well, returning 9.9 percent.

Finnerty broadened the review to all insider transactions, not merely clustered buying and selling. He used more than 30,000 insider decisions (9,602 purchases and 21,487 sales) between January 1969 and December 1972. That period included two sharp market declines separated by a recovery. Finnerty found that stocks which insiders bought tended to rise more than the market and fall less, while stocks being sold by insiders tended to rise less than the market and fall more than the market. Finnerty concluded: "The results for both the buy and sell portfolios bear out the fact that insiders, because probably of their access to privileged information, can outperform the market in their stock selections." Insiders' above-market return, in fact, showed up most strongly in the very month they bought or sold. Says Finnerty: ". . . [T]his may indicate either that the information on which insiders act soon becomes public knowledge and is discounted by the market quite quickly or that the knowledge that insiders have been accumulating certain stocks prompts the public to acquire the same stocks and thereby bid up the prices." In the first month, insiders earned an excess return of 3.68 percent on their purchases, while stocks they sold performed 0.90 percent worse than the market. For a typical twelve months, insider buys acted 8.34 percent better than an average portfolio, while stocks they sold performed 4.82 percent worse than an average portfolio.

Lorie and Niederhoffer found striking continuity in insider trading. Successive transactions tended to be the same, producing long sequences of buying and selling. In their sample of 3,973 purchases and 3,277 sales, occurring in 105 randomly selected NYSE companies between January 1950 and December 1960, "the odds in favor of a purchase followed by a purchase were three times as great as a purchase followed by a sale." Thus, "one purchase indicates that other purchases are likely to follow." The authors found that stocks bought by insiders were more than twice as likely in the next six months to have large price increases than to suffer declines. The odds also favored a large gain more than twice as often after insiders bought than after they sold. The two University of Chicago authors further turned up evidence that insider exercise of stock options is a bearish phenomenon—the opposite of popular assumptions. Insiders seldom exercised options in the same month they bought or sold stock. But when the events coincided, the insiders sold shares four times as often as they bought. This suggests that exercising options is a form of selling, of taking profits with a six-month time lag (the required holding period for stock obtained via options), rather than a form of purchasing stock in anticipation of future price gains.

Kerr, a proponent of the "efficient market" theory, attempted to determine whether outsiders could earn above-market returns by purchasing stocks that insiders had bought. His conclusion was negative—that by the time information becomes public via the *Official Summary of Security Transactions and Holdings,* it is fully reflected in stock prices. Kerr's sample was limited to 120 stocks that had drawn three or more insider purchases (and no sales) during 1976. While the stocks outperformed the market, Kerr found that the gains were not significant. (Kerr employed a different statistical model for determining market risk-return than did most other analysts, and he counted only price changes after insider reports had appeared in the *Official Summary.*) One of Kerr's central implications, that information about insider transactions (or about the reasons for the transactions) reaches the market ahead of the *Official Summary* (which often lags transactions by months), supports findings by Finnerty and others that much of the insider gains comes soon after their purchases. This explains why market advisory services attract subscribers by providing fresher data, drawn directly from the insider filings. But Pratt and DeVere, whose study drew upon a much broader sample, reported that outside investors could still do pretty well even if they bought two months after insiders had done so.

Nunn, Madden, and Gombola examined the most recent data, 850 purchases and 606 sales between February 1974 and August 1978. Stocks that insiders bought, adjusted for volatility, performed on average 9.3 percent better than the market in the next twelve months. The study found chief executive officers and directors the most prescient (with above-market returns of 10.8 and 10.2 percent, respectively), followed by vice-presidents (8.8 percent) and beneficial owners (7.5 percent). An interesting anomaly vis-à-vis other studies was the results for stocks that insiders sold. While these stocks underperformed the market in the early months, they *outperformed* the market after twelve months by 1.1 percent. The authors worked from single insider transactions. The sample was limited to larger trades ($10,000 or more) and by the authors' screen, which used only a portion of the trades by directors and vice-presidents. This may have distorted results by underrating the importance of successive purchases or sales.

# NOTES

## ONE

1. For details on the St. Joe Minerals case and other insider abuses, I have relied on court documents, *The Wall Street Journal, The New York Times,* and *Barron's.*

2. Deposition of Edgar M. Bronfman by the Securities and Exchange Commission, April 15, 1981.

3. Complaint, *SEC* v. *Banca della Svizzera Italiana, Irving Trust Company and Certain Purchasers of Call Options for the Common Stock of St. Joe Minerals Corporation,* March 27, 1981. (U.S. District Court, Southern New York, 81 Civ. 1836.)

4. Deposition of John J. Glynn by SEC, April 19, 1981. Glynn, of Baird Patrick, said that he told Tome of the SEC interest in St. Joe trading and that Tome promised to contact the agency. The next Glynn heard, Tome had left New York and returned to Geneva.

5. Julie Kosterlitz, "The Thomas Reed Affair," *Common Cause,* January-February 1983.

6. Kosterlitz.

7. Arthur J. Keown and John M. Pinkerton, "Merger Announcements and Insider Trading Activity: An Empirical Investigation," *The Journal of Finance,* September 1981, pp. 863–66.

8. "Whither Warner?" *Financial World,* November 1, 1982. Heavy breathing fogs glasses, but otherwise these analyst-company ro-

mances serve both parties. Two months before the Atari scandal broke, *Institutional Investor,* a glossy trade journal for money managers, dubbed Lee Isgur the Street's top analyst of leisure-time stocks. "Mention Lee Isgur's name to any member of his huge fan club," the report bubbled, "and the immediate, almost reflexive, response is likely to be 'Warner.' The . . . analyst leads the leisure-time pack for the seventh year in a row, and more often than not boosters attribute it to his extraordinary knowledge of Warner Communications." Isgur had projected a price of $100 on Warner by the end of 1982 and said, "It has always been my theory that the upside potential is so great that to risk not owning it will cost far more than a temporary decline." ("The 1982 All-America Research Team," *Institutional Investor,* October 1982.)

9. "Who Gets the Most Pay," *Forbes,* June 6, 1983. Warner chairman Steven Ross ranked fourth, including stock gains, in the magazine's survey of top-paid managers. If stock gains aren't counted, Ross was No. 1, with salary, bonus, benefits, and contingent payments of $3,681,073.
10. Gene G. Marcial, "Insider Trading: Warner Sweats in the Spotlight," *Business Week,* January 10, 1983.
11. *The Wall Street Journal,* December 24, 1982.
12. Complaint, *SEC* v. *Raymond E. Kasser,* September 26, 1983. (U.S. District Court, Northern California, 83 Civ. 20267.)
13. Complaint, *SEC* v. *Dennis D. Groth,* September 26, 1983. (U.S. District Court, Northern California, 83 Civ. 4534.) In reconstructing the chronology of insiders' knowledge, the SEC noted that as early as November 17, 1982, Atari advised Warner executives that fourth-quarter net income would be only half of what the company had hoped. As the situation at Atari deteriorated, insiders sold.
14. Complaint, *Steven Becket et al.* v. *Warner Communications Inc. et al.* (U.S. District Court, Southern New York, 82 Civ. 8288.)
15. Richard V. Norell, SEC Division of Enforcement, Washington, to author, September 22, 1983.

## TWO

1. John Brooks, *Once in Golconda* (1969), p. 66.
2. Thomas Gibson, *The Pitfalls of Speculation* (1916), pp. 28–31.

3. Frederick Lewis Allen, *The Great Pierpont Morgan* (1949), pp. 182–83; and Dana L. Thomas, *The Plungers and the Peacocks* (1967), p. 68.

4. John Durand and A. T. Miller, *The Business of Trading in Stocks* (1933 ed.), p. 16.

5. Brooks, p. 73.

6. Robert Irving Warshow, *The Story of Wall Street* (1929), pp. 67–68.

7. Gustavus Myers, *History of the Great American Fortunes* (1936 ed.), pp. 299–302; and Warshow, pp. 90–97. Details vary in these and other accounts, but the common thread is that on the New York City Common Council and in the legislature, office-holders who demanded bribes weren't honorable enough to stay bribed.

8. Myers, pp. 307–8, 408–13; Warshow, pp. 109–33.

9. Warshow, pp. 116–17.

10. Clarence W. Barron, *More They Told Barron*, edited by Arthur Pound and Samuel Taylor Moore (1931), p. 9.

11. James Grant, *Bernard M. Baruch: The Adventures of a Wall Street Legend* (1983), p. 58.

12. Grant, p. 58.

13. H. L. Wilgus, "Purchase of Share of Corporation by a Director from a Shareholder," *Michigan Law Review*, February 1910, p. 297.

14. Roberts Walker, "The Duty of Disclosure by a Director Purchasing Stock from His Stockholders," *Yale Law Journal*, May 1923, p. 637.

15. Henry G. Manne, *Insider Trading and the Stock Market* (1966), pp. 34–35. Professor Manne's book, long out of print, provides a reasoned critique of much of the theory behind prohibitions on insider trading. Manne earned high marks for prescience; the problems he foresaw in 1966, such as analysts' potential liability, grew into a legal jungle by the 1970s

16. Quoted by Manne, p. 35.

17. Manne, pp. 35–36.

18. Quoted by Manne, p. 38.

19. Quoted in "A Current Assessment of the Law Proscribing Insider Trading," Theodore A. Levine, Thomas A. Ferrigno, Nancy Watters, Michael D. Mann, 1983. The authors of the paper were attorneys for the SEC Division of Enforcement.

20. Quoted in "A Reasonable Amount of Time," John Brooks, *Business Adventures* (1969), p. 142.

21. "The Conscience of Insiders," *Great Business Disasters,* edited by Isadore Barmash (1972), p. 182.

22. The assumption was debated by legal scholars. Manne (pp. 12–13) argues that nothing in most employment contracts implies such constraint, as long as an insider's use of his knowledge doesn't injure the company.

23. Manuel F. Cohen, SEC chairman (1964–68), cited in "Street of Fear?" Robert M. Bleiberg, *Barron's,* September 1, 1969. Bleiberg also quoted a dissenting judge in the Texas Gulf Sulphur case on the need for definitions of illegal trading: "The resolution, if such be possible, of the many problems presented in this field should be by rule, as definite as possible, formulated in the light of reality and not retroactive in effect as here. . . . Presumably the Commission will make recommendations to the Congress to give that body an opportunity to accept or reject after thoughtful debate such proposals as may be made. The companies, . . . their employees and the investing public alike should have some knowledge of the rules which will govern their actions. They should not be forced, despite an exercise of the best judgment, to act at their peril or refrain *in terrorem* from acting."

24. Roberta S. Karmel, *Regulation by Prosecution* (1982), p. 211.

25. Karmel, p. 226.

26. Levine, Ferrigno, Watters, Mann, p. 5.

27. Quoted in "The Equity Funding Scandal," Isadore Barmash, *Great Business Disasters,* p. 291.

28. Raymond L. Dirks and Leonard Gross, *The Great Wall Street Scandal,* 1974, pp. 278–79. See also William E. Blundell, "Equity Funding: 'I Did It for the Jollies,' " *Swindled! Classic Business Frauds of the Seventies,* edited by Donald Moffitt (1976); and Ronald L. Soble and Robert E. Dallos, *The Impossible Dream* (1975).

29. John C. Boland, "Dirks vs. the SEC: Round Two," *Barron's*, June 18, 1979. The SEC counsel, Donald N. Malawsky, later became SEC regional administrator in New York and then joined the New York Stock Exchange as a senior vice-president in member firm regulation.

30. Raymond L. Dirks, "Freedom of Information in the Market," *The New York Times*, July 17, 1983.

31. Stanley Sporkin, "Setback to the SEC's Enforcement Drive," *The New York Times*, July 17, 1983.

32. John M. Fedders, "A Call for Stronger Deterrents," *The New York Times*, July 17, 1983.

33. Fedders.

34. Studies finding that insiders regularly do better than the market have been performed by Shannon P. Pratt and Charles W. DeVere; Joseph E. Finnerty; James H. Lorie and Victor Niederhoffer, and others. Their work is described in Appendix II.

35. Robert B. Blackburn, SEC New York regional office, to author, October 3, 1983.

36. Arthur J. Keown and John M. Pinkerton, "Merger Announcements and Insider Trading Activity: An Empirical Investigation," *The Journal of Finance*, September 1981, pp. 863–66.

37. *The Wall Street Journal*, September 27, 1983.

38. Daniel Seligman, "An Economic Defense of Insider Trading," *Fortune*, September 5, 1983.

39. Manne, pp. 131–45.

40. Levine, Ferrigno, Watters, Mann, p. 24. The authors cite a 1982 New York case *(Camelot Industries Corporation* v. *Vista Resources Inc.)* in which a federal judge ruled that a broker had not violated Rule 14e-3 in tipping a stock while knowing that another company planned to buy the shares and that a tender offer had been mentioned. The judge said that it had not been proved that the broker "knew of Vista's tender offer plan from any statement or document, despite his own internal certitude on the subject." State the authors: "The court thus held that actual knowledge of a tender offer is required to impose liability under Rule 14e-3."

## THREE

1. John C. Boland, "Canny Insiders," *Barron's*, January 26, 1981.
2. Dick Griffin, "The Big Play in Chicago Milwaukee," *Fortune*, May 22, 1978.
3. Boland, "Canny Insiders." See also *Barron's:* Bernard Shakin, "Better Dead Than Red?" July 23, 1979; Shakin, "Trustee Sees Smaller Line," August 27, 1979; Boland, "October Scoreboard," November 10, 1980.
4. Proxy Statement, Avatar Holdings Inc., April 10, 1981.
5. Boland, "Ugly Ducklings," *Barron's*, June 22, 1981.
6. Boland, "Insider Favorites," *Barron's*, February 8, 1982.
7. Boland, "Ahead of the Crowd," *Barron's*, December 27, 1982.
8. Boland, "Ahead of the Crowd."
9. Boland, "Insider Favorites."

## FOUR

1. Prospectus, Gulfstream Aerospace Corporation, April 8, 1983. See also John R. Dorfman, "Just Like the Good Old Days," *Forbes*, April 25, 1983.
2. Kathryn M. Welling, "New Kid on the Block," *Barron's*, April 9, 1979.
3. Rodger W. Bridwell, *The Battle for Financial Security* (1980), pp. 136–40. Bridwell, a money manager, wrote on insider trading for *Barron's* in the 1950s and 1960s.
4. The SEC voted unanimously in 1983 to lift the requirement that companies disclose such executive perquisites as use of company airplanes, cars, apartments, and so forth, as well as extensive details on options and incentive pay. The old rules were adopted, noted *The Wall Street Journal* (September 23, 1983), after SEC investigators "uncovered huge hidden perquisites at major corporations. Since then, corporations have repeatedly urged a rollback. . . . many companies contend that detailed pay reporting is an unwarranted invasion of corporate managers' privacy." They also complained about the expense of gathering the data for proxy statements. SEC chairman John Shad said the broader disclosures

weren't "material to an investment decision" though there was "a lot of curiosity" about executive pay among financial analysts and shareholders. Shad dismissed such interest: "Gossip columns are more carefully read than hard news." The SEC said it wanted to make proxy material easier to read. About the same time, the commission proposed a new rule to limit another kind of information. The rule would bar "pink sheet" quotations for inactively traded stocks by brokers who lack current financial statements from the companies. As *Forbes* noted (December 19, 1983), this would be a boon to insiders trying to soak up undervalued shares because it would remove competing bids.

5. Ralph Nader, letter (December 2, 1983) to John M. Fedders, director of enforcement, SEC. (Nader's role in the stock market hasn't always been as a critic. In 1979, Gannett News Service exposed a series of stock transactions by Nader organizations including a short sale of ITT Corporation shares in 1970 while Nader was taking ITT to task over a merger.)

6. To author, December 29, 1983.

7. *The Wall Street Journal,* December 5, 1983. The article contends that strict enforcement of insider reporting rules has never been high on the SEC's priority list. Asked if that was true, Andrew L. Rothman, the agency's public affairs director, said: "I guess I wouldn't argue with it."

8. What disclosure? Consider the following excerpts from monthly reports in *Barron's* on top-performing stocks: "Oscar Mayer . . . jumped 31 percent, to 21, in a few hectic days. . . . When the New York Stock Exchange asked the company what was up, according to *The Wall Street Journal,* an Oscar Mayer official reportedly said he didn't know of anything. After an SEC query, the company and General Foods disclosed . . . that they were discussing a possible takeover" (February 9, 1981). "On March 18, word moved on the Dow Jones wire that Horn & Hardart knew of 'no adverse news' to account for the slump in its shares. Next day came the fourth quarter earnings, off 8 percent" (April 6, 1981). "The action in Four Phase System underscored traders' ever-remarkable knack for sniffing out impending takeovers. Coincidentally or not, the board of directors . . . met on Tuesday, December 1, a day the stock closed up 1⅛ points on 39,800 shares. The next day, the issue shot up 5¾ points . . . as volume ballooned to 302,000 shares. Part way through the run, R. Frederick Hod-

der, Four Phase's treasurer, told Dow Jones that he knew of no corporate reason for the move. But a week later, Motorola disclosed that it had agreed to acquire Four Phase. . . . Of his December 2 disclaimer, Hodder now says: 'There had not been negotiations at that time. There had been some contact.' He [wouldn't] say whether it had been discussed at the December 1 board meeting'' (January 11, 1982). Other examples may suggest the scope of late or misleading corporate disclosure. After six marketing executives quit Prime Computer to join another firm, the shares plunged. Prime said it hadn't planned to announce the resignations but issued a press release because of the heavy trading in the stock. Obviously someone had already heard (*The Wall Street Journal,* July 18, 1983). In three weeks late in 1982, the price of HRT Industries crumbled from $8.38 to $4.50 on unusually large volume. On November 10, HRT said that ''there aren't any internal developments that would account for the recent activity in the company's stock.'' Twelve days later, trading was halted for the company to announce that it was filing for bankruptcy under Chapter XI (*The Wall Street Journal,* October 14, 1983). There are other episodes not on the public record. A major East Coast railroad quietly increased its stock holdings in another line shortly before announcing a higher-priced tender offer for the rest. Another rail corporation kept mum on litigation for settlement of bond claims—while brokers who knew what was going on bid the bonds from $74 to $163. This catalogue could be expanded. Companies and their executives like to keep secrets. Although misleading disclosure is illegal, there's more of it than the SEC seems able to prosecute. None of the above episodes yielded complaints. As for material disclosure in general, the SEC has issued no guidelines; it's up to management to determine whether a ''contact'' from a potential suitor is ''material.'' The standards, such as they are, have been set in the agency's usual fashion, by unpredictable litigation.

## FIVE

1. Some of the nation's best proprietary products are carried on corporate books for token sums. These may or may not constitute ''hidden values.'' Such arguments have been put forth with mixed success, for example, for movie studios' film libraries.

2. Benjamin Graham, David L. Dodd, and Sidney Cottle, with Charles Tatham, *Security Analysis,* 4th ed. (1962), pp. 172–78.

3. Richard Greene and Paul Bornstein, "A Better Yardstick," *Forbes,* September 27, 1982.

4. Graham and Dodd, p. 543.

5. Form 10K, Horizon Corporation, September 27, 1983.

SEVEN

1. Cary Reich, "Has Allen Got a Deal for You," *Institutional Investor,* April 1983.

2. Reich.

3. Leslie Wayne, "A Daring Dealmaker Piles Up Profits," *The New York Times,* June 12, 1983.

4. John Train, *The Money Masters* (1980), p. 12.

5. Annual Reports to the Stockholders (1982, 1983), Berkshire Hathaway Inc. Warren Buffett's letters to shareholders are noted for fluency and common sense. A compilation of past letters is available from the company: 1440 Kiewit Plaza, Omaha, Nebraska 68131.

6. Carl C. Icahn, "Stop the Oppression of Shareholders," *The New York Times,* May 22, 1983.

7. Offer to Purchase, Icahn Acquisition Corporation, September 8, 1982. The SEC later complained that Icahn had not fully disclosed to shareholders the ramifications of breaking the company's status as a tax-sheltered realty trust. Icahn settled the complaint, neither affirming nor denying guilt.

8. *The Wall Street Journal,* February 12, 1981; April 7, 1981.

9. Michael Brody, "Back to the 'Sixties," *Barron's,* October 24, 1977.

10. Leon Levy, "Inside the Battle Over Trans World," *Fortune,* June 13, 1983.

11. Michael Brody, "Cloak and Suit," *Barron's,* April 5, 1982.

12. Jean A. Briggs, "How the Rich Get Richer," *Forbes,* February 14, 1983.

13. *The Wall Street Journal,* April 7, 1981.
14. John Brimelow, "The Posner Touch," *Barron's,* November 19, 1979.
15. Gigi Mahon and John C. Boland, "The Pulte Caper," *Barron's,* September 4, 1978.
16. *The Wall Street Journal,* July 29, 1981.

## EIGHT

1. *The Wall Street Journal,* November 3, 1983.

## NINE

1. Dan Dorfman, Chicago Tribune Syndicate, May 5, 1983; Anne Crittenden, "Reaping Big Profits from a Fat Cat," *The New York Times,* August 7, 1983. "I'm the happiest man who ever lived," William Simon told *The Times.* He isn't always such a great sport. After bad investments in Amarex Inc., an oil and gas concern that sank into Chapter XI, Simon and others sued broker Donaldson, Lufkin & Jenrette Inc., to make good their losses (*The Wall Street Journal,* June 9, 1983).
2. Martin J. Pring, *Technical Analysis Explained* (1980), p. 266.
3. Joseph E. Finnerty, "Insiders and Market Efficiency," *The Journal of Finance,* September 1966, pp. 1141–48. Other researchers have reached similar conclusions.
4. Kenneth Nunn, Gerald Madden, and Michael Gombola, "Are Some Insiders More 'Inside' Than Others?" *The Journal of Portfolio Management,* Spring 1983, pp. 18–22.
5. *The Wall Street Journal,* February 4, 1982.

## TEN

1. Priscilla S. Meyer, "The Boiler Plate Defense," *Forbes,* April 25, 1983.
2. Jean A. Briggs, "I Like It Here," *Forbes,* March 15, 1982.
3. *The Wall Street Journal,* March 26, 1982.

4. *The Wall Street Journal,* March 26, 1982.
5. *The Wall Street Journal,* April 1, 1982. Ford was a member of the Amax board at the time of the SoCal bid; Brown joined the board in June 1981.
6. *The Wall Street Journal,* March 9, 1982.
7. Proxy Statement, RCA Corporation, March 8, 1982.
8. *Business Week,* March 22, 1982. Having friends helps. When the chairman of Statesman Group Inc., a Midwestern insurance holding company, resigned, the board agreed to have the company buy his stock for about three times its market value. ''It was a friendly negotiation,'' said the former executive's successor (*The Wall Street Journal,* August 13, 1982).
9. Ann M. Morrison, ''Those Executive Bailout Deals,'' *Fortune,* December 13, 1982. The tally on golden parachutes was updated on November 14, 1983.
10. *The Wall Street Journal,* August 11, 1983.
11. Jean A. Briggs, ''Shoot-out at Rorer Gulch,'' *Forbes,* June 20, 1983.
12. John C. Boland, ''Who's After Rorer?'' *Barron's,* July 5, 1982.

# INDEX